NEED,
SPEED,
AND GREED

ALSO BY VIJAY V. VAITHEESWARAN

Zoom: The Global Race to Fuel the Car of the Future
(co-authored by Iain Carson)

Power to the People: How the Coming Energy
Revolution Will Transform an Industry, Change Our
Lives, and Maybe Even Save the Planet

NEED, SPEED, AND GREED

How the New Rules of Innovation Can
Transform Businesses, Propel Nations to Greatness,
and Tame the World's Most Wicked Problems

VIJAY V. VAITHEESWARAN

HARPER
BUSINESS

An Imprint of HarperCollinsPublishers
www.harpercollins.com

HarperCollins books may be purchased for educational, business, or sales promotional use. For information, please write: Special Markets Department, HarperCollinsPublishers, 10 East 53rd Street, New York, NY 10022.

FIRST EDITION

Designed by Jaime Putorti

Library of Congress Cataloging-in-Publication Data has been applied for.

ISBN 978-0-06-207599-4

12 13 14 15 16   OV/RRD   10 9 8 7 6 5 4 3 2 1

For Michelle and Keila

CONTENTS

Part Three

GREED: How to Win in the Age of Disruptive Innovation

NEED,
SPEED,
AND GREED

INTRODUCTION

Welcome to the Ideas Economy

"I have worked in over sixty jobs in my life," says Trevor Rose, an Australian tinkerer, describing a lifetime of frustration in the workplace. "I couldn't think of a line that says 'I am this,' because I have done a million and one tiny little things, none of which was really a career in the way most people experience—meaning the money was absolute rubbish."

Yet Trevor is a born innovator. He has always had bright ideas, and he loves solving problems. He even put himself through most of a university course in engineering and computer science a few years ago, until the money ran dry and he had to drop out. But employers often do not take him seriously, so he has not had the chance to shine. After all, if you got a résumé at your firm from a prospective hire that said the candidate had dropped out of college and had gone through dozens of jobs, would you give him the benefit of the doubt?

A decade ago, that would have been the end of the Trevor story. He would have remained just another bright spark whose talents withered on the vine thanks to the elitist approach to innovation taken by the world's corporations, governments, and leading universities. But there is a happy ending, thanks to today's global innovation revolution.

As *Need, Speed, and Greed* will show, there is a powerful change under way in how innovation happens. This new approach is transforming how intellectual capital connects with financial capital, knocking down ivory towers along the way. Thanks to the globalization and Googlization of the world economy, clever ideas from every corner of the world now have the chance to be taken seriously—even if they come from people without fancy credentials. Governments, charities, and corporations alike are increasingly turning to open and networked models of innovation, such as the use of incentive prizes, to solve difficult problems.

An American company that has pioneered this approach is InnoCentive, a spin-off from the pharmaceutical giant Eli Lilly. The company has developed an Internet platform that allows organizations grappling with thorny technical problems to post them as challenges on its website. Because the InnoCentive site is open to all comers, regardless of academic credentials or job title, it attracts millions of creative people from around the world. The one who best solves a given challenge wins a cash prize, which can range from a few thousand dollars to millions of dollars.

After his money troubles forced him to drop out of his college courses, a forlorn Trevor Rose was browsing the Web one day when he encountered InnoCentive. He stumbled across a challenge posted by a private charitable foundation looking for a better method to deliver banking services in the developing world. He knew absolutely nothing about that industry, but he was intrigued enough to work on the problem. But so did many others around the world, including actual experts in development issues and in finance.

Astonishingly, the Aussie outsider beat them all to the punch. According to the officials in charge, his winning entry "proposed a mobile software application that batch processes expected spends and syncs those predictions up with actual expenses on a transaction basis." Put simply, he worked out how simple software could match up what people are likely to spend with what they actually end up spending using their mobile phones in banking. How did he do it? "When I read the further details, it just started me thinking, and before I knew it, there I was writing down the solution that came to mind. OK, it took a bit of scribbling on paper and drawing diagrams and nutting things over . . . but that's part of the process I get hooked on and why I love to solve problems."

He won the challenge and took home $2,000. But the modest prize was not the only bounty on offer, explains Alpheus Bingham, a cofounder of InnoCentive. The ability to get one's ideas connected with organizations that can scale them up and make a difference in the real world matters, he argues. So too does the recognition that comes with the prize.

Trevor warms up to the idea of making a difference: "I do like the possibility that something I thought of might help someone in a country where the economy is very tough already, and perhaps make their lives easier in some way . . . I hope so." But he goes on to explain that this wasn't the main reason he attempted the challenge. For him, the main motivation was the chance to overcome a lifetime of frustrated attempts at innovation. That's why he continues to tackle other people's problems. He even won another InnoCentive cash award recently, for figuring out a better method for removing hair roots for a commercial client.

Trevor sums up the Ideas Economy nicely: "I like the idea of being an InnoCentive solver because for me it's like a little billboard that will say to those who doubted me in life that maybe they are wrong and I am a lot cleverer than I look."

Something New Under the Sun

Innovation matters, now more than ever. With manufacturing accounting for less than a third of economic activity in many rich countries, knowledge—the currency of the Ideas Economy—is now paramount. The United States and the rest of the rich world will not be able to compete with rivals offering low-cost products and services if we all do not learn to innovate better and faster. But if we do so, there is every reason to think that the world may yet embark on a postindustrial revolution, one that will put the world economy on a much more sustainable footing for the future.

Innovation is the key to global competitiveness, but it is not necessarily a zero-sum game. Those wailing today about the rise of China and the loss of America's innovation edge give you only half the picture. Yes, our own failure to invest in infrastructure, education, and other pillars of the innovation economy hurts our economy—but the rise of the East need not. On the contrary, because the well of human ingenuity is bottomless, innovation strategies that tap into hitherto neglected intellectual capital and connect it better with financial capital can help both rich and poor countries prosper. This rising tide can indeed lift all boats, but only if we make the effort to patch the holes in our vessel first.

Although the word *innovation* is often used to refer to new technology, many innovations are neither new nor involve gadgets. The self-service concept of fast food popularized by McDonald's, for instance, involved running a restaurant in a different way rather than making a technological breakthrough. So innovation is not the same thing as invention. These days much innovation happens in processes and services.

Novelty of some sort does matter, although it might involve an existing idea from another industry or country. For example, Edwin Drake was not the first man to drill for a natural resource; the Chinese used that technique for centuries to mine salt. But one inspired morning in 1859, Colonel Drake decided to try drilling (rather than digging, as was the norm back then) for oil in Titusville, Pennsylvania. He struck black gold, and from his innovation the modern oil industry was born. A useful way to think about innovation is that it's *fresh thinking that creates something valuable*, whether for individuals, firms or society at large.

According to the popular notion, innovation is something that men wearing white coats in laboratories do. And that's the way it used to be. Companies set up vertically integrated R&D organizations such as AT&T's Bell Labs, and governments fussed over innovation policies to help them succeed. This approach had its successes, so many companies still spend pots of money on corporate research and bureaucrats still obsess over industrial policy. But this old-fashioned process is slow and insular and unsuited to a world economy that moves at an ever-accelerating pace.

The good news, as this book explains, is that the centrally planned approach is giving way to more democratic models of innovation. Clever ideas have always been everywhere, of course, but companies and societies were often too closed to pick them up. The nascent move to an open approach to innovation is far more promising. An insight from a bright spark in a research lab in Bangalore or an avid mountain biker in Colorado now has a decent chance of being turned into a product and brought to market.

The generation and handling of ideas can make or break jobs, companies, and entire national economies. "We firmly believe that innovation, not love, makes the world go round," insists John Dryden of the Organization for Economic Cooperation and Development (OECD), the official think tank for rich-country governments. Corny, perhaps, but studies do show that the most important driver of economic growth—and with it living standards—over recent decades is innovation. Innovative firms and countries also tend to outperform their peers. After all, mankind is not discovering new continents or encountering vast deposits of new minerals.

Most innovation over the past few decades has been caused by global economic integration and disruptive new technologies—in other words, the breathtaking globalization and Googlization of the planet. In the coming decades, the quest for environmental sustainability and the need to meet the health demands of a fatter, sicker, and older global population may prove to be the greatest engines of innovation—and, therefore, the great economic opportunities of our lifetimes.

The tools and rules of innovation are changing at an unprecedented pace today. It was once the preserve of elites, but innovation is becoming more democratic as open and networked approaches take off. Countries and companies are rethinking the role of incentives, as a richer world population finds motivation in purpose and not only profit. And entrepreneurs and company bosses alike are realizing the vital need to embrace risk taking and fast failure in order to keep up with the accelerating pace of global change. There even seems to be a happy confluence of technological advances, market expansion, rising prosperity, and a freer flow of ideas that promises to usher in a new golden age of innovation.

But to unleash that potential, whether as an entrepreneurial policy maker or as an aspiring employee-of-the-month, you need to face an increasingly risky world with courage. Is your community or country ready to be agile, keeping pace with a world that is moving at double speed? Is your company really open and networked, and do you know how to be a beacon for good ideas from which your firm can extract value? And most important, are you willing to fail, fail, fail, and fail again—learning the right lessons quickly and moving on to the next experiment— until you succeed?

A Reality Check

This book challenges some widely held views about innovation, the role of government versus business, supposed global crises, and the future of the world economy. Among the popular notions that we'll put to a reality check:

- Invention, intellectual property rights, and cutting-edge technology are the key to innovation.

- The rise of China and India as innovation powerhouses will inevitably come at the West's expense.

- The most difficult global challenges the United States faces today are fixing Wall Street and dealing with terrorism.

- The best way to bring about a clean energy transformation is to launch a well-funded, government-run "moon shot" like the Apollo lunar mission.

- Resource wars, be they over petroleum or fresh water, are unavoidable.

- Global trends point to a "population bomb" that will make sustainable development impossible.

- Free markets would solve even difficult global problems such as climate change if only meddling politicians kept out of the way.

- Western health firms and systems are so well financed and technologically superior that they have nothing to fear or learn from poor-world upstarts.

- Innovation is always good for society.

- Today's world economy is no riskier than yesterday's.

- When it comes to innovation, there's nothing new under the sun.

In debunking these notions, the chapters that follow will build the case for a rethink of how the world approaches innovation. And the concluding section of the book will present a manifesto for the coming age of democratic innovation—"The Disruptive Dozen: The New Rules of Global Innovation."

My central argument is that thanks to ways in which innovation is rapidly evolving, the world stands on the cusp of a post-industrial revolution. This is a very good thing if you can learn the new rules of innovation. This book will reveal the principles and practices—and introduce the good gurus and go-getters—now reshaping the world economy. The most influential of the small handful of innovation experts who really matter is Clayton Christensen, a soft-spoken Harvard professor with some hard-hitting ideas. In his best-selling book *The Innovator's Dilemma,* he argued that there are two different kinds of technological invention that drive businesses. The most common are "sustaining technologies," which lead to incremental improvements to products and services that sustain the business models of incumbents and preserve the status quo. Most companies end up focusing on such incremental innovation, as this is what pleases the existing base of customers and makes short-term economic sense.

Far less common are "disruptive technologies," which offer radically new ways of meeting customers' needs that do not fit neatly into old business models and which often come from unexpected quarters. Such breakthroughs are often shunned by existing companies, as they see them as threats to existing, profitable lines of business—or as not nearly good enough to satisfy existing customers. Christensen observed such behavior among the big technology firms that cornered the market several decades ago with very expensive technologies for data storage; when cheap and small disk drives first arrived, the incumbents scoffed that this would never be good enough. In fact, the scrappy upstarts managed to produce devices that were very affordable and good enough for the needs of most people—including many who could never afford the expensive, gold-plated storage devices.

Christensen warned that most established firms get trapped into making better and pricier products for their best customers, leaving them vulnerable to attack by nimble disruptive innovators from below. That is precisely what happened to the traditional computer firms, which made large and expensive systems for corporate users, when microcomputers arrived: firms such as Digital Equipment Corporation and Wang ignored gadflies such as Apple and ultimately went bust, though IBM found a way to survive. Kodak and Polaroid were sideswiped by the arrival of digital photography, which they too discounted as a fringe business. And online retailing continues to wreak havoc on those bricks-and-mortar businesses that do not have a radical strategy for embracing the digital disruption. Some of those dinosaurs—such as IBM, Kodak, and Walmart—did learn how to dance to a new tune, while many others went bust. That points to Christensen's next great contribution: reflecting further on his observations, he realized that the really disruptive force was not the technology, but the business model embraced by the upstarts. In his next book, *The Innovator's Solution*, he changed the term of art from "disruptive technology" to "disruptive innovation."

Christensen, a strikingly tall and imposing figure, is now in his sixties, and battles with cancer and a stroke have slowed his speech a bit. But his mind remains as razor sharp as ever, and the great man now has bigger game in his sights. He has been examining the rise of various Asian economies over the past few decades and thinks the argument about disruption applies well to the rise of China. What about the Southeast Asian "tiger" economies such as Taiwan and Japan, which rose much earlier? The rise of the tigers was impressive, but they simply lack the scale needed to pose a threat to the West. As for Japan, he argues that it really had the chance to be disruptive but ultimately became trapped by the innovator's dilemma. In industry after industry, Japanese firms rose to the global lead by disrupting comfortable incumbents in Europe and the United States. But once they reached the technology frontier, he argues, they themselves got captured by their own best customers into gold-plating inventions—the classic trap he identified. The United States got out from that trap because of its dynamic entrepreneurial economy, which allowed uncompetitive steel and textile mills to fail and car plants to relocate in order to redeploy financial and human capital into newly disruptive industries such as the Internet.

Alas, Japan's ossified corporate sector, debt-laden banking sector, and top-heavy government policies have all prevented such a rejuvenation. That, thinks Christensen, has exposed Japan to disruption by an even more potent rising star, one that possesses both the economic heft that Singapore will never have and the entrepreneurial nimbleness that Japan lacks: China. And coming a few years behind it, one could add, are India and Brazil. That suggests the global economy and its comfortable incumbents are in for a rocky ride.

That is one important reason to think the world economy is entering a riskier period. However, this is not to say all of the advantages of incumbency are gone. It may be no easier to disrupt incumbent technologies or business models than in the past. However, thanks to the democratization of innovation described in this book, lots of new kinds of disruptive entrepreneurs from all over the world are now able to get access to markets, capital, and connectivity. That allows them to try out many more wild and crazy ideas than in the past, in effect, getting many more shots on goal, making it more likely that a genuinely disruptive force such as mobile telephony will emerge again in the future.

Over the past few decades, globalization and Googlization have kicked off the first phase of an innovation revolution more profound and powerful than any economic force since the arrival of Europeans on American shores half a millennium ago. This has brought such advances as the World Wide Web, social networking, 24/7 connectivity, and global markets. This book peers inside the minds of the winners and plants red flags on the black holes they avoided so that you can raise your game. Innovation is evolving from being a fuzzy notion to being a proper discipline, much as the total-quality movement in manufacturing management did a few decades ago. Drawing on the best of the academic and field work in this emerging area, this book will teach you the new rules that you need to know and point to the skills you need to develop to profit from the shifting global economic order.

Need, Speed, and Greed will describe the urgent need for new solutions to twenty-first-century crises, profile cutting-edge innovators as they disrupt established business models and upend entire industries at breakneck speed, and show how greed can do good if the broken rules of capitalism are fixed so that entrepreneurial firms and markets are rewarded for solving socially important problems.

Need: Why Innovation Matters

The first section of the book frames the innovation question by looking at the big picture and argues that today's challenges mean innovation is more important than ever. After enjoying decades of seemingly effortless prosperity and unprecedented material progress, we are now entering a complex and risky economic era laden with potentially devastating global threats. This demands an entirely new approach to innovation in response.

This section of the book picks up on the current debate between the techno-optimists, who argue that a confluence of disruptive technologies make these the best of times, and the eco-pessimists, who point to a perfect storm of demographic and ecological forces that could lead to cataclysms ahead.

The real trends that underlie today's global challenges are unprecedented urbanization, rapid aging, and the spectacular rise of emerging economies and a global middle class. These forces are mostly to be applauded, as Chapter 1 explains, for they are the result of rising global prosperity and improving health conditions for billions of people. The problem arises because the same trends also add pressure to health, environmental, and other systems.

Some of these impacts are global, as seen in emerging crises ranging from climate change to pandemic diseases. Others lead to local troubles like resource scarcity and air pollution. The chapter points the way forward on these grand global challenges.

It is not just planetary-scale problems that demand an innovation revolution: corporate-scale problems do too. Established companies in the developed world are today facing disruptive threats from emerging markets that could put them out of business altogether—and in the future, today's emerging champions from the BRIC countries (Brazil, Russia, India, and China) will themselves face challengers from the rising countries of CIVETS (Colombia, Indonesia, Vietnam, Egypt, Turkey, and South Africa) and other acronym-bearing hot spots. Chapter 2, which examines the trend toward frugal engineering, explains why this poses such an existential challenge to the West's storied multinationals. It also makes the controversial argument that this very same trend could actually turn out to be good for ordinary people in the very same developed economies.

The most important reason the world needs fresh thinking on innovation is the fact that many people are being left behind by the advance of the knowledge economy. There are signs of a growing backlash because many even in the middle classes of rich countries feel they do not have the tools needed to participate in the ongoing transformation of the world economy. The elites of Mumbai are today closer to the elites of Manhattan than they were two decades ago, it is true, but what about Kansas? The hard-working salarymen of the developed world are not getting richer, are definitely getting angrier, and may well be getting shafted by the economic elites who have mastered the new rules of global innovation.

Even as rural women in Africa have seen their lives transformed by mobile phones and the Internet, the middle classes and blue-collar workers in rich countries everywhere have been squeezed by the new global realities. As the first phase of the innovation revolution gives way to a much more profound transformation in the next decade, the United States and other rich societies must find a path to inclusive growth or risk being left behind by history.

That points to one of the central political and economic questions of the age: how can the extraordinary benefits of the innovation revolution be shared more equitably? The good news, as Chapter 3 reveals, is that the more open, bottom-up nature of innovation today lends itself to more widespread participation by those without fancy doctorates or MBAs. However, many still lack the skills and savvy to take advantage of these opportunities the way the intrepid Trevor Rose did on InnoCentive.

Speed: Where Innovation Is Going

Humanity can tame this century's grand global challenges, but only if it embraces the trend toward the democratization of innovation. This will require learning new skills—and leaving old habits and misconceptions behind. The second section of the book describes the three powerful ways in which meta-innovation—that is, innovation in the very ways in which we innovate—is changing fast. If you want to succeed in this brave new world, you must be agile, open, and willing to embrace risk.

There is a quiet but powerful confluence of technology trends upending business that could accelerate the pace of meaningful innovation. As Chapter 4 explains, some influential thinkers even argue that this confluence amounts to a "singularity," which will lead to a postbiological civilization in which the line separating man and machine disappears over time. That seems a bit far-fetched. Even so, the confluence of multiple technologies advancing at an exponential pace promises to accelerate global innovation and speed the global economy toward a postindustrial world.

What is more, the creative process is being prised apart in astonishing, even frightening, ways. One is the emergence of net-worked and user-driven business models. Chapter 5 scrutinizes the open-innovation movement in detail and finds that there is much to celebrate here. However, it warns that this approach has been over-hyped and argues that there is peril as well as promise in openness.

Another factor changing the way innovation works, explored in Chapter 6, is the evolving nature of risk and changing attitudes toward failure among the world's leading innovators. Simply put, the downside of globalization and Googlization is that individuals, firms, industries, and even entire economic systems the world over are now much more interconnected. As the recent financial melt-down revealed, that makes life riskier in ways that many people have yet to grasp fully. Leaders can build resilience into organiza-tions and countries by rethinking how to trade off benefits and risks in evaluating new policies, technologies, and methods. At the very personal level, each of us needs to embrace experimentation, calculated risk taking, and fast failure in our own lives, educational tracks, and career choices.

Greed: How to Win in the Age of Disruptive Innovation

It is fashionable, in this post-Enron and post-Lehman era, to decry the failings of rapacious capitalism. Capitalism is indeed flawed in important ways that are making it difficult to tackle the demographic, economic, and environmental challenges ahead. But the final section of the book argues that to rail against capitalism without acknowledging the power of markets, the profit motive, or Schumpeterian "creative destruction" is to miss the greatest opportunity to solve the world's problems.

The short-term obsessions of shareholder capitalism, for example, have led corporations in the past to ignore the opportunities for sustainable profitability to be had by investing in natural assets over the long term. Because the true or life-cycle costs of market activities, such as environmental or social costs, are typically not reflected by market prices or government policies, managers and entrepreneurs do not have sufficient incentive to favor clean energy technologies, say, or prevention-oriented medical treatments over costlier, less efficient, unsustainable alternatives.

Despite the prevailing antimarket sentiment, greed can be good—if, *and only if,* a more muscular government plays its proper role so that the playing field of capitalism is no longer rigged in favor of dirty industries, inefficient markets, and short-term payouts. Market forces and profit are powerful incentives for change, after all. Rather than wish them away or demonize them, we need to harness them and redirect the creative energies of entrepreneurs and corporations to take on—and profit from solving—the world's wicked problems.*

The greatest fallacy in innovation circles is the notion that innovation is a zero-sum game. But China's rise does not have to come at the expense of the West, just as Japan's peaceful rise several decades ago did not come at America's expense—despite widespread panic and gloom-mongering at the time. Chapter 7 explains what governments should and should not do to fix market failures, end perverse subsidies, and realign incentives in favor of sustainable capitalism.

How should bosses and aspiring bosses at established companies respond to the new global threats? History suggests that many such firms will be unable to adapt to new realities and therefore will bite the dust. But farsighted leaders and nimble workers can transform organizations—even ones that are many decades old and have tens of thousands of employees—if they figure out the new rules of innovation. Chapter 8 highlights the need for traditional industries to capitalize better on the intangible capital within their organizations by connecting it with the knowledge economy outside their firms.

There is a dramatic U-turn now getting under way in corporate boardrooms, moving them away from short-termism and dishonest accounting and toward that level playing field. Dynamic social entrepreneurs and "philanthrocapitalists" are now harnessing market forces in new ways to achieve social goals. Chapter 9 argues that what motivates idea generators in the new age of innovation is not mere profit: it is profit inspired by the passionate pursuit of purpose.

That is the foundation stone of the Ideas Economy and the path to inclusive growth, the new paradigm for sustainable economic development in the twenty-first century. The answers lie in the dynamic interplay of the three great forces that are turning the world you know on its ear: need, speed, and greed.

PART ONE

NEED:

Why Innovation Matters

1

Wicked Problems, Wiki Solutions

Are these the best of times or the worst of times? On one hand, today's grand global challenges, the consequence of unprecedented interdependence and resource guzzling, are daunting. But on the other hand, new ways of innovating promise robust solutions to such problems, solutions that may yet create the profitable industries of the future.

The advance of technology and the spread of globalization have helped improve the health of the world's population in numerous ways, ranging from the spread of HIV medicines and vaccines to the remote provision of care via telemedicine. Unfortunately, globalization and the march of development have also made it harder to tackle some global problems that experts thought they had gotten under control—such as pandemic superbugs that have the potential to wipe out much of humanity.

Bacterial superbugs are a good example of what economists call a tragedy of the commons. The problem arises

because a shared global resource (in this case, the effec-
tiveness of antibiotics) is being diminished selfishly or unwit-
tingly by some people to the detriment of all—including future
generations.

The classic problem of this sort is climate change. Most en-
vironmental problems, be that smog in the air or pollution in
waterways, are local and reversible. In time, as countries get
richer and as technologies improve, these problems are gener-
ally tackled successfully: the air in Los Angeles and London,
for example, is far cleaner than it was in the hazy 1970s, never
mind how filthy London's was back in Dickensian times. In con-
trast, carbon pollution does not automatically reverse itself the
richer a country or region gets. Worse yet, there are irreversible
triggers in the climate system that may be crossed off in coming
years, leaving mankind unable to return to a safe climate no
matter how great the willpower or how deep the pockets of
future generations.

Getting a handle on such global public goods, which often
fall between the cracks of national regulations and an imperfect
system of global governance, promises to be one of the grand
challenges of this new century. This chapter sounds the alarm
bell about such scourges, examining in particular the threat of
deadly pandemics, but it also brings good news from the front
lines of many such battles. Bottom-up approaches, building
on democratic technologies such as the Internet and mobile
phones, offer hope that the world may yet overcome pervasive
market and government failures in dealing with such challenges.

Can you change the world by changing your underwear? That
is what Jeff Denby believes. A lanky young man with a fashionably
disheveled look and little money in his pockets, he hardly seems

like a revolutionary. But he is armed with a few things more important than money alone in today's innovation-driven world: passion,
purpose, and a provocative idea.

While getting his MBA at the University of California at Berkeley, he realized that there was one essential industry that was just
crying out for fresh thinking. He observed that the underwear business, a billion-dollar enterprise, is dominated by two types of firms:
those that peddle cheap commodity briefs (think store-brand tighty-
whities) and those that market underwear using fantasy hunks and
babes (think Calvin Klein and Victoria's Secret).

Denby and Jason Kibbey, a fellow MBA from Berkeley, realized
that there was a huge market opening. Informal polling and their
intuition suggested that many people wanted underwear that was
nicer than plain-vanilla briefs, but were nevertheless deeply un-
happy that their only high-quality choice was underwear marketed
with a frat-boy mentality. So they came up with the idea of socially
responsible underwear and founded a company called PACT.

The firm's philosophy of ethical business starts with the sourc-
ing of its raw materials. Denby spent months researching the entire
supply chain for undergarments. He settled on a supplier in Turkey
who uses only cotton that is certified to be organic and who pays
workers a living wage. In addition to the product being ethically
produced, PACT also donates 10 percent of the profits of every sale
to charity. The most striking aspect of the firm's business plan is its
marketing approach. The firm sells its products using not images
of waifs but pictures of real people (including Berkeley graduate
students) with realistic bodies wearing its stylish underwear.

The start-up's novel approach so appealed to Yves Behar, a de-
signer who runs a hip consultancy known as *fuse*project, that he
agreed to invest in the firm and to design its products. Noting that
he has won numerous honors from design societies, the *New York*

Times recently raved that Behar "has helped create some of the most memorable designs of recent years." He has worked for firms ranging from Herman Miller to BMW to GE, but he is best known for designing the rugged little computers distributed by the One Laptop per Child program—a charitable effort that distributes extremely cheap computers for use in schools in the developing world.

Now Behar's team is coming up with a variety of novel and ever-changing designs for PACT. He explains that by bringing together sustainability and great design, the firm has been able to create an entirely new reason for people to purchase and wear a product that goes beyond traditional marketing. "Advertising," he insists, "is the price companies pay for being unoriginal." Each design (his firm comes up with new ones every six weeks) is associated with a different charity that benefits from its sales. One style of underwear benefits the green charity started by Wangari Maathai, the Kenyan Nobel Peace Prize winner, for example, while another supports Oceania, a nonprofit that works to conserve marine ecosystems. Other designs support literacy projects, endangered forests, and so heartwarmingly on.

Unlike multinational clothing giants with rigid supply chains, the firm's nimble manufacturing platform is able to make small batches of underwear in those unique patterns. That allows it, like the Swiss watchmaker Swatch, to change its designs frequently. Denby hopes that this encourages customers to change their underwear just as frequently, improving the world a little bit as they do so.

Sustainable underwear may seem trivial in the grander scheme of things, but in fact the PACT story gives a glimpse into the way that the new tools and rules of innovation promise to tackle the world's grand problems. Globalization and Googlization are essential enablers, of course, as Denby would not be able to manage his foreign supply chain and market his wares globally from California without them. However, the essence of this firm's strategy is to persuade customers that its purpose is worth supporting. That purpose, as demonstrated by the firm's embrace of sustainable agriculture and its no-sweatshops policy, is the improvement of the planet and respect for people everywhere. People plus planet means purpose, the firm is betting, and they hope this will translate into profits too.

Greed for Good

The rise of social entrepreneurs like Denby, a theme explored in full in the final chapter of the book, is but one facet of the ongoing innovation revolution. However, any celebration must be tempered by the fact that humanity is also entering a period of dramatic global challenges. The world economy is undergoing unprecedented changes due to several powerful trends that are amplifying the disruptive impact of 24/7 global connectivity and rapid technological change.

One such trend is the transformation of humans into a primarily urban species. For the first time in human history, more than half of mankind lives in urban areas. Within a few decades, that figure will approach three-quarters of the global population. Most of these people will live in the sprawling megacities of the developing world, not just the familiar Shanghais and São Paulos but the dozens of other less well-known cities in China with a population already bigger than Philadelphia's.

Mass urbanization will both demand faster and deeper innovation and provide the means for getting it. It will demand innovation because crowding ever more people into megacities will strain urban infrastructure, political systems, and civility to the breaking point. That requires imaginative responses. Happily, this migration promises to spark many new waves of innovation, as cities have long proved essential crucibles of creativity. Geoffrey West of the Santa Fe Institute has found that the average city slicker is three times as creative as the average country bumpkin. He also found that the creative output of a city scales nonlinearly. A city that is 50 times the size of a village nearby is, on the average, 130 times as innovative on such measures as creative output, research budgets, inventions, and so on.

Another of the big trends demanding a global innovation response is the rise of China, India, and other giant economies of the emerging world. The striking economic gains posted by the BRIC economies and their less-famous emerging brethren are surely to be applauded, for two reasons. Within one generation, more than a billion people have been lifted out of the most grinding poverty imaginable into lives of relative comfort. That is something unprecedented in human history. More amazingly, the rise of those economies raises the tantalizing prospect of eradicating of global poverty within the lifetimes of those born today. And the rapid rise of the middle classes in those countries could prove the salvation of companies in stagnant or slow-growing economies of the developed world.

But again, that silvery cloud comes with a dark lining. The economic growth in these developing economies is guzzling precious resources such as oil and commodities, raising concerns about food scarcity and greatly fueling global warming and local environmental crises. If this astonishing demographic and geographic transformation happens on business-as-usual trends—if development follows the worst examples from the rich world (think

American-style exurban sprawl)—this is an ecological and human tragedy waiting to happen. That is because public policies, technologies, and markets are not organized to deal with the kind of stress that is about to be put on the world's essential infrastructure, ecosystems, and resource base.

The most difficult aspect of the resource puzzle is that many different pieces of the puzzle actually fit together in ways that make simple, siloed solutions irrelevant. Energy issues could be more easily solved, for example, if many forms of energy conversion did not consume and pollute huge amounts of water. Water scarcity could be dealt with by desalination, but the equipment for removing salt from seawater uses enormous amounts of energy. Lack of fresh water and freakish droughts (aggravated by climate change) are a big reason food prices are up—but in turn, most of the world's fresh water is consumed in highly inefficient fashion by the agricultural sector, not by heavy industry or thirsty urban households. The World Economic Forum has dubbed this the "water-energy-food-climate nexus" and has set up a high-level group of experts, government leaders, and corporate bosses to come up with possible solutions. One of those heavyweights is Indra Nooyi, the chairman of Pepsi, and she argues that "the only way to measurably and sustainably improve this dire situation is through broad-scale collaborative efforts between governments, industry, academia, and other stakeholders around the world."

These grand global challenges certainly add up to a mighty headwind for the global economy, but Nooyi is right to suggest that these challenges can be overcome if creative and collaborative solutions are advanced to identify and reward innovations that tackle society's big problems. This distinction matters, because innovation is not always a good thing. For example, a lot of technological invention is directed at coming up with gadgets and gizmos of negligible business or social value. And the drug lords and mafias of the world are often highly entrepreneurial, but their business-model innovations are hardly to be applauded.

William Baumol, a distinguished economist at New York University's Stern School of Business, has spent a lifetime studying this topic. He argues that, without innovative entrepreneurship, the growth miracle of the last two centuries would not have happened—but he hastens to add that entrepreneurial activities are not always productive and growth-enhancing. In fact, across almost all of history, most such efforts were directed at redistribution rather than at producing new wealth: aggressive warfare, larceny, bribery, and rent-seeking litigation, among many others. Autocracy, the absence of the rule of law, and prevailing cultural norms allowed elites and free riders to capture most of the gains produced by innovative entrepreneurship throughout history. But starting at some point before the industrial revolution, most notably in Florence and Antwerp, attitudes and institutional arrangements changed so that productive capitalism—which enhances the general welfare, even as it enriches the individual entrepreneur—rather than rent-seeking and deviant entrepreneurship came to be prized and rewarded. That as much as anything explains the transition from millennia of stagnation, disempowerment, and oppression to the economic dynamism, social mobility, and democratic advances seen in the last few centuries.

Now it is time to double down on that tried-and-true pathway to growth by using the tools of innovation to turn the world's grand challenges into this century's greatest economic opportunities. The key is for society to find ways to reward socially useful innovation. That is not to say that the inventor of the next Pet Rock or erection pill should not be handsomely rewarded: if such inventions satisfy unmet consumer needs, they do represent value-creating innovations and therefore deserve market success. But plenty of other unmet human needs also require urgent attention, ranging from fresh water and affordable food to protection from climate change and pandemics. Unfortunately, the free market does not currently provide adequate returns for innovators who work on such difficult problems.

That argues for a rethink of public policies, which need to roll in the externalities of such actions as burning fossil fuels through carbon pricing and other mechanisms that will reward investments in clean energy. It argues for corporations to think beyond quarterly results to creating long-term value, which can be done only if the true social and environmental impacts of business are taken into account. And it calls for individuals to be more mindful of their consumer choices, which can have unintended ripple effects across the global supply chain. If the growth to come in this century follows such a thoughtful path, one that is mindful of ecosystem impact and human health concerns, one that leads with innovation rather than blundering and blustering ahead with business as usual, then the current challenge turns into an extraordinary opportunity for economic growth and human advancement.

For that to happen requires a radical rethink of why and how to innovate. Today's understandable concerns about managing security and fixing finance must be seen through that prism. The world has spent the first decade of this new century fighting conventional battles, looking in the rearview mirror. The two grand global challenges taken on thus far are terrorism after 9/11 and the financial crisis after the collapse of Lehman Brothers. These are necessary battles, of course, and at the moment they seem to be the most important ones imaginable. But they are not, in fact, new ones: political terrorism has been around for more than a millennium, and capitalism has always gone hand in hand with global financial crises—just think of the South Seas bubble and tulip mania of yore.

Look from the perspective of the children born today, and it becomes clear that terrorism and financial panic are not the most difficult of the global challenges. Seen from the vantage point of 2050 or 2100, the big challenge for current generations is the handling of the unprecedented demographic, economic, and environmental transformation that is happening on this watch.

Larry Brilliant is a big believer in innovation. He should be, given the fact that he is a medical doctor who used a powerful vaccine to help eradicate smallpox in India. He later started Google's philanthropic division, known as Google.org, and now runs the Skoll Global Threats Fund (started with money from Jeff Skoll, the cofounder of eBay). His career progression telegraphs his view of the world. He is very concerned today about the prospects of interlinked global challenges that he considers catastrophic risks. "We live in an uncertain, complex age," he says, "and the problems of water scarcity, climate change, and pandemics all have the same root cause: too many people living unconsciously." He believes global governance must change to acknowledge the growing number of existential threats. In early 2011, that view received an endorsement from a surprising quarter: China, the aspiring global innovation champion. Zhou Shengxian, the country's environment minister, declared that "in China's thousands of years of civilization, the conflict between mankind and nature has never been as serious as it is today."

That juxtaposition of a new golden age for innovation with wicked global problems again raises that important question: are these the best of times or the worst of times? One could argue that the question itself is irrelevant; it's always a bit of both. Perhaps, but occasionally humanity also reaches inflection points in history when the decisions people make, as individuals and together as societies, propel the species decisively in one direction or another. This is one of those inflection points.

There have been occasional periods of history when peace and progress brought tremendous prosperity (think Pax Romana and the Victorian age of invention) or when death and destruction doomed unfortunates to lives of grinding misery (as during the Dark Ages and the Great War). The world is approaching such a crossroads today. The decisions made in the next decade about how to live, the direction economies will take, how resource-intensive development will be, and whether society will do more to reward socially useful innovation will have profound, planet-altering consequences that will last a century or more.

There is now a great race under way between the forces of development and those of degradation. The fate of people and the planet hangs in the balance, and the outcome is not preordained. Even so, mankind can tip the scales in favor of a positive outcome—if the pace of global innovation is accelerated. How to do that, exactly? Part of the answer lies in better-coordinated, scaled-up, and patient efforts at innovation at the global level.

Investing in the Global Commons

John Kao is one of the world's leading innovation gurus. He is sunny by disposition, and quick with a smile and a warm anecdote. He has been known to bring down the house at corporate meetings by belting out a couple of jazzy numbers on the piano (he toured with Frank Zappa in younger days). Indeed, his breakthrough book is called *Jamming*, and it compares the art of innovation with the controlled chaos involved in making great jazz music. He is not so cheerful anymore. He is convinced that the core dilemma today is that more and more people are competing over the world's resources, so mankind has to find innovative ways to make more from less. Doing this will require "an unprecedented marshalling of intellectual energy and of innovation capacity."

What the world needs, he argues, is a new operating model of innovation itself—what he calls large-scale innovation. He argues, intriguingly, that individual and corporate efforts are no longer enough. Dealing with the world's wicked problems will require societies themselves to become engines of innovation. Rather than putting out fires when they flare up, he says, countries must organize themselves to innovate at scale so as to build resilience, prevent meltdowns, and invest in nurturing the industries of the future. He points to Finland's evolution from a focus on mobile telephony to health and wellness services as one example. Another is Singapore's thoughtful and multipronged strategy for dealing with water scarcity. Kao's Institute of Large Scale Innovation, which counts policy makers and official advisors from several dozen countries around the world as members, spreads such best practices in the belief that "a global vision of innovation . . . may be how we save our increasingly crowded, fragile and interdependent planet."

Bill Gates is also convinced that the world's wicked problems require bold new approaches. He is doing his part by using the heft and resources of his Gates Foundation to stimulate global-scale innovation. For example, the charity's Grand Challenges program awards cash prizes and publicity to clever thinkers anywhere who can come up with novel solutions to the problems it is trying to tackle. He is convinced that society greatly underinvests in innovation, and he wants to see greater outlays on education, research and development, and other bits of societal infrastructure that boost innovative capacity. He also thinks private sector investors need to take a longer-term view if they are to fund the breakthrough technologies and industries of the future. He points approvingly at the strategies undertaken by two novel investment outfits, Intellectual Ventures and Khosla Ventures, as models for how the private sector can help scale solutions to those wicked problems.

"On the face of it, why should the Gates Foundation bother with us?" asks Edward Jung rhetorically. "They have access to the best minds and technology already." Yet, he insists, his firm is needed by outfits such as the foundations that are seeking fresh ideas to deal with incredibly difficult challenges, including the eradication of malaria or polio. Jung is a cofounder of Intellectual Ventures, an outfit that is an odd mix of investment fund, technology developer, and (by Jung's own admission) patent troll. Because the firm has a very long view on its investments—he says twenty years is the shortest investment window his fund considers—it has the patience to invest in complex technologies in fields such as low-carbon energy (it is funding the development of radically different nuclear plants) and public health (it has come up with lasers to zap malarial mosquitoes) that take time to mature.

The firm gained notoriety when the book *SuperFreakonomics* made much of its radical geoengineering approaches to dealing with climate change, which many environmentalists took to mean it was not serious about dealing with the causes of global warming on the ground. But Jung insists the authors of that book picked just the most eye-catching of the many alternatives his firm is working on in this area. He explains that because the firm is not a peddler of any given technology, unlike multinational engineering giants, it has the freedom to develop a variety of possible solutions based on a set of scenarios. Most efforts at taking on wicked problems fail, so Jung believes such problems require a patient portfolio approach that builds in failure as part of the business model: "Unlike a venture capital fund, who takes ten shots a year, we take hundreds a year . . . but our wide portfolio means we don't have to pick which technology and application will come first." The firm is willing to make less money by taking less risk in the aggregate, and in doing so is paving the way for many others who will profit handsomely from taking the technologies it nurtures to market.

One of those who intends to profit by saving the world is Vinod Khosla. "I have a religious belief in the power of ideas propelled by entrepreneurial energy," he declares. Coming from some businessmen, such talk might sound self-serving or plain nutty. But Khosla helped to found Sun Microsystems, a company that pioneered such essential bits of Internet technology as network servers and Java, a programming language. He then made his name and his fortune as a partner at Kleiner Perkins, a Silicon Valley venture capital firm famous for its early investments in AOL, Amazon, Compaq, and Google.

His eyes have turned toward a new target, the oil industry, and he is now busy plowing his billions into esoteric clean-energy technologies. Why is Khosla taking on this particular crusade when he could concentrate on the technology investments that have served him so well, or even opt for a gilded retirement? Like many very rich men, he now wants to improve the world: "Just starting another Sun doesn't do it for me anymore." As an engineer turned venture capitalist, Khosla has a healthy respect for the power of new technologies to create disruptive innovations. And the free marketeer in him clearly relishes the prospect of really taking on the big, rich, and well-entrenched firms that dominate the oil industry.

Another part of the explanation lies in his complex relationship with India. Like several of Silicon Valley's most successful people, Khosla boasts a degree from the Indian Institute of Technology. When he tried to start a project to help the mother country, he was initially frustrated by its bureaucracy and corruption. His first attempt to start a traditional top-down charity failed, so he now funds only charities embracing microenterprise approaches. A lesson he learned from India, he says, is that one has to think big: "Unless you influence the lives of at least a million people, it simply doesn't matter."

His plan is to use technology and entrepreneurship to tackle big social and environmental problems at scale. "In venture capital, we fail far more often than we succeed," he says. "I've decided that I'd better focus on taking on problems that really matter, so that when I win, it makes a difference to the world." He has developed an investment strategy that pours pots of resources into high-risk but potentially game-changing energy technologies—what he calls black swans—in hopes that one or two of these neglected ideas may one day save the planet. He pooh-poohs fashionable areas of green investment such as hybrid cars and photovoltaic cells as mere greenwashing, choosing instead to put his money into radical technologies that can transform huge markets such as engines, lighting, cement, water, and buildings. He insists that any such technology, when scaled, must pass what he calls the "Chindia test": prices must be low enough to be attractive in China and India.

Tackling the grand, and thus far, mostly ignored challenges of the twenty-first century—what some have called the most wicked of the current problems—will require better tools, smarter approaches, and, most important, much more *ambition*. Given that these are global problems, it only makes sense that part of the solution lies in better global coordination, pushing for worldwide economies of scale, and taking the very long view. However, top-down solutions will simply not be enough, no matter how clever or benevolent the visionary behind them.

In fact, tackling the twenty-first century's most difficult problems will require a completely different approach that also taps into the wisdom of crowds and uses bottom-up innovation. If you doubt it, consider the threat posed to humanity by just one of these wicked problems: pandemic disease.

Beware the Superbug

"There is simply no greater threat to humanity than a viral pandemic," declares Nathan Wolfe. Though he is young and dashing—the *New Yorker* declared his demeanor to be "a cross between a pirate and a graduate student"—Wolfe is no armchair alarmist. He is one of the world's leading virologists, fighting on the front lines to save the world from the next deadly wave of HIV, SARS, or influenza. From the Mekong delta to the strife-torn jungles of the Congo, he and his team are building a global "viral surveillance" network that he hopes will monitor the tropical hot spots that have in the past produced such deadly viruses so that investigators can nip them in the bud.

Monitoring the blood of bush-meat hunters in Africa and chicken farmers in China may seem an esoteric or academic exercise to those sitting in comfortable homes in faraway places such as New York or London. In fact, it's not. Because of the astonishing growth of globalization, air travel and container shipping now connect each corner of the world to every other. The rapid advance of urbanization and deforestation is whittling away the last of the truly wild places on earth, which have always been the greatest source of disruptive and deadly new human viruses such as HIV.

Gabriel Leung knows this all too well. Leung is one of Asia's leading experts on infectious diseases and even served for a time as the Hong Kong government official in charge of pandemic preparedness. That city is especially important to the rest of the world for two reasons. First, it is close to the Pearl River delta, one of a handful of viral hot spots that, thanks to close contact between humans and wild animals, are sources of many potential viral threats. Second, Hong Kong is a major hub for air travel, so a deadly bug that passes undetected by the city's health officials could quickly travel around the world and cause a potential pandemic, as SARS did a few years ago. "We are the world's sentinel for pandemics," Leung says.

It is no longer implausible that a new virus would leap from a remote farm in rural China to the "wet markets" outside Hong Kong and onto an international jetliner bound for Europe or North America. That sort of leapfrog is exactly what happened when SARS appeared out of nowhere in Asia and within weeks shut down large parts of the Canadian economy. So big was the economic blow that the Rolling Stones even headlined a huge benefit concert in 2003 for Toronto that attracted some half a million people. Such a leap is probably what happened in 2009 with the appearance of the H1N1 flu that surfaced in Mexico but which turned into a global pandemic. The virulence of that particular viral cocktail was not as deadly as it could have been. But the world almost certainly dodged a bullet with H1N1, given the global lack of preparedness, and next time things may not go so well.

Africa is the hot spot for blood-borne diseases, but the hot spots for respiratory killers such as SARS and H1N1 include China and Southeast Asia. To take just one example, globalization, rising prosperity, and increased meat consumption mean that the number of chickens raised for food has increased manyfold in the past few decades. The problem is that in parts of this region, humans and animals live so close together that an exchange of viruses (called "viral chatter") is almost inevitable.

Adding to this deadly formula are the side effects of rapid economic growth. As reckless development leads to depleted aquifers and diminished agricultural yields, farmers chop down ever more trees. But those trees used to serve as essential buffers between mankind and the zoonoses, as scientists call diseases that jump from animals—bats, monkeys, wild cats—to humans. The rising temperatures and ecosystem changes that are coming with climate change are driving wild animals closer to human settlements too, exacerbating the problem.

In short, the world is now entering a dangerous new age of pandemic diseases. Zoonoses are on the rise in the world's hot spots. These already account for the lion's share of all new infection threats. Some of these are familiar already—West Nile virus, Ebola, SARS, H1N1. But the really scary part of this tale is that these are but the tip of the iceberg. There may be a million or more viruses waiting to be discovered in Africa alone, and the world may well see the sudden emergence of a new such virus with deadly global pandemic potential each and every year this century. In *The Viral Storm*, Wolfe argues that "the historical approaches to dealing with pandemics—wait and see followed by a rush to diagnostic and vaccine development—will not be sufficient and will fail as they have with HIV." What is needed, he argues, "are radical new approaches and a paradigm shift away from response and toward pandemic prevention."

Fleming's Prescient Warning

If that's not scary enough, consider the threat posed by superbugs of the bacterial, not viral, variety. These are on the rise because many antibiotics—which, along with vaccines, are probably the technological innovations that have saved the most lives in human history—are losing their effectiveness. Alexander Fleming, who helped discover antibiotics, issued this stark warning during his Nobel Prize acceptance speech in 1945: "There is the danger that the ignorant man may easily underdose himself and by exposing his microbes to nonlethal quantities of the drug make them resistant."

Today, antibiotic resistance is a costly and dangerous problem. Yet those who misuse these wonder drugs mostly do not pay the cost. Patients pressure their doctors to give them pointless antibiotics for viral infections such as colds or the flu, and courses are often left unfinished. In some parts of the world, antibiotics can be bought without a prescription. Analyzing official figures from the Food and Drug Administration, Louise Slaughter, an American congresswoman who is a microbiologist by training, calculates that four-fifths of the antibiotics used in the United States are given to livestock—often to get perfectly healthy animals to grow faster.

Antibiotic resistance causes longer and more serious illnesses, lengthens stays in hospitals, and complicates treatments. Occasionally, people have died when they need not have. Today, resistant bacteria mostly threaten children, the elderly, cancer patients, and the chronically ill. However, the reason to worry is that this is likely to be a harbinger of worse things to come. Each year there are nearly 450,000 new cases of tuberculosis that is resistant to multiple drugs, causing at least 150,000 deaths. More than a quarter of new cases of TB identified recently in parts of Russia were of this troublesome variety.

Added up, the costs are enormous. In the United States alone, the Alliance for the Prudent Use of Antibiotics, a nonprofit group, calculates that resistance to antibiotics causes $17 billion to $26 billion per year in additional costs to the health care system. In one study, a random sample of 1,400 patients at an American teaching hospital found such resistance in 188 people; twelve additional deaths resulted.

The problem, however, is a global one, and there is another, less obvious cost. In many poor countries, the cost of drugs gobbles up half or more of the total health budget. As resistance grows, points out a task force organized by the Center for Global Development, patients are forced to turn from failed front-line therapies to second-line drugs. These are scarcer and much more expensive. For the cost of treating just one patient with extensively drug-resistant TB, a hospital could treat two hundred with the ordinary variety of TB. So the burden is in the form of greater ill health for the poor and higher health care costs for the rich as proven therapies fail and new superbugs—that is, drug-resistant strains of bacteria—take off.

Some skeptics argue that the global rise in drug resistance, while a problem for those with weakened immune systems, is not a problem for healthy adults. A related argument maintains that overuse of antibiotics does not necessarily lead to an increase in resistance. Herman Goossens, a prominent microbiologist at the University of Antwerp, vigorously disagrees. He conducted a double-blind, placebo-controlled trial, the results of which were published in the respected medical journal *Lancet*, which debunked both arguments. His team divided healthy volunteers into three groups and randomly gave them either azithromycin or clarithromycin, two common antibiotics, or a placebo. Researchers then checked the streptococcus bacteria that naturally reside in throats.

What they found proved what doctors and researchers had claimed for many years. The patients taking the placebo had no drug-resistant strains of streptococcus, but within days those on either antibiotic suddenly had streptococcus with sharply elevated levels of resistance to those same two antibiotics. Goossens explains that exposing healthy patients to antibiotics leads to nonresistant bacteria acquiring the genes that provide resistance. In his view, the fact that the streptococci retained this resistance for over a year, during which period they replicated many times over, challenges the theory that bacteria do not want to be drug resistant. "This argument is no longer valid in real life, as some bacteria do get resistance and we have shown they are fit—indeed, the bugs select for resistance fast and stay fit for over a year."

No surprise, then, that new superbugs are now emerging at a steady pace, and the media are noticing. At the end of 2010, a genetic mutation, NDM-1 (quickly dubbed the "New Delhi superbug"), was identified in India. This new bacterial strain led to panic because it was resistant even to powerful antibiotics often used as treatments of last resort. Resistance was found to be able to transfer between different species of bacteria. The immediate backlash in the British media held that Indian hospitals were to blame, and even credentialed experts argued that British "health tourists" should think twice about getting cheap surgeries done in India. But Srinath Reddy, head of the Public Health Foundation of India, offered this chilling observation about NDM-1: "Antibiotic resistance is a global problem, there's no need to finger-point India . . . thanks to international travel, we now have a virtually inexhaustible supply of human hosts so they can easily mutate into more virulent forms."

Alarmed by the crisis at hand, the World Health Organization declared that the annual World Health Day for 2011, celebrated on April 7, be devoted to the topic of antimicrobial resistance. "No action today, no cure tomorrow" was the motto. And to be fair, there has been some action of late. The Infectious Diseases Society of America has issued its 10 × '20 Initiative, which calls for the development of ten new antibiotics by 2020. A transatlantic task force has been formed to look into this problem. Bills were also introduced in the U.S. Congress that would address some parts of the puzzle, such as curbing the use of antibiotics in healthy livestock (to get them to grow faster).

However, these efforts miss the point, argues Ramanan Laxminarayan of Princeton University and the Center for Disease Dynamics, Economics and Policy, a think tank. He was an early advocate of thinking about drug resistance as a global-commons problem. For one thing, simply paying for new antibiotics is an expensive proposition that does not ensure they will be managed effectively in the future. Also, he argues they fail to deal comprehensively with the incentives that lead to overuse of this global shared resource—antibiotics effectiveness—on both the demand and supply sides of the equation.

First, to demand. According to an opinion piece published in 2010 in the *Journal of the American Medical Association*, as much as 50 percent of antibiotic use is unnecessary or inappropriate. Overuse, misuse, improper dosing, and the use of substandard or diluted medicines all contribute to the rise of resistance. But so too do weak health systems and governance: unless a strict code of practice forbids overuse and systems are in place to monitor behavior, doctors have every incentive to treat the patient in front of them rather than worry about the theoretical patient a decade hence who may suffer from the consequences of antibiotics overuse.

Many Bugs, Few Drugs

The supply side of the equation is equally gloomy, as the pipeline is drying up. From 1983 to 1987, sixteen new antibiotics won approval from the U.S. Food and Drug Administration (FDA). From

2003 to 2007, only five won approval. Pharmaceutical firms have not come up with a new first-line TB drug in many years. Penicillin, still considered something of a miracle drug, is now much less useful than it used to be thanks to the rapid growth of resistance. That frightens Barry Bloom, a former dean of the Harvard School of Public Health, who sighs, "I can't even imagine what we'll do if we lose penicillin."

Why did the industry hit such a dry spell? Kim Lewis of Northeastern University argues that the pharmaceutical industry "overmined" this resource during the golden era of antibiotics half a century ago. Having picked the low-hanging fruit, goes the argument, the science has simply gotten harder.

Ah, but even if the science has gotten harder, surely scientific progress over the past few decades has helped? The drug industry did pour hefty sums into applying genomics, proteomics, and high-throughput screening to this problem. Alas, it did not work. Despite spending millions of pounds on this effort, argued David Payne of GlaxoSmithKline, a British pharmaceutical giant, in a striking paper he coauthored a few years ago, his firm and others came up empty-handed: "It was clearly very hard to find targets, so we stopped." Other drug research chiefs share his frustration. Mark Fishman of Novartis, a Swiss rival, met with similar frustration at the lack of big breakthroughs in genomics. So now, he says, "we've gone back to the brute-force method of screening millions of candidates that kill a bug—and then evaluating them for safety in humans."

There are signs that the pipeline crunch at Big Pharma may be worsening, but some biotechnology firms are coming up with novel approaches. Theravance, an American company, has come up with an antibiotic that treats skin infections, including some caused by MRSA—an especially nasty type of bacteria that is resistant to many antibiotics. Cubist, another American biotech, took a chance on a new antibiotic that also targets MRSA. The drug, derived from a compound found at the base of Mount Ararat in Turkey, had serious side effects, so it was discarded by Eli Lilly, a big pharmaceutical firm. Cubist worked out how to adjust its dosing so that it no longer causes permanent muscle damage, and now the antibiotic is a commercial success.

"We want to regreen the tree from the golden era of antibiotics research!" exclaims Andrew Myers, a Harvard chemist whose ideas are being developed by Tetraphase, a biotechnology firm. Tetracyclines are a class of antibiotics that have been around for decades. However, research into this area slowed down and few new drugs were approved in this class in the past thirty years. But a dozen years of research led Myers to a novel way to synthesize new drugs in this class—a process that Tetraphase is now hoping to commercialize. He is convinced that such scrutiny of other existing classes of antibiotics may also lead to similar breakthroughs.

Kim Lewis of Northeastern is working on radically different approaches. For example, bacteria are typically grown in a petri dish. Only 1 percent of the microorganisms collected from the natural environment can actually be cultured in the laboratory—a precondition to developing useful new drugs from them. Lewis's research, published in *Chemistry and Biology,* fingers a culprit. His team found that the bacteria in question lack siderophores, compounds that bind iron for them, so the microorganisms fail to grow in the petri dish despite swimming in nutrients. He thinks there are many more growth factors for previously uncultured bacteria. If he is right, it may open up a new way to discover antibiotics. "This will give us tools to access biodiversity that have been hidden from us," he thinks.

Roger Pomerantz of Merck, another giant American pharmaceutical firm, vows that his company is committed to research in this area for the long haul. And it is not after just incremental improvements, as "we are looking for clear major leaps," he insists. Pushed on the matter, though, he concedes it will not be easy: "As this area matures, it gets harder to hit the innovation threshold, as we are victims of our own success."

A Tragedy of the Commons

The sad truth is that this industry is a victim of misaligned economic incentives that make it hard for private sector firms to justify plowing billions into long-term research in this area, even though it is very clearly in the interests of society for such work to be done— and done now. For example, even if a company comes up with a great new anti-infective, such a drug will likely earn it far less than remedies for chronic diseases or even those for mundane problems such as erectile dysfunction. That is because a good antibiotic works in a week to two weeks and may never be needed again; it is therefore far less profitable than, say, a statin that must be taken every day for years on end. Many government-run health systems unfairly reward anticancer and central nervous system drugs more handsomely than antibiotics, even though the latter offer more bang for the buck in terms of reducing mortality and morbidity.

That is why it is probably too much to expect the pharmaceutical industry alone to solve this problem, says Ramanan Laxminarayan, given the legion of market and regulatory failures involved in this global resource problem. That argues both for bigger carrots, in the form of financial incentives for the development and use of both new antibiotics and companion rapid-diagnosis systems (it is suspected that only a tenth of TB cases globally are diagnosed properly and in a timely fashion), and for bigger sticks in the shape of treatment and dispensation guidelines for doctors and pharmacists. It also suggests that novel forms of open innovation, be they Web-based collaborations between academia and pharmaceutical firms or public-private partnerships, may be necessary to shoulder the developmental risk involved in such long-term research.

Bottom-up approaches are attractive for another reason. Even coming up with breakthroughs in antibiotics would be akin to wasting precious water by pouring it into a leaky bucket. Tackling this problem requires fixing the bucket by dealing with the demand side of the equation.

Reining in overuse, misuse, and abuse will be difficult and will require concerted action by governments, companies, and health care providers. Well-meaning aid agencies and charities dispensing drugs freely in poor countries should ask themselves whether the necessary safeguards and patient education are in place for proper use of powerful drugs. Governments in some countries, such as China, that link financial reimbursement for doctors and hospitals with the amount of drugs dispensed must abolish that perverse practice.

Regulators must do better in their monitoring and public health surveillance, so that counterfeit or substandard drugs (containing less than the proper dose of active ingredients, for example) do not get to unwitting patients. Companies that hope to profit from antibiotics can do more to encourage the development of rapid and portable diagnostics—a mushrooming field—so that their pills are popped only when they will actually help the patient.

Ultimately, it is the doctor-patient relationship that is paramount. Because both doctor and patient have a legitimate self-interest in curing the crisis apparent today, not the one that may come tomorrow due to growing drug resistance, both have incentives to overuse antibiotics. Medical associations can put in place more rigorous training and drug dispensation protocols that, for example, insist that doctors follow up with patients to make sure they have completed their entire course of antibiotics.

All of the top-down solutions will come to naught, however, if patients continue to abuse these drugs. In the end, solving this problem probably requires the ordinary person to behave just a bit less selfishly. In this, the superbugs problem is much like climate change and other tragedies of the commons: the greatest hope may be offered by bottom-up solutions that start with individual responsibility and are enriched by top-down coordination and democratic technology.

The Perfect Storm

The good news on the antivirus front is that pioneers are starting to answer this call to arms. To see how, travel with Nathan Wolfe to Cameroon, where his Global Viral Forecasting Initiative has set up a world-class virus-monitoring center. His team ventures into the deep jungle, setting up networks of relationships with people who hunt bush meat (such forbidden wild animals as gorilla and chimp), as they are most prone to the viral chatter between species that leads to zoonoses. They take blood specimens from both the hunters and their game, run the samples through advanced gene-sequencing machines, and try to predict which deadly virus will be the next to make the jump into humans.

Now Wolfe wants to go further. He believes that a combination of mobile telephony and information technologies, deployed in a robust global surveillance system, can catch the next SARS or

HIV long before it turns into a global pandemic. The key, he says, is early detection and early response, based on information fed in from the grassroots.

One relatively new tool in the box is digital detection. Researchers at Google, MIT's Media Lab, IBM, and other outfits are applying sophisticated software tools to try to predict outbreaks of disease. For example, software can crawl the Web and look for press reports in many languages that point to the outbreak of an unusual disease. This is valuable, as countries suffering outbreaks of potential pandemics—China and Thailand are recent examples—typically are not eager to advertise this fact out of fear of hurting tourism or exports. Google has demonstrated how this technique was able to predict outbreaks of plain-vanilla seasonal flu in the United States a week or more before the government's Centers for Disease Control did.

Overcoming its initial skepticism, the public health establishment is now coming around to the use of such communications technologies in the quest to predict, prepare for, and possibly prevent the next great pandemic. John Brownstein of the Children's Hospital Boston and colleagues published a thoughtful endorsement of these technologies in the *New England Journal of Medicine* in 2009. They argued not only that the adoption by health officials of distributed communications technologies and Web-crawling software would be useful, but also that ultimately they "expect that patients' contributions to disease surveillance will increase. Eventually, mobile phone technology, enabled by global positioning systems and coupled with short-message-service messaging (texting) and 'micro-blogging' (with Twitter), might also come into play." Strikingly, the researchers concluded that "Internet-based systems are quickly becoming dominant sources of information on emerging diseases."

The catch is that while such "rumor registries" are useful, any leads must still be validated by boots on the ground—such as Wolfe's shock troops. Public health surveillance systems are increasingly using mobile phones and smart handheld devices for this task too. When Kenyan officials suspected in 2008 that Somali refugees might have brought polio into the country for the first time in twenty years, they alerted health workers in the area, who used their mobile phones to log patient symptoms, medications dispensed, and so on. By analyzing those data remotely, health officials in the capital were able to contain the outbreak.

Building on that success, Wolfe now wants to transform surveillance into a predictive tool rather than wait for signs of trouble. One technology he considers promising is the "lab on a chip." Researchers around the world are now rushing to develop portable, fast, and affordable ways of analyzing samples out in the field. At the moment, samples often need to be sent to distant laboratories for analysis, a process that can take days or longer. Wolfe thinks he will soon have a device that will identify an unknown bug by using advanced genetic analysis. Think of it as a crude form of tricorder, the handheld gizmo used on *Star Trek* to scan alien environments.

He also sees great potential in the mobile phone. When he visits remote parts of Congo not connected by road or electricity grid, he often finds that there is cellular service. Locals are able to use their mobile phones, recharging them at night using portable generators. His team is developing a software system to offer hunters an incentive (it might be a tiny financial payment, or perhaps some sort of nonmonetary reward) to send an SMS message letting him know when they are ill, which would provide a useful early warning. Health workers would then be sent to test the ailing hunter to see if there is cause for alarm.

Global health visionaries are now pondering a much more

interactive smart grid that can make sense of that hunter's initial warning. One possible technology is FrontlineSMS, a free application that allows health officials to analyze a huge flood of text messages without the need for central servers or Internet access. For a global surveillance system to be robust, though, it must provide the people closest to the trouble with the information and authority they need to act swiftly. There are now open-source applications such as Ushahidi (created by Kenyan activists during that country's recent political strife) that put together data from disparate mobile sources and combine them with maps and other data to be used by field workers to act on a warning. The Rockefeller Foundation, along with the United Nations Foundation and others, is now encouraging such mobile innovators to agree on best practices and common standards to allow the most promising ideas to spread easily, quickly, and widely.

That, in short, is how a band of brave and mostly unsung innovators is beginning to prepare humanity for dealing with one of the gravest risks of this new century. Dealing with such global threats will be difficult, as both governance and market failures need to be overcome, but it need not be impossible—especially if governments get help from the private sector. The next section of the book takes up that very question: how companies should respond to such threats and opportunities.

In the case of superbugs, as with other potential disasters, getting economic incentives right and deploying decentralized technologies will help. And the early successes suggest that while the world may indeed be getting riskier, today's innovation revolution means mankind need not enter such a future unarmed. As Wolfe puts it, "If the Internet is humanity's planetary nervous system, we are now building our planetary immune system."

2

Cheap and Cheerful

The dramatic rise of China, India, and other emerging-market powerhouses to date has been driven by cheap labor and low-cost manufacturing—but they are no longer content with being the world's workshops. These countries are rapidly moving up the value chain with indigenous and often ingenious approaches to innovation. The resourceful engineers of the East need to be taken seriously, for their frugal innovations are starting to leapfrog their firms to the top of the global heap.

Developing economies are fertile terrain for breakthrough innovation. Booming middle classes with disposable income and rising expectations are creating lucrative markets. Legions of fresh graduates in technical disciplines such as software engineering are providing the brainpower needed to design the future. Add to that the fact that most people in these countries still remember what it means to be poor—meaning firms must operate frugally, producing affordable goods while using fewer resources—and it produces the perfect conditions for creative, clever, and occasionally brilliant products and services.

This chapter shows why the rise of Asia's frugal innovators puts established firms in health care, energy, automotive, and other historically dominant but now troubled sectors of the rich world on notice. That is forcing these industries to look for fresh approaches to innovation in order to survive. Here's why this disruption could actually be good news for the middle class in the United States and other parts of the rich world.

Enter the principal cardiac operating room at Bangalore's Wockhardt Hospital early any given morning, and you are likely to find a patient lying on the operating table with a privacy screen hanging between his head and chest. During a recent visit, the table was occupied by a middle-aged Indian man whose serene look suggested that he was ready for the serious heart operation to come. Asked how he was, he smiled and answered in Kannada that he felt fine. It was only when his visitor stood on a stool to look over the screen did it become apparent that the patient's chest cavity was already cut wide open.

It turns out that while the patient was chatting away, Vivek Jawali and his team of surgeons had nearly completed the complex bypass operation. Because such "beating heart" surgery causes little pain and does not require general anesthesia or blood thinners, patients are on their feet much faster than normal for this procedure. This approach, pioneered by Wockhardt, has been so safe and successful that medical tourists now come to Bangalore from around the world.

This is but one example of India's extraordinary innovations in this sector. Private health entrepreneurs are now directing the country's rich technological and medical talents toward frugal engineering approaches that should make the rich world's bloated health systems envious. He is fêted today as a pioneer, but Jawali remembers how Western colleagues for years publicly ridiculed him for advocating his inventive surgical techniques.

He thinks that snub reflects an innate cultural advantage enjoyed by countries such as India. Unlike the hidebound health systems of the developed world, he says, "in our country's patient-centric health system, you must innovate." He makes clear that this does not mean the adoption of every fancy new piece of equipment. Over the years, he has rejected surgical robots and laparoscopic kits because the costs did not justify the supposed benefits. Instead, he has looked for tools and techniques that spare resources while improving outcomes.

Shivinder Singh, boss of Fortis, a rival Indian hospital chain based in New Delhi that has since acquired Wockhardt as part of a grand pan-Asian expansion strategy, provides more evidence that Western technology multinationals have forgotten the art of frugal engineering. The Duke-educated MBA observes that most of the expensive imaging machines made by such firms are only marginally better than older models. Meanwhile, vast markets for poorer hospitals go unserved. "We got out of this arms race a few years ago," he says. Fortis now promises its patients only that its scanners are "world-class," not necessarily the newest. He asks a sensible question: "Why can't these firms make more of less and less of more?"

He is not alone in thinking that the many medical centers and multinationals of the developed world are looking at innovation the wrong way. Paul Yock is head of the biodesign laboratory at Stanford University. He argues that in the past, medical technology giants such as Europe's Philips and the U.S. company Medtronic have "looked at need but been blind to cost." Given growing concerns everywhere about runaway inflation in health care costs, he insists, the business model that has so handsomely benefited

Medtronic and other Western med-tech firms "is not going to work any longer."

He is convinced the only way forward is to turn the industry's innovation process upside down. He teaches his graduate students to put cost effectiveness much earlier in the invention process. The key, he reckons, is *first* to identify a gap in the marketplace, rather than coming up with nifty technologies that must then go looking for a need. He finds inspiration in India. Convinced that the country's combination of technical talent and financial constraints will produce a world-class devices sector, he has recently extended Stanford's design program to the subcontinent.

Though generic drugs probably come to mind first when thinking of health innovation in India, the country's health system is actually bursting with many less familiar examples. Inventive firms are coming up with novel devices and information technologies, clever business models, and the integration of all these into radically different approaches to delivering affordable health care. The catalyst is the combination of a vast and poor population suffering from huge unmet health needs and a dynamic private health sector eyeing a huge market opportunity.

Leapfrogging to the Top

How did the also-rans of the corporate world become the new leaders of global management? The answer lies in leapfrogging. Unlike rivals in the industries of developed economies, companies in the developing world are often free of legacy. As Gary Hamel and C. K. Prahalad have written, "The most effective weapon new competitors possess is probably a clean sheet of paper. And . . .

an incumbent's greatest vulnerability is its belief in accepted practice." These burdensome legacy systems can range from antiquated infrastructure (such as the aging fleet of coal-fired power plants in the United States, which still provide over half of the country's grid electricity) to outmoded and inefficient management practices (such as some European medical device firms' insistence on gold-plating every new scanner and testing device).

Frugal engineering is about much more than just cost cutting. Prahalad, the management thinker most closely associated with this thesis, famously argued that there was a fortune at the bottom of the pyramid—but that in order to profit by selling to customers in the developing world, Western firms had to reinvent their business models from the bottom up. Trying to peddle the wares developed for rich markets without the frills will fail, he argued, because costs will still be much too high. Rather, companies need to start from scratch, figure out what the frugal consumer actually wants from a product or service, and strip away all of the extra costs ruthlessly. In one of his last writings before his untimely death in 2010, he argued that elegant frugality will come to trump conspicuous consumption even in rich countries. The recent recession made clear, he argued, that "affordability and sustainability, not premium pricing and abundance, should drive innovation today."

That is a lesson that third-world innovators have taken to heart. They are reinventing the entire value proposition of business today, from supply chains to talent management to product marketing and distribution. Many of these breakthroughs do not involve snazzy technologies or new patents, though: the advances are often incremental improvements in processes and products. However, because these firms started out by putting the needs of poor consumers first and building business models around them, they do much better than rich-world counterparts that have tried to rejigger Western business models to fit local conditions.

Better Business Models

If you want a motorcycle, go to Chongqing. Although this dusty central Chinese city of drab office buildings and perpetually gray skies is better known as the gateway to the enormous Three Gorges Dam, it is also the two-wheeler capital of the world. Led by the region's pioneers, China now makes half the world's motorcycles. But more important than the numbers produced is the way these motorcycles are made—especially the way designers, suppliers, and manufacturers have organized themselves into a dynamic and entrepreneurial network.

Unlike state-run firms, the city's private sector upstarts, such as Longxin and Zongshen, did not have big foreign partners with deep pockets and proven designs, such as Honda or Suzuki. So they came up with a different business model, one that was simpler and more flexible. Instead of dictating every detail of the parts they want from their suppliers, the motorcycle makers specify only the important features, including size and weight, and let outside designers improvise.

This so-called localized modularization approach has been very successful and delivered big cost reductions and quality improvements, says John Seely Brown, an innovation expert who used to head the legendary Xerox Palo Alto Research Center (PARC). It is one example of the sort of business model innovation that he insists is far more radical than conventional product or process innovation.

China Moves Ahead

Examples of these business model innovations are now bubbling up from developing economies to threaten the established global giants. Seely Brown and his collaborator John Hagel argue that the activity of private entrepreneurs means "China is rapidly emerging as the global center of management innovation, pioneering management techniques that most U.S. companies are struggling to understand."

Frugal innovators are reinventing business models in several powerful ways. One of them is by outsourcing many activities—and you thought jobs went only one way, from your home state to Indian call centers! It turns out Chinese and Indian bosses also need to worry about cheaper competitors, be they close to home or in cheaper places such as Cambodia and Vietnam. Rather than have vertically integrated business models, for example, Indian telecom operators often outsource many parts of their value chain—and are able to offer among the lowest rates in the world as a result.

Another tactic is the inventive use of hybrid business models and cross subsidies to achieve massive economies of scale. Aravind, a pioneering Indian eye hospital chain, uses a tiered pricing structure that charges wealthier patients more (for example, for fancy meals or air-conditioned rooms), so it is able to cross-subsidize free care for the very poorest. G. Venkataswamy, the firm's deceased founder, was inspired by McDonald's, and set off to achieve the same sort of scale in eye care. Aravind staff screen more than 550,000 patients a year via outreach camps in remote areas, referring more than 86,000 per year for surgeries at its hospitals. International experts have confirmed that the care offered is of the highest caliber, not least because its doctors perform so many more surgeries than they normally would in the West that they become extremely good at them. And it is profitable, without donor aid or subsidies.

Indeed, the most vibrant of these third-world entrepreneurs are those who escape the heavy hand of government. Entrepreneurs in China must compete with privileged state firms with access to cheap credit as well as the local arms of multinationals. That makes China's "bamboo capitalists" extraordinarily resourceful in trying to reach global markets. India has been less integrated into the world economy, so many of its innovative firms have initially concentrated on reaching poor consumers in the domestic market. For instance, Selco, an Indian solar energy pioneer, found that because many of its customers were living in remote areas, it had to set up local networks of trained technicians to sell, install, and repair its products, and it had to provide customers with small loans.

Most of these Chinese and Indian innovators are not well known, but it is only a matter of time before some will be. For example, there are now more than four hundred firms designing integrated circuits in China. So far they produce pragmatic, copycat designs, but some will in time become world-class innovators. One guru who forecast the rise of enterprise in the Asian giants long ago is Tarun Khanna of Harvard Business School. In *Billions of Entrepreneurs,* he observes that it is now almost commonplace to imagine that one could build a billion-dollar corporation from scratch without having to visit such erstwhile temples of high finance as London or New York, whereas two decades ago such a notion would have been laughable. "Entrepreneurship has truly gone global," he concludes.

The emergence of Asian world-beaters exemplifies the two forces driving innovation: a new wave of globalization and the spread of information technology. These two forces allow the creation of unexpected and disruptive business models, such as the one used by

Chongqing's motorcycle makers. Other examples include the design networks established by Taiwanese contract producers in the textile industry. Groups of innovative just-in-time suppliers abound in Asia, feeding Western fashion and consumer goods companies.

They are often managed by supply chain experts, such as Hong Kong's Li & Fung. Unlike Japan's *keiretsu*, which bound companies and their suppliers together with interlocking shareholdings, these firms are free to leave their alliances. They stay together only if they continue to learn and profit from the experience. In some ways they resemble the nimble networks of firms that underpinned Silicon Valley's success.

Low labor costs may have given such firms a head start, but that is a transitory advantage. India's software innovators were once sniffed at as merely low-cost offshoring and back-office operations. But firms such as Infosys, Wipro, and Tata Consultancy Services (TCS) have become world leaders in business software services. S. Ramadorai, who led TCS to greatness, says his firm sees "innovation as a key enabler of its productivity edge." He points out that it has been investing in R&D for twenty-five years and holds numerous patents and copyrights. TCS has won praise for its global innovation ecosystem, which brings together academic labs, start-ups, venture capital firms, large independent software firms, and some of its most important customers.

Scourge or Savior?

Innovation is also changing the pharmaceutical industry. Small biotechnology firms, using networked approaches, are getting ahead of Big Pharma. This too opens the way for Asian competitors, such as India's generic-drug champions. These firms were once copy-cats, trampling on Western patents to make cheap generic versions of drugs. But increasingly such firms are shifting to process innovation and even the discovery of new drugs, as an intriguing recent Indo-American pharmaceutical deal reveals.

Generic drugs have long been considered a scourge by Western pharmaceutical firms. So it is ironic that the next great opportunity for Big Pharma may lie in doing to Big Biotech exactly what the generic-drug firms have done to traditional pharmaceutical companies: decimate margins with cheaper copies.

Pfizer, the world's biggest pharmaceutical firm, and Biocon, India's largest biotechnology outfit, announced in late 2010 that they will work together to bring "biosimilar" insulin treatments to market. Biosimilars are generic impersonations (though, it must be noted, not identical copies) of complicated biotech drugs. Revealingly, it is the Indian upstart that will come up with the original drugs and manufacture them; the American firm will only market them. David Simmons of Pfizer explains that this venture is part of his firm's new strategy to become a "one-stop shop" for biosimilars.

His enthusiasm is understandable, given that this is the next frontier for the industry. Biotech-based drugs account for only a fifth or so of global drug sales, but sales are projected to grow at double-digit rates. In contrast, many conventional drugs now face declining sales and a steep cliff of patent expirations. Add the fact that many biotech drugs enjoy enormous margins—some treatments cost $100,000 or more per year—and it is easy to see why this looks like a juicy target for generic assault.

The example of biosimilars shows how the innovators of the emerging world could, just possibly, end up rejuvenating rather than burying the bloated industries of the West—if only, like Pfizer, the big multinationals of the West swallow their pride and accept they have much to learn from the brash upstarts.

Growing Global

The resourceful engineers of the East need to be taken seriously. Their frugal and frantic innovations are leapfrogging their firms toward the top tiers of the global heap. Roughly a tenth of the Fortune 500 list of the world's biggest companies is now Chinese. One of those companies, Huawei, is now one of the most important manufacturers of telecommunications equipment in the world. Tata, an Indian powerhouse, has not only come up with an attractive small car that costs less than $4,000 (the Nano, which it plans to export to Europe from India) but also shocked the car industry by taking over Britain's Jaguar Land Rover.

And though China and India are in the lead, rich-world innovators would also be wise to keep an eye on Brazilian rivals. While the developed world saw economic growth shrivel during the great recession of recent years, Brazil has grown robustly of late. This will come as a shock to some, but it could overtake Britain and France to become the world's fifth-biggest economy by 2020.

The Latin American country's mining and agribusiness giants are among the world's best, putting established multinationals such as Rio Tinto and Cargill on the back foot on global markets. Its huge and growing middle class already makes it one of the world's five biggest markets for mobile phones, computers, automobiles, cosmetics, and fizzy drinks. And just as China did a few years ago with the Beijing Olympics and the Shanghai World Expo, Brazil is opening up to the world for the FIFA World Cup (2014) and the

Olympics (2016) with a massive infrastructure plan expected to top $50 billion.

While some Western multinationals have clearly understood that an economic tsunami is coming, many others—especially in asset-heavy, slow-moving industries such as steel and energy—seem convinced their particular industries are not so vulnerable. But even those "old economy" industries are now rapidly becoming knowledge industries, whether they realize it or not, and thus are also ripe for disruption, as the case of American health care shows.

Competition Is Good for Your Health

Rather than fear the frugal engineers of the East, consumers in the West should rejoice. By injecting a healthy dose of competition and commonsense innovation into these industries, they may be doing rich countries a favor. If you doubt it, travel an hour and a half northeast out of Beijing on a winter work day. There you will find a research and manufacturing facility built by Weigao, a Chinese med-tech firm that started as a township enterprise. The neatly manicured exterior gives way to a tidy but surprisingly chilly complex of laboratories and shop floors. Only the clean room, it seems, is fully climate controlled. That offers the first lesson in frugal innovation: unlike in the comfortable corporate campuses of the rich world, people shiver here while fancy equipment stays warm.

Brave the cold, though, and you will find such seemingly obscure local labs to be hotbeds of frugal innovation attracting investment from the world's most successful multinationals. Medtronic, an American med-tech giant, is a good example. After years of selling high-end products, the firm entered into a joint venture in

2009 with Weigao. Now, local and foreign-trained designers and engineers work side by side in the facility outside Beijing. They have already launched half a dozen inexpensive, novel products that Medtronic would not have made on its own.

Impressive, but what led to the U-turn? Simon Li, the well-connected head of the joint venture, says three things persuaded Medtronic's executive committee to see China "not as a host but as a home." The growth of secondary cities creates enormous opportunities for less-expensive technologies. The Chinese government's big push on "indigenous innovation" gives the edge to local firms in tendering, procurement, and so on. (An engineer gleefully points out that as a local entity, the Medtronic joint venture has affordable access to valuable metals such as titanium; to widespread outcry from global manufacturers, the Chinese government now restricts exports of rare-earth metals.) But the most important reason his firm "just had to localize," says Li, is the astonishing rise of local rivals.

Beyond Frugality

A decade ago, the American med-tech sector towered over all others and China's was of little relevance. But by the reckoning of PricewaterhouseCoopers (PWC), the U.S. lead will suffer on every important innovation metric in this industry over the next decade, while emerging giants will start catching up. China, in particular, could become a bigger force in this sector than Europe as of 2020—by both creating and consuming med-tech innovations.

First, to creation. For example, says Christopher Wasden of PWC, the traditional approach taken by big multinationals to sutures is to sell disposable versions on the cheap-razor/costly blade business model. But, he observes, local rivals beat them by developing reusable sutures, a frugal and less wasteful option that appealed to local sensibilities and pocketbooks. The local takeover of the market for heart stents is another straw in the wind. Not so long ago, says Li, Western firms such as his thought their dominant market position was unassailable. When Microport came out with products that were 40 percent cheaper, he recalls, doctors were initially skeptical. "But they did hundreds of clinical trials and now they own 70 percent of the Chinese market!" he exclaims.

Similar tales are unfolding in other parts of the industry, and investors are taking note. Microport and Lepu Medical, another local rival in the stent market, have both had successful public placements (the former on the Hong Kong market and the latter on the Shenzhen market). Mindray Medical, which makes inexpensive patient monitors and related equipment, is listed on the New York Stock Exchange; it has substantial exports into developed markets already. Trauson, a local firm specializing in orthopedics, went public on the Hong Kong Exchange.

Not in My Backyard

Consider consumption next. China's med-tech market is forecast to grow 15 percent a year to 2015, reaching $43 billion by 2019; India's is galloping at 23 percent and should top $10 billion by the decade's end. And China is now spending $125 billion in a massive push to expand health care outside the major cities. That creates vast new markets for inexpensive medical technologies.

The dual-track strategy taken by Philips, a Dutch multinational, confirms that there are really two Chinas: one fancy and one frugal. Ronald de Jong of Philips reveals that his firm now sells more high-end CT scanners in China each year than it does in the United States. But, mindful of China's big push to expand health care into rural areas, Philips has also made numerous local acquisitions. He says the chief benefit is not access to cheap labor but rather access "to a culture of frugality."

Omar Ishrak, a senior executive at GE for many years, argues that the term "frugal innovation" underplays the revolution at work, as price is only one advantage. The local innovation approach often leapfrogs to the latest technologies, be it miniaturization or mobile communications or advanced materials, that produce devices both cheaper and better than rich-country models. He points to GE's locally developed Brivo line of MRI and CT machines, which provide "just what is needed."

All impressive stuff, but this is not to say that Chinese firms are about to take over the med-tech world tomorrow. For one thing, points out Rajesh Parekh of McKinsey, local firms do well only in less-complex and noninvasive fields such as imaging and engineering; they have yet to penetrate highly risky and sophisticated markets such as those for implanted defibrillators. What is more, says Rachel Lee of the Boston Consulting Group, the in-country laboratories set up by foreign firms are doing better at cutting-edge research than are the local rivals, who are focused on development. That suggests the Western giants may have a few years in which they can master frugal innovation overseas and bring home those lessons before the eventual but inevitable Asian assault.

Will the storied multinationals really dance to a new tune? The Western med-tech firms vigorously insist they are already doing this and trot out a few colorful examples of frugalista products they offer in rich countries. Scrutinize their claims, though, and it becomes clear that this—thus far, at least—is a mere trickle.

This is extremely shortsighted, for the sort of frugal innovation now bubbling up in China could yet save American health care. That may seem an extraordinary claim, given that the United States remains the Goliath of the $350 billion medical technology industry. American med-tech firms, historically the world's most innovative, still make up thirty-two of forty-six firms in this sector with annual sales over $1 billion. And their home market still accounts for some 40 percent of global sales.

It is to their credit that the Western giants have responded to Asia's rise by investing furiously in those booming emerging markets, and they clearly are learning useful tricks from the thrifty natives. What the giants are reluctant to do is to bring those cheap and cheerful technologies back into developed markets. But that is precisely the dose of competition that bloated health systems such as America's really need.

Disruption Ahead

To be fair, there are several obstacles to frugal innovations entering the United States that must be swept aside. One is red tape. Since a safety scandal led to the withdrawal in 2004 of Vioxx, a blockbuster painkiller made by Merck, the FDA has grown excessively risk averse. It now often takes twice as long for firms to get new medical technologies approved in the United States than it does in Europe. This discourages upstarts, as they typically lack the army of regulatory experts and deep pockets required to navigate the tricky FDA process.

Another needless barrier holding back the tide of cost savings is the convoluted system of health care payments in the United

States. It is not enough for a clever device to be safe and economical. To succeed in the United States it must also be blessed by the official Centers for Medicare and Medicaid Services (CMS). But getting a CMS payment code can take years—again, cosseting the incumbents who drove costs up in the first place.

That points to the most self-interested obstacle—the big Western firms themselves. It's true that they are not in a defensive crouch the way Detroit's carmakers were when confronted by the rise of Asia's car industry several decades ago. But firms such as GE, Philips, and Medtronic are not rushing to sell their frugal inventions back in the United States or Europe. Part of the explanation is structural: salespeople operating on commission and distributors set up to peddle scanners costing $100,000 or more do not know (and do not want to know) how to hawk portable versions costing just $10,000 or even $1,000. The bigger obstacle, confesses one senior executive, is the belief that customers in the United States simply "have more ability to pay."

A disarmingly honest Omar Ishrak explains that America's risk-averse regulators and its complex payment system are a problem, but he offers that "manufacturers are also to blame." The sales and distribution systems at firms such as GE, set up to sell $100,000 scanners, are not suited to sell versions at a tenth that price. And, he confesses, manufacturers "do not present comprehensive evidence of value" before the sale; rather, he thinks, they rely on "an emotional kind of sale."

That may have worked in the past, but as health budgets get squeezed in the West and cost-effective technologies emerge from the East, emotion will surely yield to economics in time. History suggests that this strategy will ultimately fail, as the eventual assault of well-engineered, affordable Japanese cars taught Detroit's carmakers—and that Western consumers should welcome the newcomers with open arms. Jeffrey Immelt, GE's chairman, coauthored a case study published by the *Harvard Business Review* in 2009 describing the challenges and ultimate triumphs encountered by the dynamic Ishrak, then a rising star at his firm, in developing health care innovations in Asia. In mid-2011, the GE boss was challenged with this question: what about Ishrak's confession that GE's own sales and commission structures greatly hindered the flow of frugal innovations to markets such as the United States? Immelt laughed and revealed that on that very day, Medtronic had poached Ishrak to be its new chief executive. As for GE, he accepted the critique: "We're just going to have to find another way to pay our salesmen."

That is a sobering insight, especially for those concerned about the middle class squeeze—the subject of the next chapter. But if American firms do not eat their own lunch (Silicon Valley jargon for replacing one's own business model with a better one), Asia's rising stars of med-tech will do it soon enough. Technology is advancing at such a breathtaking pace that innovation simply can no longer be suppressed by cozy multinationals keen on milking their assets. That's why the only real question left is whether the frugal innovators that will come out on top will use forks or chopsticks.

3

Of Stagnation and Rejuvenation

Today's innovation revolution is making the world a wealthier and better place in many ways. So why is it that many ordinary people in developed countries feel that their lives are getting worse? There is even a chorus of experts now arguing that the children born today may be the first generation of Americans to be worse off than their parents.

The explanation for this malaise, which was evident even before the recent financial crisis, is the middle-class squeeze. Thanks to the forces of globalization and Googlization, the elites of Mumbai now lead lives as good as or better than those enjoyed by the elites of Manhattan and Munich. With the transformative power of mobile telephony and microfinance, rural women in Rwanda and slum dwellers in São Paulo's favelas now have economic opportunities unimaginable just a decade ago. But what about Kansas?

The disruptive forces overturning the old economic order are creating enormous opportunities, but many in the struggling middle classes are not benefiting. There are various

*explanations for this trend, but it is at least in part because
even educated, white-collar workers in many rich countries
lack the skills to capitalize on those opportunities. As the broad
middle of the developed world watches elites capture much of
the gain from the new global order, anger and resentment are
growing. Unless leaders from both the public and private sectors take steps to widen access to the economic opportunities
made possible by the Great Disruption, a dangerous backlash
against globalization, immigration, and innovation looks to be
in the cards.*

*The critics of today's economic transformation are right in
suggesting that there is an indefensible inequity in how the
fruits of revolution are being shared. There is even evidence to
support the assertion that the United States, long the most dynamic big economy in the world, may be headed for stagnation.
However, it is wrong to suggest that such a decline is inevitable
or that the disruptive forces behind the global economic rise of
recent decades have run out of steam.*

*The good news is that the new economics of innovation
points to a creative set of tools, rules, and social norms to
tackle this problem. The road from stagnation to rejuvenation
runs through innovation.*

Arianna Huffington is an optimist in general and a big believer
in the future of the United States in particular. Growing up in
Athens, Greece, she walked past a statue of Harry Truman every
day and dreamed of moving to the land of opportunity. She had the
chance, at the age of sixteen, to spend the summer with American
families, and she loved it so much she vowed to come back. When
she did, in 1980, she came for good and made the most of her
opportunities. The flamboyant and witty migrant has grown her

Huffington Post into one of the only financially successful online journals and has become an influential social and political commentator. By any measure, the United States has been good to her, and her faith in the country has been amply rewarded.

So why is she now warning that her adopted homeland is on its way to becoming a third-world country? The reason is simple. She worries that the extraordinary economic squeeze that middle-class Americans have experienced in recent years will turn the country into a place with just two classes—the rich and everybody else. That, after all, is how famously unequal societies such as Brazil and India have long been (at least until the remarkable rise of the middle classes in emerging markets of late). But now, she explains in *Third World America*, the warning signs are unmissable: "Our industrial base is vanishing, taking with it the kind of jobs that have formed the backbone of our economy for more than a century; our education system is in shambles, making it harder for tomorrow's workforce to acquire the information and training it needs to land good twenty-first-century jobs; our infrastructure—our roads, our bridges, our sewage and water and transportation and electrical systems—is crumbling."

Huffington does not want to be a Cassandra. However, she observes sadly, the other Greek woman sounding the alarm was proved right, as the Trojans discovered to their detriment. And so too may be this one, if U.S. leaders do not act. The confluence of economic and political forces squeezing the middle class today in developed countries, not just the United States, is all too real. Huffington worries that the American dream of achieving a better life for one's children through hard work and discipline is now in peril. Though some dismiss any talk of a middle-class squeeze, many on both sides of the political aisle share her concerns. President Barack Obama declared in 2010 that "the class that made the twentieth century the American century . . . has been under assault for a long time." And Ronald Haskins, who served as the senior White House advisor on welfare policy to President George W. Bush, stated recently, "We've had a dramatic increase in inequality in the country. There's no question about that. Some people try to argue that point that it isn't true, and I think that, you know, it's crazy for anybody to do that. Every data set that I'm aware of shows that there's huge, increased inequality."

Consider the evidence. The richest 1 percent of Americans took home less than 9 percent of the country's income in the late 1970s. By 2007, the richest 1 percent took in 23.5 percent of total national income. The last time income was that concentrated in America was back in the 1920s. Rising inequality does not have to translate automatically into a squeeze on the middle class, of course: it is possible for the very rich to get much richer even as the ordinary Joe makes a wee bit more. But in this case, the squeeze was indeed on. The modest gains in income that average American households saw in the years before the recent financial crash were often more than wiped out in practice by soaring debt payments, rising insurance premiums, out-of-pocket health care charges, and other substantial increases in the cost of living. Alan Greenspan, the former chairman of the Federal Reserve Board of Governors, warned as far back as 2005, "This is not the type of thing which a democratic society—a capitalist democratic society—can really accept without addressing."

What is more, the squeeze is not a uniquely Yankee phenomenon. Branko Milanovic, a World Bank economist, has crunched the numbers on inequality in and among countries. He makes the important observation that global income distribution was actually made more equal by the extraordinary rise of India and China in recent decades. Indeed, judged on a global scale, the past few decades have produced something of a great leveling across the world—which is surely to be applauded. However, offsetting that were forces that led to greater inequality within important countries. He points out that while the United States is among the most unequal of developed countries, "inequality has risen decisively in Western nations over the past twenty-five years."

If that were the end of the story, it would be merely a moral outrage. However, while some inequality in income is inevitable and even desirable (most reasonable people will agree that hard work and brilliance should be rewarded more generously than sloth and stupidity), extreme inequality strains the social compact and risks propelling societies into chaos. That is why the bigger worry is the prospect of a backlash sparked by growing inequality, as this could do much to harm the economic outlook for everyone—including the struggling middle classes. There are already signs that the stagnation and malaise seen in the United States and other developed countries is fueling anti-immigration and antitrade sentiments. If the engines of innovation that have produced extraordinary global prosperity (albeit in inequitable form) over the past few decades were to be gummed up by a halt in the flow of ideas, people, and goods, then the result may well be much slower economic growth or worse for all of society. And history shows that the battle over how big a slice of pie one gets becomes much uglier when the pie is shrinking rather than growing.

The challenge of yawning income gaps within countries threatens to undermine the innovation-driven transformation that has done so much good for so many in the global economy. A backlash is already under way in various countries, as seen in the local resentments against job-grabbing immigrants, rapacious capitalists, "socialist" big government, and other presumed enemies of the middle class—as well as the global difficulties encountered by the Doha round of trade liberalization and the latest negotiations under the UN's Kyoto treaty on climate change. Robert Reich, a former Clinton administration official who is now at the University of California at Berkeley, argues that change is coming, for good or ill: "The question is not whether the pendulum will swing back. It surely will. The question is *how* it will swing—whether with reforms that widen the circle of prosperity, or with demagoguery that turns America away from the rest of the world, shrinks the economy, and sets Americans against one another."

So what to do? Most of the explanations for the middle class squeeze involve distributional arguments: yes, the pie is growing, say critics, but greedy or well-connected elites are grabbing unfairly large shares of that pie. There is certainly truth to this argument, as Jacob Hacker and Paul Pierson show in their book *Winner-Take-All Politics*. Whether it is by securing income tax cuts that benefit mostly the very wealthy, lobbying for federal funding for pork-barrel projects in favored industries, or keeping in place tax breaks for employer-provided health care (which subsidizes the privileged while forcing higher insurance rates and out-of-pocket health costs on poorer working people), American elites have clearly managed to gobble up an ever bigger piece of the economic pie.

Indefensible as these are, at least such distributional problems can be addressed by the political system, if and when the two political parties in Washington decide to get serious about the country's future. For example, one of the biggest reasons ordinary families feel poorer is the fact that an ever-increasing share of their monthly compensation (which, put simply, is a mix of cash income and health benefits) is going to pay for rising health premiums. Big business often huffs and puffs about health care inflation, which is roaring at rates much higher than the overall inflation rate for the economy, but here's the dirty little secret: companies do not actually care too much about this issue. The federal tax code allows them to write off the total compensation paid to workers, regardless of the split between health benefits and cash income. The sharp rise in health insurance costs in recent years has not put individual companies (especially those in sectors, such as retail, that do not face foreign competition) at much of a competitive disadvantage. However, it has been a big factor behind the stagnation in the level of inflation-adjusted wages paid to the ordinary worker. That is why meaningful health reforms, going beyond President Obama's recent efforts, that check the inflation in health care costs could help alleviate the middle-class squeeze.

This may seem difficult, but it is actually easier to carry out such reforms, which rejigger how the economic pie is divided, than it is to address another possible cause for the middle-class squeeze: that the pie has stopped growing altogether.

Is the Low-Hanging Fruit Gone?

Tyler Cowen, an iconoclastic economist at George Mason University, makes this much more disturbing argument in *The Great Stagnation*, the most talked-about book on economics in many years. Looking at shrinking real wages and weakening purchasing power for ordinary Americans, he observes that typical individuals in earlier generations saw a doubling of living standards every few decades. Americans today, he argues, are sinking into a great stagnation and must get ready for an era of diminished expectations. The reason, he argues, is not just because the elites are taking the biggest pieces of pie. It is, he argues controversially, because the pie itself is no longer growing as it used to. And, he adds for good measure, none of the tricks in today's innovation tool kit described in this book will come to the rescue of the current generation of middle-class families.

That is an astonishing claim, and one that is worth scrutinizing. His central proposition is that the United States has been "living off low-hanging fruit for at least three hundred years." Whether this was cheap immigrant labor, free land (though the Native Americans would bristle at that notion), or powerful new technologies, the country's economic rise can be explained in large part by such gifts. Rates of economic growth in the United States have slowed down since about 1970, he thinks, because the benefits of the previous momentum were exhausted before new sources of growth were discovered.

That assertion seems to fly in the face of conventional wisdom and everyday experience, which suggest that the world is living through an extraordinary economic boom fueled by new information and communication technologies. After all, is this not the age of the personal computer, the Internet, mobile telephony, and other marvels that have done so much to improve lives and propel economic growth? His stunning answer is no: "Apart from the seemingly magical Internet, life in broad material terms isn't so different from 1953." He argues that earlier technologies such as electricity and railroads were much more transformative than today's. The Internet, he claims, is a marvelous invention that has dramatically improved the quality of people's lives—but, he insists, it has yet to make much of a contribution to jobs, productivity growth, or economic output. Many Internet products are free and Internet firms profitless; even goliaths of the sector such as Facebook and Groupon employ pitifully few people compared, say, to the automobile industry a century ago. Worse yet, he argues, these technologies will not do much to revive growth or help ease the middle-class squeeze: "We are at a technology plateau and the trees are more bare than we would like to think." In short, innovation will not ride to the rescue anytime soon.

What should one make of this extraordinary, if deeply distressing, assessment of the future? Cowen is certainly right about a few things. The big Western economies could stay stuck in a quagmire for some years even as developing economies boom, for a couple of reasons. In the short term, the overhang of the financial crisis will keep the middle class squeezed for a while yet. High levels of unemployment and recessionary cutbacks mean that lots of workers and factories are idle. It may be difficult for many of those now unemployed to find new jobs, as evidence suggests long-term unemployment leads to the degradation of skills, creditworthiness, motivation, and marketability. The OECD estimates that just closing this "output gap" and putting the rich world back where it was before the financial crisis, never mind put the great stagnation behind, could take till 2015.

A longer-term factor is demographics. Most developed economies are aging rapidly, so the supply of new workers is about to decline just as the number of retirees (whose benefits are usually paid for by working people) is about to surge. Unless countries embrace more liberal policies on working-age immigrants from developing countries, this will precipitate a pension crisis and also lower the potential economic growth rate. Other ways out of this problem would be for workers to toil until later in life or for lots of new native-born workers to enter the workforce after receiving a decent education, but those factors seem unlikely to ease the squeeze soon. Any whisper of pushing back the age of eligibility for Social Security or government pensions prompts ugly public rows in the United States and Europe, while the biggest potential pool of unpaid workers in recent history—women—has already entered the workforce of wealthy countries in droves over the past few decades.

In addition to battling those headwinds, the economies of the developed world have a problem with productivity growth. This matters for several reasons. First and foremost, it matters because economic growth is driven by two chief factors: population and productivity. In emerging economies, the first factor can play a big role, as populations are often young and labor forces are expanding rapidly. But that is unlikely in mature economies, which tend to have stable and aging workforces. That is why in the advanced world, improving productivity—that is, producing ever more valuable goods and services with each unit of labor—is the most powerful way to grow faster. The arrival of information technology fueled a productivity boom in the late 1990s in the United States, as did the wider adoption and diffusion throughout the economy of related software and productivity tools in the early 2000s. Europe also improved, but not nearly as much as the United States, perhaps because its markets are less competitive. So companies there invested less in improving services and business processes in such sectors as retailing. The upshot is that productivity growth was losing steam in developed countries before the global financial debacle.

So Cowen is right to sound the alarm about the productivity engine sputtering, as this engine is the closest thing governments have to a silver bullet when it comes to revving up economic growth and creating the good jobs that will end the middle-class squeeze. But he goes further, postulating that no new productivity miracle is in the offing. The 30 percent or so of workers that benefit directly or indirectly from the rise of the Internet and computing (be they Google software engineers and high-end content providers, Geek Squad technicians who install high-tech equipment in the homes of the technologically challenged, or artists who design funky iPad cases) will thrive, he guesstimates, while the rest of society will be relegated to an underclass that will fall ever further behind.

Is he really right in suggesting that rapid productivity growth will become impossibly difficult because the low-hanging fruit is gone? More to the point, is he right in arguing that today's remarkable innovation revolution will do little to ease the middle-class squeeze anytime soon? Only time will tell for sure, but there are good reasons to be more optimistic if—and this is a very big *if*—governments take the right steps to kick-start growth and fuel innovation.

The Only Silver Bullet

The *New Yorker* ran a lovely cartoon in 2011 that captured thousands of years of economic history in a snapshot. The artist sketched a Stone Age scene, with a small family huddled together around a big rock. The only material possession in sight is a stick held by a child. The father looks at his son and says somberly, "When I was your age, things were exactly the way they are now."

It is hard for people in the developed world to believe this, but through almost all of mankind's history, economic stagnation was the norm, not the exception. Until about three hundred years ago, the per capita income of all but the very elite (think pharaohs and kings) remained grindingly small. That is why the lives of sons were remarkably similar to those of their fathers. But the industrial revolution sparked a surge in economic growth that raised living standards and disposable income dramatically. Angus Maddison, an economic historian, has calculated that the average European was four times richer in the middle of the twentieth century as his counterpart was in the early part of the nineteenth century. Revealingly, the average American got eight times richer over that same period but—thanks to government policies of the day that were hostile to the diffusion and adoption of new technologies and ideas (in other words, the essence of innovation)—the average Chinese person actually got poorer.

So could the past turn out to be prelude for the middle class? First consider the notion that the days of rapid productivity growth are gone. The McKinsey Global Institute (MGI) has done a detailed investigation of the matter. Asked if Cowen is right, James Manyika, a director at MGI, replies yes and no. Without a productivity boost, today's younger generation will see slower increases in living standards. By his group's calculations, Americans born in 1960 saw their GDP per head grow 2.5 times by the age of forty; those born in 2000 can expect to see it grow only 1.6 times by that age on current trends. That is hardly stagnation, but it is fair to say America may be entering an age of diminished expectations unless productivity growth speeds up. And that will not be easy: MGI estimates that U.S. productivity growth needs to accelerate by nearly a third from current levels to sustain past GDP growth rates over the next decade, assuming no increase in labor inputs.

Nevertheless, there is reason to think productivity growth can pick up. For one thing, the argument that there is no low-hanging fruit may be wrong. The United States may have one of the most efficient big economies in the world, but there are still plenty of corners of inefficiency and waste. For example, health care gobbles up some 18 percent of U.S. GDP, far and away more than what any other rich country spends on this, but international comparisons show that the country gets only mediocre health outcomes. There is plenty of evidence that money is wasted, inventions are needlessly gold-plated, and costs are merely shifted around from one part of the sector to another. Similar arguments can be made about the U.S. public education sector, which is crying out for innovation and efficiency gains.

MGI has scrutinized the American economy and found that there is "plenty of headroom" for future productivity improvements. About three-quarters of those gains look to come from the private sector, and a quarter from government and quasi-public sectors such as health care. Even if Cowen is right that the lowest-hanging fruit is gone, there are surely plenty of lowish fruits that can be reached, albeit with a bit more effort. That suggests the tree is not bare. What is more, the MGI work debunks the perception held by some that productivity gains inevitably come with massive job losses—an understandable sentiment given the mass layoffs undertaken by employers during the recent financial crisis under the guise of productivity enhancement. The think tank looked back across the past century and found that for every rolling ten-year period but one, productivity improvement went hand in hand with rises in employment.

Ah, but what about Cowen's bolder claim—that technology has run out of steam and that innovation will not come to the rescue of the United States anytime soon? If that were true, that would cast doubt on the central arguments of this book: that the world's grand challenges, as well as the middle-class squeeze, could be tackled by a wave of socially useful innovation. One pillar in his argument is his assessment that Internet companies, which are giving many things away for free, are not producing much economic value. That is a questionable assertion. While it is true that lots of things appear free at the point of use—think of Google searches or coupons from Groupon—in fact there is value being created discreetly. The personal data that Google collects from searches allow it to tailor its lucrative online advertising, just as the "vapor trail" of data left by (mostly unwitting) users of location-based services such as Four-square allows such firms to profile users and create data analytics that investors believe to be hugely valuable. And this Big Data goldmine is unlikely to be tapped out anytime soon: astonishingly, Google estimates that some 15 percent of the search requests it receives every day are new and unique.

Another pillar in Cowen's argument is that previous revolutionary technologies have taken many decades to transform societies. Since the Internet is relatively young, he argues, this means that any big economic dividends are a long way off—and therefore innovation will not save the middle class anytime soon. He points to deep economic analysis done by Alexander Field in *A Great Leap Forward*, a book that overturns conventional wisdom by demonstrating that the decade that saw the greatest productivity advance in the twentieth century was the 1930s. (Previously, many argued that it was the wartime efforts at resource mobilization that kick-started the golden economic era of the 1950s and 1960s.) Field shows that during the Great Depression, companies adopted dramatically better processes and technologies that eventually led to such marvels as streamlined cars with automatic transmissions, diesel locomotives, and a world-beating film industry in Hollywood. The point about the long cycles of innovation is surely right: invention often comes in a fast and furious flurry, but the real economic gains are usually realized only decades later as those inventions are adopted and adapted throughout society.

But this argument ignores the fact that lots of money has been invested in fields other than the Internet over the past few decades and it is quite possible that those long-term investments will pay dividends in the next decade or two. Bill Gates has little time for talk of stagnation: "Bah—would you rather live in the 1950s?" Thanks to those decades of investments in research and development, Gates says, he sees extraordinary progress coming soon in fields ranging from energy storage to advanced materials to genomics. The first problem with the techno-pessimistic view, he argues, is one of time horizons. If one speaks of just a few years, the view may be right, but if one speaks of the long term, it is surely wrong, he thinks. The second problem, he argues, has to do with the inadequacy of metrics such as productivity and GDP, which do not capture many ways in which technology is improving lives. For example, how does one calculate how much humanity's lot has improved because of the arrival of Wikipedia, which puts more information into the hands of schoolchildren in the world's poorest villages than the American president commanded just a few decades ago? And, asks Gates mischievously, "who changes flat tires anymore?"

Beyond Stagnation

This debate is likely to rage for some time yet, and eyes are sure to glaze over as the economists and technologists clash, but here is why everyone needs to pay attention. The concerns voiced today by Tyler Cowen about the United States may soon ring true for other countries too if governments fail to fix bad policies that retard innovation and implement good ones that boost it (a topic taken up by a later chapter, "The Sputnik Fallacies"). Even before the financial crisis, Europe had a problem with productivity growth worse than that of the United States, and Japan's lost decade of economic malaise has already produced a lost generation of youth. The Middle East desperately needs to create new jobs too, if the hopes raised by the democratic uprisings of the Arab Spring are not to be cruelly crushed: the World Bank estimates that the region needs to create eighty million more jobs by 2020 just to absorb new entrants into the labor pool without loss of living standards. And even China, the source of much of the dynamism in the world economy of late, will face a crisis in time thanks to its one-child policy. Unlike India, which looks to enjoy a "demographic dividend" as lots of young workers enter the economy soon, China's workforce is aging and there are not enough children to fill the void.

The surest path from stagnation to rejuvenation runs through innovation. To see why, consider the lessons offered by the new economics of innovation and "intangible" capital. In early 2011, Ben Bernanke, the current chairman of the Federal Reserve Bank's Board of Governors, gave an important but little-noticed speech at a conference at Georgetown University that sketched out the relationship between innovation and growth: "Innovation and technological change are undoubtedly central to the growth process; over the past 200 years or so, innovation, technical advances, and investment in capital goods embodying new technologies have transformed economies around the world . . . in addition, recent research has highlighted the important role played by intangible capital, such as the knowledge embodied in the workforce, business plans and practices, and brand names. This research suggests that technological progress and the accumulation of intangible capital have together accounted for well over half of the increase in output per hour in the United States during the past several decades."

Bernanke's praise for the role of innovation in sparking economic growth heralds the triumph of the new economics of innovation. Traditionally, economists did not think too much about technology and its impacts on economic growth. That began to change as research by a camp of economists, most prominent among them MIT's Robert Solow (who later won a Nobel Prize for this work), suggested that technical progress dwarfed the role played by labor and capital in determining economic growth in modern economies. That laid the foundation stone for new growth theory, an influential update on Solow's work that was pioneered by Paul Romer, a longtime Stanford economist who has recently moved to New York University. The essence of this philosophy is the notion that the source of economic progress is ideas.

That is a radical departure from classical economic thinking, which focused on traditional means of production such as land, labor, and capital. But research and elaborate calculations done by economists in Romer's camp show that growth is driven not merely by physical objects but mostly by smarter ways of manipulating physical objects that create new goods and services that satisfy society's unmet needs: in short, by innovation. As Romer puts it, "The classical suggestion that we can grow rich by accumulating more and more pieces of physical capital like forklifts is simply wrong . . . any kind of physical capital is ultimately subject to diminishing returns." In contrast, he observes, knowledge is subject to *increasing* returns.

That is the essential insight of the age of innovation. Because more than one person can make use of such knowledge-economy goods as software at one time, such goods are tremendous drivers of productivity. After all, though it may cost Microsoft hundreds of millions of dollars to produce the first copy of a new software program, it costs the firm next to nothing to produce the millionth or billionth copy. Romer invokes the analogy of a kitchen to explain his theory. Mixing inexpensive ingredients according to a recipe creates valuable new dishes. Most people believe the limit on growth is the number of ingredients available to cook according to a given set of recipes. Ah, but if ingenious new chefs devise better recipes, then society could generate more economic value per unit of raw material.

The new economics of innovation offers a powerful rebuttal to the notion that resource scarcity limits growth and dooms mankind to stagnation. As Romer puts it: "Every generation has perceived the limits to growth that finite resources and undesirable side effects would pose if no new recipes or ideas were discovered. And every generation has underestimated the potential for finding new recipes and ideas. We consistently fail to grasp how many ideas remain to be discovered. Possibilities do not add up. They multiply."

This is not to say that innovation is easy, of course, or that the current pace of progress is unprecedented. The great Victorian age of invention brought the world many marvels, including the telegraph, which lifted productivity at the time and laid the foundations for progress in the century to follow. Hal Varian, the chief economist at Google, has observed that technology changes, "but economic laws do not." He notes that even in today's Internet economy such age-old factors as inflation, business cycles, profits, and monopolies all still matter.

Romer himself offers the most powerful note of caution. Ask him about Cowen's thesis on the great stagnation, and he offers a surprising response at first: "I agree with him that something big has gone wrong in the United States since the 1970s." He agrees productivity is not growing as fast as it should be, but he strongly disagrees that the reason is the rate of arrival of new technologies. Rather, he argues, the problem is rules: "New technologies absent the right rules can be harmful." He points to the example of fisheries, where new technologies in netting and trawlers have led not to greater economic value or sustainable productivity gains but to overfishing, declining stocks, and industrial decline. By rules he means more than a static set of regulations or the rule of law; his "rules" can range from bankruptcy codes to government regulations to social norms around corruption. He insists they need constantly to adapt to keep pace with changing technologies, societal mores, and the effects of scale. Intellectual property is another set of rules that influence the pace of innovation. Romer acknowledges the importance of issuing patents as an incentive for inventors, but argues that current rules may need to be softened to allow for greater and more rapid dissemination of ideas.

Societies that get these rules right will benefit more from the invention and adoption of new technologies than will those with rules that are distorted, perverse, or captured by elites. He worries, for example, about the lobbying power of incumbent industries to defend the status quo and win such perks as outsized executive compensation. To help developing countries accelerate their development process by leapfrogging to good rules, he is now campaigning for special charter cities to be carved out of developing countries. Some call it neocolonialism, but he insists these newly created zones would operate independent of local elites under the authority of benevolent foreign overlords applying time-tested rules and good governance (rather as Britain did in Hong Kong). As for the malaise of the United States, Romer believes that the wrong rules allowed such sectors as health care and finance to suck in huge resources without producing much value for society.

The rules that a society adopts influence not just the total amount of effort that goes into innovation, he argues, but also the types of problems that all this innovative effort is trying to solve: "If some of the best minds of the current generation are spending their time trying to figure out innovative ways to engage in rent-seeking instead of creating value, human progress will suffer." This is what happened as the financial sector in many Western countries, most notably in the United States and Britain, became increasingly disconnected from the real economy. The American financial industry grew dramatically during the bubble years preceding the recent crash, with its size soaring to historical highs of nearly 8.5 percent of U.S. GDP; in 1990 it was under 6 percent and in 1970 roughly 4 percent. But this growth was based on illusory innovations and unsustainable gains, as the collapse later revealed. Worse yet, there is some reason to think that the lure of easy money on Wall Street sucked some of the brightest and most enterprising people away from careers in other fields that have traditionally produced socially useful innovation and entrepreneurship.

That, in sum, is why innovation matters so much at the level of the ordinary person. Today's middle-class squeeze is not just the result of the Great Disruption of the global economy: it is also the result of countries clinging to the wrong rules for encouraging innovation and sharing its gains. The final section of the book investigates what the right rules are by asking what governments, companies, and individuals can do to encourage innovation in the first place. But before turning to that question it makes sense to consider, as the next section does, the dramatic ways in which innovation itself is changing. After all, as Ben Bernanke pointed out, it is intangibles such as the know-how inside the minds of innovators that are increasingly driving innovation.

PART TWO

SPEED:

Where Innovation Is Going

4

The Singularity
and Its Discontents

The world is undergoing an unprecedented demographic, economic, and environmental transformation today. The rapid aging of the global population comes just as mankind has become a primarily urban species for the first time in its history. Adding to this mix, of course, is the forceful arrival of giant emerging markets onto the world stage.

As a result, there is now a great race under way between the forces of development and those of degradation. The fate of people and the planet hangs in the balance, and the outcome is not preordained. Even so, society can tip the scales in favor of a positive outcome—if somehow mankind could find ways of accelerating the pace of innovation directed toward the grand global challenges (as opposed to, or at least in addition to, coming up with yet another triple-decker bacon-taco burger).

But can we really speed up innovation in this way? Actually, some of the world's leading entrepreneurs and thinkers—including leading lights of Silicon Valley—are convinced that today's disruptions herald the arrival of a new golden age of innovation. This chapter describes the quiet but powerful confluence of technologies accelerating innovation today that could help tame the world's most wicked problems.

Some prognosticators claim these trends will inevitably lead humanity to a glorious postbiological future, and perhaps even to immortality. That seems fanciful, if not absurd. But one does not have to believe such claims to acknowledge that the convergence of key technology trends, in fields ranging from materials science to synthetic genomics to artificial intelligence, is accelerating global innovation and speeding the global economy toward a postindustrial world.

Thirty years ago, Julian Simon and Paul Ehrlich entered into a famous bet. The former, a libertarian at the Cato Institute think tank, was skeptical of the gloomy claims made by the latter, a Stanford University ecologist best known for his predictions of environmental chaos and human suffering resulting from gross overpopulation. Thumbing his nose at such notions of resource scarcity, Simon wagered that the price of any five commodities chosen by Ehrlich would go down in price over the following decade. History shows that the supposed "population bomb" did not explode, and the world did not, in fact, run out of resources. Simon handily won the bet.

Ah, but that did not silence the nabobs of negativity. A growing chorus of doom now argues that the world cannot possibly feed ten billion mouths, that Africa is destined to fail, and that the world is heading for an unavoidable climate calamity. Those are genuine crises confronting the world, but is humanity's fate really so gloomy?

Nonsense, argue the techno-optimists. Matt Ridley, a noted British science writer, boldly predicts that in 2110, a much bigger world population could enjoy more and better food produced on less land than is used by farming today—and even return lots of farmland to wilderness. The key, he insists, is continued technological progress.

And some think the floodgates are about to open on such progress. Ray Kurzweil, an accomplished inventor and author of *The Singularity Is Near*, argues that there is an unprecedented confluence of disruptive technologies coming—in fields ranging from communications to synthetic genomics—that will dramatically improve the human condition. He even predicts that machines will surpass humans in intelligence in a few decades when the species will cross a momentous and irreversible point: the Singularity. This will herald not a posthuman world, he insists, but rather a post-biological one: "As we gradually learn to harness the optimal computing capacity of matter, our intelligence will spread through the universe at (or exceeding) the speed of light, eventually leading to a sublime, universe-wide awakening." Imperfect memories and extinguishable bodies will then be beautifully augmented by spiritual machines that enhance and prolong lives—perhaps, he dares to say, raising the prospect of immortality.

Time even put the Singularity on its cover in early 2011, declaring in large letters that 2045 will be "the year that man becomes immortal.*" Careful readers would have noticed the asterisk, which offered caveats, but the flattering profile of Kurzweil inside the magazine only reinforced the view that his notions are to be taken seriously. To Kurzweil's claim of immortality, the article's author added this additional eye-catching promise: "So if computers are getting so much faster, so incredibly fast . . . all that horsepower could be put in the service of emulating whatever it is our brains are doing when they create consciousness—not just doing arithmetic very quickly or composing piano music but also driving cars, writing books, making ethical decisions, appreciating fancy paintings, making witty observations at cocktail parties."

Shortly after that cover story came out, John Kelly, the head of research at IBM, declared that "we are at a moment where computers and computer technology now have approached humans." That grand claim came on the eve of a major test of computing prowess. His firm had shocked many back in 1997 when its Big Blue computer beat Garry Kasparov, a Russian grandmaster, at chess. But winning at chess is a trivial task compared to understanding the complexities and idiosyncrasies of human speech.

So the firm developed Watson, a supercomputer it thinks is capable of understanding natural language. To put this claim to the test, the firm arranged for its creation to compete (without accessing the Internet) on *Jeopardy!*, the television game show known for using clever clues and coy wordplay that even humans struggle to understand at times. In the contest, televised in late February 2011, Watson trounced the two most successful previous champions of that game on its way to a convincing victory.

One man who was not at all surprised by this was Kurzweil, who has long predicted the rise of intelligent machines. It turns out that he leads an influential cabal of techno-optimists—a group that includes leading figures in Silicon Valley, scientific grandees, and even the first chief information officer of the Obama administration—that believes mankind is headed for a glorious, postbiological era that will follow the Singularity. On this view, humans will coevolve with machines until artificial intelligence inevitably surpasses the human kind (by 2029, on his calculation).

That is heady stuff, but what exactly is the Singularity? The week that *Time* put Kurzweil on its cover, Wikipedia—the current avatar of collective human insight—offered this reasonable definition for the term, which is borrowed from astrophysics:

"a hypothetical event occurring when technological progress becomes so rapid that it makes the future after the singularity qualitatively different and harder to predict. Many of the most recognized writers on the singularity, such as Vernor Vinge and Ray Kurzweil, define the concept in terms of the technological creation of super-intelligence, and allege that a postsingularity world would be unpredictable to humans due to an inability of human beings to imagine the intentions or capabilities of super-intelligent entities."

Everyone knows about Moore's law, which holds that the number of transistors that can be squeezed cheaply onto a computer chip will double every eighteen months to two years. This rule of thumb has held good for five decades, and thanks to a confluence of technological advances, magically seems likely to hold good for at least another couple of decades. Kurzweil's journey as a futurist began when he examined the progress in other realms of modern technology, and found that they too have been quietly improving at such astonishing rates. Whether it is the speed of microprocessors, the cost of computing power, the volume of DNA sequencing, the growth in Internet connectivity, or a host of other variables, he found the same explosive growth.

This law of accelerating returns, as it is known, underpins the modern digital economy and provides the strongest scientific support for his forecasts for the future. This idea of an ever-expanding universe of opportunity is widely held in technology circles. Kevin Kelly, a cofounder of *Wired* magazine and leading technology futurist, agrees with Kurzweil on this rather radical notion of increasing returns. In his book *New Rules for a New Economy*, he argues that as the interconnectedness of people and objects increases "the consequences of those connections multiply out even faster, so that initial successes aren't self-limiting, but self-feeding."

Dystopians, Unite

Even in the heart of Silicon Valley, though, there are some who are skeptical that these impressive trends actually add up to the Singularity. The naysayers even dared to gather once inside the Googleplex, the quirky California headquarters of the search firm, to ventilate their objections to this notion. At that private meeting held in 2010, which included leading scientists and technologists as well as science fiction writers, some argued that the movement had become New Age kookery rather than serious science. Geoffrey West, a theoretical physicist and former president of the august Santa Fe Institute, has even publicly dismissed the Singularity as complete "bullshit."

Other critics, such as Bill Joy, a cofounder of Sun Microsystems, agree with Kurzweil about the rapid technological change to come, but warn that this could lead to a dystopia of nanobots run amok and other techno-horrors. Eliezer Yudkowsky, a theorist in the field of artificial intelligence (AI), has put the danger this way: "The AI does not hate you, nor does it love you, but you are made out of atoms which it can use for something else." He and a band of like-minded futurists are working on developing a first generation of AI creatures that are explicitly friendly toward human beings, reasoning that they would get an evolutionary head start on any malicious superintelligent creatures that might follow.

Transcendent Man, a documentary released in 2011 about Kurzweil and his ideas, gave voice to a number of such critiques. To his credit, Kurzweil has been open to criticism over the years. Indeed, much of his recent writings has been devoted to responding to challenges and to putting his earlier predictions to a reality check. A recent essay on his website devotes some 150-odd pages of analysis to weighing up his earlier predictions and critiques of them, and argues that he got 78 percent of his predictions right. Had he left it there, it might have persuaded many fair-minded observers, but he could not resist adding that "most of the rest was wrong only by time frame."

On the worrisome point about technology's unintended dangers, he readily accepts that innovation can be a double-edged sword—just look at man's taming of fire, he says. But he insists that the risks, if properly managed, are more than outweighed by the rewards—just as man's mastery of fire has brought us much more gain than pain. He serves as an advisor to the American government on bioterrorism (he has been honored by several presidents for his innovations), and he acknowledges that a biological attack by some rogue group is inevitable. The way forward, he insists, is to develop rapid response systems to tackle new threats—much as global Internet SWAT teams now crush nascent computer viruses as quickly as they emerge. "The Internet has never been taken down by such attacks—not even once—and we can do the same for other threats," he insists.

That seems sensible enough, but push Kurzweil a bit more and one reaches trickier terrain. In response to questions about the religious implications of his confidence in science's ability to extend human life indefinitely, Kurzweil provides the provocative closing line of that documentary film: "Does God exist? I would say not yet." That smacks of insufferable hubris, scoffs one critic, who denounces him as a "pseudo-religious crackpot." One renowned futurist who counts herself as Kurzweil's friend says, "Ray's just having the world's most public midlife crisis."

Such notions send even techno-spiritualists such as Kevin Kelly into fits. He thinks the Singularity vision is a useful inspirational myth, but the God talk has him denouncing Kurzweil as a "modern-day prophet" who simply gets it "wrong." His magazine ran a damning critique of the Singularity notion back in 2008, offering numerous scientific arguments to suggest that superintelligence will prove far harder a nut to crack than imagined by the Singularitarians: "An algorithm is only a set of instructions, and even the most sophisticated machine executing the most elaborate instructions is still an unconscious automaton. Philosophy aside, a constellation of recent scientific findings indicates that no matter how fast CPUs become in future decades, they'll be no more aware than a toaster."

Ouch. Clearly, even the best-informed scientists still disagree about the rate at which artificial intelligence will encroach on human intelligence. Still, even if the bigger claims made for the Singularity are not realized, there is good reason to think Kurzweil is right in his most important argument: the world is entering a period of accelerating global innovation. If these efforts are directed at problems such as climate change and chronic diseases, then it is just possible that the human condition could improve dramatically this century. After all, that is precisely what happened over the twentieth century thanks to such technological marvels as electrification and vaccination.

Hail, *Homo Evolutis*

But what if the biggest breakthroughs come in improving the species itself? Some technology experts think humans might even evolve into a fitter, stronger, smarter, and better-looking species in coming decades—a mere blink of an eye in evolutionary terms. "Forget the Singularity—biology will trump technology!" insists

Juan Enriquez, an author and biotechnology expert. Enriquez and Steve Gullans argue in "Homo Evolutis," a striking essay, that the breathtaking advances seen today in biotechnology, gene therapy, epigenetics, proteomics, and myriad related fields are turbocharging evolution itself. "The idea of a rapid evolution of our species into a species that directly and deliberately guides its own evolution, and that of other species, is no longer completely outlandish because it is not one technology, government, company, region or discipline that is driving speciation."

They predict that this will force a rethink of politically correct nostrums maintaining that all humans are created the same. Instead, they posit that "a robust moral position embraces diversity as one of humanity's greatest assets." As genomics advances, for example, scientists are discovering that some humans (often in some parts of the world) are born with the ability to be superior sprinters, high-altitude climbers, and so on. If one's rival in the Tour de France inherited such a genetic trait through sheer dumb luck of parentage, is it really cheating if one uses gene therapy to obtain such a trait (in a manner that cannot be traced)? What if your child's classmate genetically inherited a superior ability to do higher-order math or to master complex languages and you had the chance to give your hardworking child a painless treatment that would level the playing field?

As with Kurzweil's forecasts for machine superintelligence and postbiological bodies, this argument raises hackles from some in the scientific establishment. Even if the prognosticators are wrong about the pace of change, though, they may turn out to be right about the direction. What is more, any such hyperevolution will raise uncomfortable questions about what it means to be a human.

There is reason to think all of this talk about exponential progress in technology and biology is not just the stuff of science fantasy.

The OECD, a research body not given to flights of fancy, recently published a detailed look at trends in science and technology. It argued that "converging trends in nanotechnology, biotechnology, robotics and computing are creating unprecedented capacities to manipulate nature. This is even changing what 'natural' means." The agency's experts note that the Korean government now has a robot ethics charter, and that a study commissioned by the British armed forces concludes "an implantable information chip could be wired directly into the human user's brain by 2035 . . . in the longer term, technology convergence may permit enhancement of healthy people."

William Nordhaus, a Yale economist, has analyzed productivity growth in computing over time. He observes that there has been a phenomenal increase in computing power over the past century. Depending on the standard used, it has skyrocketed since the days of manual computing by a factor of 1.7 trillion to 76 trillion. Looking to the future, he observes that "aside from humans, computers and software are the ultimate general purpose technology . . . with the potential for penetrating and fundamentally changing virtually every corner of economic life." At current rates of improvement, he says provocatively, computers are approaching the complexity and computational capacity of the human brain.

The OECD's Andrew Wyckoff points out why this matters so much in an age of wicked problems. While governance and other underlying factors matter greatly, he argues that technological innovation can and must play a critical role in tackling thorny societal challenges. For example, the 2030 Water Resources Group, an independent nongovernmental outfit, has estimated, based on current trends, that in two decades the world's thirst for fresh water will exceed likely supply by 40 percent. Better end-use efficiency of the sort already seen in some parts of the agricultural and industrial sectors could help, as would new supply infrastructure, but a big shortfall still seems likely.

New technologies can help close that gap: "The outputs of biotechnology research [such as genetically modified crops] are helping to meet the challenge of doubling food production sustainably by 2050 while using approximately the same area of arable land, fewer resources (particularly fossil fuel, water and nitrogen), and at the same time mitigating climate change." Though the technology for genetic modification of crops is denounced by environmentalists, it is estimated to have delivered net economic benefits in 2008 of $9.2 billion, evenly split between farmers in the rich world and the poor world.

Such a level-headed endorsement of today's technology revolution should make clear that the world stands on the cusp of a new golden age for innovation. After all, it is precisely such a culture of continuous improvement—which began in earnest with the industrial revolution and which promises to speed up yet again if Kurzweil's predictions of a new postindustrial revolution are correct—that explains the astonishing improvements in the human condition over time. It is easy to forget that the twentieth century marked a period of unprecedented economic growth that lifted masses of people out of abject poverty. It also brought technological marvels such as modern pharmaceuticals and other advances in public health that tackled many preventable diseases. The result has been a great enhancement of human welfare and longer, better lives for most people living in most places on earth.

But of course the twentieth century's advances did not solve all of the world's problems—and there are plenty of new, twenty-first-century global challenges now confronting humanity. Mindful that market forces may not necessarily direct the coming innovation revolution at those wicked problems, Kurzweil has decided to help forge the future. With help from the founders of Google and other Internet-age figures, he launched Singularity University in 2009. This remarkable interdisciplinary institute, housed on a NASA campus near Silicon Valley, aims to churn out inventors, entrepreneurs, and investors who will tap into tomorrow's disruptive technology trends to take on such problems as water scarcity, neglected tropical diseases, and climate change. Every summer, the school takes in several dozen extremely bright, entrepreneurially minded students for its accelerated graduate program. The students are dynamos from a variety of backgrounds and geographies, and they are exposed to some of the world's leading technologists with the aim of accomplishing "ten to the ninth plus": coming up with technology-based solutions to big problems that will positively impact at least a billion people within ten years.

"We need to be more ambitious in taking on the world's grand challenges!" So declares Peter Diamandis, the dynamic force behind the X Prize Foundation (a charity that aims to kick-start innovation in areas such as clean energy and space travel by sponsoring incentive prizes, a topic covered in the next chapter) and a cofounder of Singularity University. The aim of the institution, he explains, is to open the eyes of the world's best and brightest to the leapfrogs made possible by exponentially advancing innovation, and to instill a passion to change the world. He shares Kurzweil's belief that humanity is on the verge of a knowledge explosion. For almost all of history, he argues, humans toiled in ignorance. But since the industrial revolution, science and technology have advanced and the human condition has improved dramatically. And we are just scratching the surface of what is possible, he insists, if only we dare to dream: "Humans have advanced rapidly for just a hundred of our 100,000 years on earth—we still know nothing!"

A Very Sexy Idea

Whenever one hears extraordinary claims being made, it is only right to be a bit skeptical. History provides lots of examples of technological marvels supposedly just round the corner—jetpacks for everyone!—that somehow fail to materialize. And even linear trends, never mind exponential ones, rarely continue forever. Rather, technological progress has often come in fits and starts, with dramatic leaps forward for a while and then a bit of wheel spinning while inventions diffuse slowly through the economy. This happens because once in a while some promising set of technologies attracts so much attention and money that it leaps forward. This happened with the space program thanks to the Apollo moon shot and nuclear science thanks to the Manhattan Project, and with computers and the Internet thanks to the investment capital that poured into this area before and after the bursting of the great technology bubble a decade ago.

So merely pointing to impressive growth trends today does not prove that technology will continue to improve in a reliably dramatic fashion. It may not. Even so, there is a deeper reason to share in the techno-optimists' view of the future: the evolutionary basis for innovation. Humans are the only species capable of break-through innovation. Some other animals do use tools, and some ants do specialize at certain tasks. But these skills are not cumulative, and the animals in question do not improve their technologies generation after generation. Only humans innovate continuously and cleverly.

Why should that be? Some have suggested that perhaps something about the chemistry of big brains leads us to tinker. Others have suggested that mastery of language or the capacity for imitation and social learning hold the key. Matt Ridley, a zoologist by training, believes the explanation lies not within the human brain but outside: innovation is a social phenomenon. In *The Rational Optimist*, he argues cheekily that the way the human collective brain grows is by "ideas having sex."

This theory is, in a way, the offspring that would result if the ideas of Charles Darwin could somehow have mated with those of Adam Smith. On this view, trade is the spark that lit the fire of human imagination, as it made possible not only the exchange of goods but also the exchange of ideas. Trade also encouraged specialization, since it rewarded individuals and communities to focus on areas of comparative advantage. And such specialists—in contrast with their generalist rivals or ancestors—had the time and the incentive to develop better methods and technologies to do tasks.

Through most of history, most people lived lives of quiet desperation, humiliating servitude, and grinding poverty. And yet, despite the pessimistic proclamations of Paul Ehrlich and many other pundits, economic growth and technological progress have come to the rescue time and again. Ample statistical evidence shows that life has indeed gotten better for most people in most places on most metrics. Whether one measures air and water pollution in California, vaccination rates in Bangladesh, or life expectancy in Japan, this conclusion is indisputable. Rising incomes played a big role in this, but even more credit must go to innovation. So argues Charles Kenny of the Center for Global Development in *Getting Better*: "The biggest success of development has not been making people richer but, rather, has been making the things that really matter—things like health and education—cheaper and more widely available. It is the invention and spread of technology and ideas that have, literally, reduced the cost of living."

The reason Ehrlich and the related Club of Rome camp of thinkers got it wrong several decades ago was because they saw worrisome trends and forecast linearly to doomsday. But such a view ignores the role of feedback loops and market responses, which inevitably lead to the robust interplay of scarcity, price signals, substitution, investment, invention, and diffusion. Once innovation is taken into account, development turns out to be a dynamic dance. And now, mankind has the chance to build on that insight in this new century as it takes on poverty, neglected and chronic diseases, climate change, and other grand global challenges.

What is most exciting about the Singularity vision is this: the hard evidence and exponential technology trends on which its extrapolations are based suggest that the current heated pace of global innovation is not only going to continue but may well accelerate dramatically in coming years. Asked if he thought the wave of technological progress brought by the Internet revolution was cresting, Bill Gates responds animatedly: "Absolutely not!"

It is hard to offer precise measurements, he notes, but the pace of technological change is more rapid today than at any point in history with the exception of perhaps the Victorian age of invention. What is more, he insists, there is no plateau in sight. Gates believes huge advances are coming in fields ranging from advanced computer modeling and materials science to communications and agricultural technologies that suggest even better days may lie ahead. When one takes into account the radical ways that innovation itself is being innovated, as the next section on open innovation explains, his big claim actually seems quite plausible. As Paul Saffo, a forecaster of large-scale change at Discern Analytics, observes wisely: "Change is never linear. Our expectations are linear, but new technologies come in S curves, so we routinely overestimate short-term change and underestimate long-term change." Never mistake a clear view for a short distance, he adds.

In the end, it seems pretty plain that the global pace of innovation is picking up today. That is the broad trend that underpins many of the other trends described in this book, especially the breathtaking move toward open innovation described in the next chapter. As the speed of change picks up, it will inevitably disrupt many lives and business models even as it creates huge new opportunities for improving lifestyles and cultivating economic growth. If enough entrepreneurs seize upon exponential technologies to come up with novel solutions to wicked problems, then today's accelerating pace of innovation could even usher in a brighter future for humanity.

On this view, the future looks bright. Still, some are taking no chances. In his final *Jeopardy!* answer, one of the human contestants conceded defeat to IBM's supercomputer by scribbling a cheeky line from *The Simpsons*: "I, for one, welcome our new computer overlords." One hopes that Watson was amused.

5

_____

So Long, Silo

Thanks to the democratization of innovation, the smartest people in your business don't work for you any longer. That, in a nutshell, explains the big move toward open and networked models of innovation at companies, nonprofits, and even governments today.

This trend promises many benefits, but caution is in order. Firms that embrace user-driven models of development risk being led down the garden trail of gold-plating offerings for the best customers, a classic trap that leaves an incumbent exposed to disruption by cheaper innovators. Crowdsourcing has produced such marvels as Wikipedia and Linux, but there is evidence that it can tap the mediocrity and stupidity of crowds, not just their wisdom. And incentive prizes, while generally an efficient way to encourage open innovation, work well only for certain types of problems.

Smart innovators should embrace open methods with gusto but keep a sharp lookout for potential pitfalls.

Berkeley seems like a fitting place to find the godfather of the open innovation movement basking in glory. The California city was, after all, at the very heart of the antiestablishment movement of the 1960s and has spawned plenty of radical thinkers. One recent sunny day not too long ago, Henry Chesbrough, a professor at the Haas Business School at the University of California at Berkeley, observed with a smile that "this is the fortieth anniversary of the Summer of Love."

Chesbrough's three books—*Open Innovation*, *Open Business Models*, and *Open Services Innovation*—have popularized the notion of looking for bright ideas outside of an organization. Firms are increasingly accomplishing this using several approaches. One way that firms, and even governments, can do this is by offering incentive prizes to those that solve specific challenges. Another approach is by using crowdsourcing, which leads firms to cast a wide net among a group—say, regular customers, or the public at large—to fish for bright ideas. Although these approaches are showing great promise, as the latter half of this chapter demonstrates, they deal only with the idea-generation part of the innovation process. Some firms are going much further by leaving behind their inward-looking, top-down innovation processes altogether.

As the concept of open innovation has become ever more fashionable, the corporate R&D lab has become ever less relevant. Studies show that many of the ideas that turn into successful products and services no longer come from there. To see why, travel to Cincinnati, Ohio—which is about as far removed culturally from Berkeley as one can get in the United States. This conservative midwestern city is home to Procter & Gamble, historically one of the most traditional firms in the country. For decades, the company that brought the world Ivory soap, Crest toothpaste, and Tide laundry detergent had a closed innovation process centered around its own secretive R&D operations.

No longer. P&G has radically altered the way it comes up with new ideas and products. It now welcomes and works with universities, suppliers, and outside inventors. It also offers them a share in the rewards. In less than a decade, P&G has increased the proportion of new-product ideas originating from outside of the firm from less than a fifth to around half. That has boosted innovation and, says its respected former boss, A. G. Lafley, is the main reason why P&G has been able to lift its long-term growth rate and boost its profits and flagging share price.

Why did the firm make the switch to an open approach, a risky move given the firm's centralized and successful past? Simply put, Lafley saw the writing on the wall. The firm's tight network of global innovation laboratories were simply not nimble enough to keep pace with the times. For one thing, multinationals such as P&G have grown so big that they need to keep generating enormous amounts of organic growth just to keep pace, which puts additional pressure on internal innovation labs that simply cannot keep up. By 2000, it became clear to Lafley that internal research productivity was stagnating even as the costs of innovation were soaring, thanks to the explosion of new technologies. Worse yet, globalization meant that markets were much more competitive than before.

The only way forward, the firm decided, was to embrace an outside-in strategy it calls Connect + Develop. Larry Huston and Nabil Sakkab, then senior innovation figures at P&G, put it this way in a seminal article published back in 2006: for every researcher inside the company, they calculated, the democratization of innovation meant there were two hundred just as good outside the firm. They also saw that the most important innovations were increasingly emerging from small and medium-size firms and even individual entrepreneurs, not from big research labs.

So the firm took the plunge. It opened its arms to outside innovators and frowned on the "not invented here" attitude common at research labs. It invited researchers from Los Alamos National Laboratory, German chemical company BASF, and other firms to sit in on the meetings of its once-secretive research advisory groups. The company invested in a number of novel efforts at open innovation, such as Yet2.com (an exchange for intellectual property) and YourEncore (a network for retired experts). It placed dozens of challenges on InnoCentive, the pioneering online platform that runs prize competitions matching firms struggling with technical problems with a wide array of clever "solvers" from around the world.

The progress has not always been even, but the results have been impressive. In the years following the launch of the scheme, research productivity shot up dramatically. The firm's innovation success rate—as measured by successful market entry of new products—doubled, even as its costs of innovation declined. Scouring the globe for "adjacent products" and tapping the distributed genius of the firm's network of suppliers (just the top fifteen suppliers employ some fifty thousand researchers, for example) has produced some dramatic winners. Mr. Clean Magic Eraser, a blockbuster product, was licensed from BASF, while the Swiffer Duster, another hugely successful cleaning product, was adapted from a product invented by Japan's Unicharm Corporation.

Not satisfied, the firm has now redoubled its efforts. It has set up a disruptive-innovation college, and expanded its program of sharing people with noncompeting firms. In 2008, for example, P&G and Google swapped two dozen employees for a few weeks; the marketer wanted more online experience, while the search firm wanted to learn about building brands. It expanded its Connect + Develop efforts, and now aims to triple the plan's contribution to innovation development (which means getting $3 billion of its annual sales growth from outsiders). As a result of all this, half of its innovation efforts meet profit and revenue targets, whereas back in 2000 only 15 percent did. The company projects that the typical new initiative in 2014 and 2015 will have nearly twice the revenue as those of 2011. Most impressively, it has managed to triple its innovation success rate. If it is able to sustain such improvements, it may justify the claim made by Huston and Sakkab that open innovation will become the dominant innovation model for this century—and that "for most companies, the alternative invent-it-ourselves model is a sure path to diminishing returns."

IBM is another iconic firm that has jumped on the open innovation bandwagon. The once-secretive company has done a sharp U-turn and embraced Linux, an open-source software language. IBM now gushes about being part of the open innovation community, yielding hundreds of software patents to the creative commons rather than registering them for itself. However, it also continues to take out patents at a record pace in other areas, such as advanced materials, and in the process racks up some $1 billion a year in licensing fees.

Since an army of programmers around the world work on developing Linux, essentially at no cost, IBM now has an extremely cheap and robust operating system. It makes money by providing its clients with services that support the use of Linux—and charging them for it. Using open-source software saves IBM a whopping $400 million a year, according to Paul Horn, the firm's former head of research. The company is so committed to openness that it now carries out occasional online jam sessions during which many thousands of its employees exchange ideas in a mass form of brain-storming. The largest one was its Innovation Jam in 2006, which involved 150,000 people from more than a hundred countries and sixty-seven companies, and it led directly to the launch of ten new businesses seeded with an initial total investment of $100 million. As a result of all this, IBM now makes more money from innova-tive, outward-facing services (which are used even by its rivals) than from traditional business lines.

Chesbrough, of course, heartily approves. He reckons that "IBM and P&G have timed their shift to a high-volume open-business model very well" and that if their competitors do not do the same, they will be in trouble. And dozens of firms ranging from Clorox, a household products firm, to Air Products, an indus-trial gases company, are, in fact, now moving toward open innova-tion. Kimberly-Clark, which sells paper products, cut its time to market with new products by almost a third using open innovation. Thanks to help from an outside collaborator, it was able to bring SunSignals, a wearable product that alerts the user when she is get-ting sunburned and needs to reapply sunscreen, to market in just six months.

Xerox's PARC laboratory in Palo Alto was long the archetype of the vertically integrated model of research, but the firm has re-cently gone the other way with a new open innovation center in Chennai, India. Usually when firms open research labs overseas, they spend lots of money on fancy equipment and hire hundreds of researchers that end up as part of its secretive global web reporting back to corporate headquarters. In contrast, what Xerox is doing is hiring a handful of "connectors" in India who are there to scan the local horizon for potential partners. Sophie Vandebroek, the firm's chief technology officer, explains that "every person we hire will partner with at least fifty or more people."

From Ivory Tower to People Power

Open innovation was not always the rage. A few decades ago, notes Chesbrough, corporate strategy gurus such as Michael Porter of Harvard Business School were advising companies to invest heavily in in-house corporate research and development as a competitive edge against their rivals. Either offer a cheaper product or invest and innovate to come up with differentiated offerings, went the mantra. In that era, a key metric of a firm's health and innovativeness was the percentage of its sales that it plowed back into research and development. This was the heyday of such legendary corporate research labs as Xerox PARC and AT&T's Bell Labs, which produced many brilliant academic papers and Nobel Prize winners. When Bill Joy, a cofounder of Sun Microsystems, declared back in 1990 that "no matter who you are, most of the smartest people work for someone else," he was viewed as a radical.

Today, firms are rushing to pare back their in-house research and beef up their open and networked innovation efforts. A big reason for this is the fact that pouring ever more money into yesterday's research model simply does not produce better results. Analysis done by Booz & Company shows that "more money is not connected to any better outcome." Every year the firm scrutinizes the amount of money spent on R&D by hundreds of leading firms, adjusting for the sector in which they compete, and gauges whether there is any correlation with metrics such as financial performance and market success. Spending nothing on research is unwise, to be sure, as the firms in the bottom 10 percent of a sector do underperform. However, even allowing for the fact that there are some minimum thresholds and benefits of scale in R&D, Booz found year after year that the lavish spenders do not get better performance.

Big-company bosses have figured out the bottom line: merely pouring more money into in-house corporate labs does not equal more innovation. In 1981, spending by firms with more than twenty-five thousand employees made up some 70 percent of all industrial R&D spending; by 2007, that had fallen to just 35 percent. Meanwhile, spending by firms with fewer than one thousand employees shot up over that same period from a 4 percent share to 24 percent. Big firms and in-house R&D still matter, as the overall spending by the big outfits did increase fourfold to $95 billion in 2007. But if you want to see which way the wind is blowing, consider the fact that R&D spending by small firms shot up fiftyfold to $65 billion during that same period. Barry Jaruzelski of Booz puts a sharp point on his firm's number crunching: "AT&T actually didn't benefit much from that Nobel-winning research back then, and today nobody has the resources or capacity to do everything on their own. Collaboration is a must."

That explains the big move in recent years toward crowdsourcing, a term popularized by Jeff Howe of *Wired* magazine. Back in 2006, he wrote an influential cover story on the topic with this provocative passage: "Remember outsourcing? Sending jobs to India and China is so 2003. The new pool of cheap labor: everyday people using their spare cycles to create content, solve problems, even do corporate R&D." In the years since, everyone from marketers to aid workers to government bureaucracies has jumped on this bandwagon.

How well has this especially sexy tool of open innovation fared? The idea is not as new as its boosters would have you believe, given that it builds on decades-old efforts at getting close to customers. And it's hardly easy to do or risk-free. For those organizations that have figured out how to use crowdsourcing properly, though, it can produce spectacular results.

Get Ready for a Wiki World

On a day in east London one recent summer, a warehouse was taken over by a company eager to make a splash. It was decked out to look like a cool New York loft. The Ministry of Sound, a London nightclub, was hired for a party afterward. The event was packed with journalists. At last the stars took to the stage. Alas, it was not the latest British rock sensation—it was a group of besuited Nokia executives there to announce a dramatic change in corporate strategy.

Nokia, a Finnish company, makes mobile phone handsets that are used by nearly a billion people around the world. However, it now wants to be a services firm. Why? Niklas Savander, of Nokia, argued that the mobile phone business "is moving so rapidly, thanks to the democratization of the Internet, that we must innovate or die." Providing people with devices alone is not enough, the company has concluded.

With half of the value and most of the innovation in a mobile phone handset now made up of software, "the leap to services is not so great as it seems," he added. After extensive consultations with its best customers, Nokia rolled out novel products offering users networked gaming, music downloads, and other services from their handsets. As customers became enthralled by the ecosystem of services on offer, went the theory, they would in turn co-create the next generation of innovations with the firm.

Visionary companies need to do even more than that, argued C. K. Prahalad, the late business professor at the University of Michigan who shot to fame with his theories about doing business with the world's poorest people. He argued that firms should cultivate a network that includes consumers in which "personalized, evolvable experiences are the goal, and products and services evolve as a means to that end." That sounds like a notion straight from the Summer of Love.

Yet despite the dangers, some companies have successfully brought consumers and others from outside the firm's R&D labs into the innovation process. Lego, the Danish maker of children's building blocks, did it successfully. Inspired by research done at MIT on how children learn, Lego launched Mindstorms, a robotics kit that allows people to design their own robots and other devices. Users—including many adults—have come up with all sorts of ways of putting together the kit to make things ranging from intruder alarms to sorting machines and even the controls for small unmanned aircraft.

Eric von Hippel of MIT, author of the influential *Democratizing Innovation*, has long advocated user-driven innovation. He says you can see it all around you. Users who feel passionate about certain products—a mountain bike, a kayak, or even a car—often fiddle around with them because the products fail to provide exactly what they want. He reckons open innovation misses the point if it's not inspired by users, because companies are then "just talking about a market for intellectual property rights, it's still the old model."

Von Hippel thinks that firms close to their lead users can come up with much better designs for new products and get them to market faster. This advice appears to contradict what Clay Christensen says (that listening to one's best customers leads firms to gold-plate assets and grow vulnerable to disruptive rivals), but in fact the two theses are compatible. Christensen's point about disruptive innovation is that firms should not uncritically cater to the demands of their most profitable current customers. They must question those demands or they could end up doing little more than gold-plating their current offerings; like von Hippel, he thinks firms should keep a closer watch on new and dissatisfied users, who are much more likely to be the source of disruptive ideas.

Invented on Facebook

Von Hippel adds that networks of hypercritical users can even help firms quickly filter out bad ideas and thus encourage the process of fast failing. The craze for social networking sites such as Facebook could be useful. Studies have shown that how people relate to the products they use, something often discussed on such sites, reveals social structure and preferences. That can help firms understand more about their customers and how to market products more effectively.

User networks operate in many businesses. OnStar, a mobile information system widely launched by GM in 2000, was initially meant only to provide safety and emergency services for drivers. But motorists wanted it to do more, and they pushed GM to innovate. Now OnStar can check if a car is working properly, open the doors for a driver who accidentally locks the keys inside, shut off the engine if the auto is carjacked, and even locate the nearest pizza place. GM believes OnStar helps to improve the firm's brand loyalty because it keeps the company in constant touch with its customers.

There is another compelling argument for firms to think hard about recruiting users to speed up and improve their innovation efforts. In rich countries much of the economic activity now involves services, but profit margins are eroding. Commoditization often occurs even faster in services than in physical products: because innovations are easier to copy, patents can provide less protection, up-front costs are lower, and product cycles are shorter.

User-driven innovation is exciting, but the full-octane blend of crowdsourcing involves all kinds of people, not just your best customers. Its poster child is Wikipedia, the online encyclopedia that has surpassed the *Encyclopedia Britannica* entirely through crowdsourced efforts.

These approaches fall into several principal categories. Firms can seek wisdom from the crowd: Quora does this by allowing people to post questions that can be answered by anyone online, with the best answers earning points or visibility. Firms can create using the imagination of the crowd: an early example of this was Threadless, a T-shirt manufacturer that gets its designs by casting a wide net among nondesigners. Firms can also allow the crowd to vote on things: eBay does this by allowing users to rate the reliability of counterparties on the site, and Amazon does this by allowing users to vote on which comments and reviews were most useful. Firms can even use the crowd to do funding: Marillion, a British band, led the way in the 1990s by getting fans to underwrite an entire tour, while Kiva, a peer-to-peer lending site, channels money from small lenders in rich countries to small entrepreneurs in poor ones. Taken together, these approaches can be an incredibly powerful way to tap into the distributed brain cells of the global population.

Novartis, a Swiss pharmaceutical giant, has put its raw scientific findings in the area of diabetes up on the Web for all to see. This seems odd at first, given that pharmaceutical firms are notoriously secretive about intellectual property rights and given that the market for diabetes drugs is, unlike the ones for neglected diseases afflicting only developing countries, hugely lucrative. It did this not out of altruism, however, but because it grew convinced that this field is so complicated that only a concerted global push, aided by crowdsourcing, will speed solutions. Because the firm still retains in-house knowledge of what all that data means, Novartis believes it still has a valuable head start on any rivals when the time comes to go for a patent or rush a drug to market.

The incumbent firms in stodgy old-economy industries such as cars and energy are reluctant to follow this trend, but newcomers in those industries are jumping in. Local Motors is an American start-up automobile manufacturer that crowdsources the designs for its specialty vehicles. When Facebook came up with a radical new way to make its servers much more energy efficient in early 2011, it made the blueprints available to all for free. That came as a shock, for the energy efficiency of one's server farms is a key competitive edge in this business. Google, for example, keeps its green techniques quiet. Being much smaller, and without the army of in-house engineers that the search giant has, Facebook decided it could benefit more from any improvements made on its designs by a global collective brain than it would by secrecy.

This is all pretty impressive, but a rather basic question seems in order. How is it possible that so many people—presumably some with day jobs and lives to lead—are now suddenly coming together to solve other people's difficult problems? Clay Shirky, a prominent technology commentator, argues that the key is the "cognitive surplus" that he claims people have these days to work on such projects. The shift to a postindustrial order gave most people lots of free time and spare thinking capacity, he argues, but until recently ordinary folk were not able to do much with it. On this view, television sucked them into a passive stupor, and for decades society wasted much of that theoretical cognitive surplus. But now, thanks to the new tools of social media and the latest iteration of Web and wireless technologies, people can connect and develop other people's products, analyze public health data in other people's cities, and send micropayments to microfinance charities in other places such as Micronesia. Donald Tapscott, coauthor with Anthony D. Williams of the provocative book *Wikinomics* and its recent follow-up *Macrowikinomics*, even makes the grand claim that mass collaboration with social networking adds up to an entirely new mode of social production.

Beyond the Wisdom of Crowds

Through much of history, crowds were seen not as a fount of wisdom but rather as a source of folly, radicalism, and even blood-thirsty excess. Investing in the Dutch horticultural industry or the Peruvian fertilizer trade are, taken at face value, reasonable propositions. But as the madness of crowds took over, though, wild-eyed speculation led to the infamous tulip and guano financial bubbles.

In other cases, reasonable men and women have been shouted down by zealots howling for blood, be they Puritans in witch-hunting Salem, crusaders in the Holy Land, or democrats in the French Reign of Terror. That explains why, for centuries, crowds were regarded with suspicion. Charles MacKay captured the excesses of the nineteenth century beautifully in his book *Extraordinary Popular Delusions and the Madness of Crowds*: "Men, it has been well said, think in herds. It will be seen that they go mad in herds, while they only recover their senses slowly, and one by one."

Ah, but that was before the age of wikinomics. With the triumph in the last decade of Internet commerce, ubiquitous connectivity, and much more democratic access to information about everything, a new theory began to take hold. Rather than herd

behavior, argued such heretics as the *New Yorker*'s James Surow-
iecki, what the new collective consciousness emerging on the Web
displayed was the *wisdom* of crowds. Thanks to the Internet, this
contrarian camp argues, a disparate bunch of strangers can make
more accurate decisions and predictions than any single person or
technical specialist. Just look, argue such folk, at how successful
this approach works online in everything from eBay vendor ratings
to Amazon book reviews even to content sites such as Wikipedia
and Digg.

The counterrevolution certainly won over big business, as many
firms have invested heavily in technologies to harvest the wisdom-
of-crowds. Greater openness and inclusiveness in decision making,
whether about what vendors are crooks or which books to read, is
probably a good thing, but could it be possible that the wisdom-
of-crowds crowd goes too far in its claims? Scrutinize some of the
celebrated examples, and it turns out there is not much of a crowd
involved—and there may not be much wisdom either.

It turns out there are limits to the magic that crowdsourcing
can do. The spin on cognitive surplus put by Shirky's argument is
an appealing theory, but it implies that people with free time only
want to do productive, socially valuable things such as saving the
rain forest or marginally valuable things such as helping consumer
products companies come up with better slogans for toilet paper.
Human nature being what it is, surely some people will use any
cognitive surplus toward unproductive or even illicit or immoral
ends. Jaron Lanier, author of *You Are Not a Gadget*, argues that
another fundamental flaw of this approach is that it could lead to a
dystopian world of "just everybody doing everything."

What's more, at times barely 1 percent of any given crowd—
say, on Amazon or on Digg—actively participates in voting or vet-
ting. Studies done by the Wharton Business School suggest that

"power users," who may be motivated by some self-interested agenda, may be skewing the results. Attempts to average out results could lead to something worse: a reversion to a bland mediocrity of answers, ignoring the truly brilliant outliers. Experts argue that some of these problems can be overcome by ensuring that a genuinely open and large crowd, as opposed to a close circle of heavy users, both participates in the crowdsourcing and shares in the profits that arise from it. But that approach produces headaches of its own, for it often takes just as much time and effort, if not more, for a firm to do crowdsourcing properly as it does just to do the job in-house.

An Open and Shut Case?

It is not just crowdsourcing that has attracted skeptics: some are unimpressed by the broader claims made for all of open innovation. Kenneth Morse, formerly head of MIT's Entrepreneurship Center, scoffs at IBM's claim to be an open company: "They're open only in markets, like software, where they have fallen behind. In hardware markets, where they have the lead, they are extremely closed."

David Gann and Linus Dahlander, of London's Imperial College, are also skeptical. They argue that firms have always been open to some degree and that the benefits differ depending on their line of business. Those using older technologies, for instance, may benefit less. They also point out that the costs of open innovation, in management distraction or lost intellectual property rights, are not nearly as well studied as its putative benefits.

Yet another critique comes from capital-intensive industries, where products take a long time to develop and remain on sale for years. Toyota's Bill Reinert laughs when asked about open innovation. With the billions of dollars his firm spends on research and on equipping its factories—not to mention a five-year product development cycle—he suggests it would be foolish to open up and allow rivals to steal its edge. "Eventually even Google will have to make something tangible, and when they do they will protect it—just like Tesla Motors [a much-ballyhooed Silicon Valley start-up that makes electric cars], which does not have an open model," he adds.

GE's boss, Jeff Immelt, observes that his firm is a leader in a number of fields, such as making jet engines and locomotives, which requires "doing things that almost nobody else in the world can do" and where intellectual property rights and a degree of secrecy still matter. Mark Little, his head of research, is even more skeptical and says outside ideas "don't really stick well here." He professes great satisfaction with the output of GE's own research laboratories. "We're pretty happy with the hand we've got," he adds.

Though it is a formidable force sweeping through business today, even boosters of open innovation agree that there are perils. One of them is that it is not easy to work with outsiders. When two firms try to tango, priorities can differ, trust may be lacking, they may have wildly differing expectations on returns on investment and risk, and they may be working on very different time horizons. Corporate cultures can sometimes clash, and some outsiders are not used to working in a business environment.

Other difficulties arise when traditional R&D centers try to work with many outside innovators, as typically happens in incentive prizes or with crowdsourcing. Alph Bingham, cofounder of InnoCentive, observes that "it takes a leap of faith for big-company R&D to believe that freelance scientists are reliable." The biggest problem is that researchers at a firm ordered to work with outsiders can fear losing control. They are also sometimes worried that successful ideas from the outside might make them look less valuable to a firm. Many also dread the workload of having to sift through thousands of suggestions of variable quality in hopes of finding that precious needle in the haystack.

Open Up and Say *Aha!*

Despite all of these legitimate concerns and obstacles, a growing number of firms are concluding that the benefits of working with people from such diverse organizations are worth the effort. For one thing, patents are becoming much less important than brands and trade secrets, given the speed at which products can be brought to market. It is true that some of the rising stars in developing economies are beginning to take out more patents, but many of their innovations are still kept quiet. So fluid are their markets, and so weak the historical patent protection in them, that bosses often prefer to keep things in the dark and come up with the next innovation as necessary to stay ahead of the competition.

Even in developed markets, the acceleration of innovation is making patents less relevant. What is more, say brand experts at P&G (which claims not even to count patents any longer), the dizzying pace of change today confuses consumers with a baffling array of choices. Such firms are increasingly turning to trusted brands to simplify things for their customers. Andrew Herbert, head of Microsoft's research center in Cambridge, England, puts it this way: "Our brand hides a tremendous amount of innovation."

Open innovation also appears to keep corporate bureaucrats on their toes, making companies better at competing. The combination of exciting new technologies and juiced-up management processes has, according to Lafley, helped P&G to reduce its rate of failed product launches from eight out of ten to just half.

Unilever's David Duncan insists that his firm—one of P&G's biggest competitors—is much better connected to its customers than it was. "Years ago, when I joined, we were very closed, vertically integrated, and owned most of the value chain—even the chemicals and software we used," he says. Now it is much more receptive to ideas and services from the outside, even posting challenges on the Internet for people to come up with new ideas. But he too confesses that there can be difficulties: "It's like the first time you used Google; it's scary and a bit tricky, but soon you see that it's great."

So how do you know if open innovation will work for a particular company? It may well depend not just on what a company does but also on how it is perceived in the market. Hal Sirkin, of the Boston Consulting Group, suggests that rather than see firms such as P&G and IBM as truly open innovators, it is better to view them as beacons. They have enough world-class experts working for them to attract outsiders who have brilliant ideas. Such firms are "open" in the sense that they are now casting a very wide net in their search for ideas. However, once they have captured the essence of those ideas, argues Sirkin, "they control them and the process of getting them to market."

Despite all the caveats, though, it is clear that open innovation done properly is a good thing and that it is here to stay. For a business that uses open and networked innovation, it matters less where ideas are invented, especially if it uses the sorts of remarkable incentive prizes that are now in the making.

Eyes on the Prize

One recent weekend, a curious cabal gathered in a converted warehouse in a fashionably grungy part of San Francisco for a closed-door conference. The group included some of the world's leading scientific experts in fields ranging from astrophysics and nanotechnology to health and energy. Also attending were leading entrepreneurs and captains of industry, including Ratan Tata, the chairman of India's Tata Group. The group was brought together by the X Prize Foundation.

What were they up to? The foundation shot to prominence with the Ansari X Prize, which offered $10 million to the first private sector outfit to fly a reusable aircraft 100 kilometers into space safely twice within two weeks. Defying skeptics, a team financed by Paul Allen, a cofounder of Microsoft, won that prize in 2004. Peter Diamandis, the mastermind behind the foundation, grew convinced that "focused and talented teams in pursuit of a prize and acclaim can change the world."

So he gathered those big shots and big brains in San Francisco to dream up more audacious prizes to tackle grand global challenges ranging from climate change to malnutrition. In the wake of the disastrous BP oil spill in the Gulf of Mexico, for example, the foundation announced a $1.4 million challenge to come up with clever ways to clean up oil spills. This came just days after the final round of competition for the foundation's Progressive Automotive X Prize, a $10 million contest designed to spur the development of the best car that can achieve a fuel economy of 100 miles per gallon of gasoline-equivalent energy.

The X Prize plotters are hardly alone. Many charities, including the Gates Foundation, are now increasing their use of incentive prizes. Industry is also growing keen on this approach and is often turning to online prize platforms. The biggest shift may be yet to come, though, as there are signs that governments are now jumping on the prize bandwagon.

The result is a dramatic surge in prize money on offer. This trend raises two questions. First, do prizes really induce innovation? And second, is it really a good use of taxpayer money for governments to be offering prizes?

Prizes in themselves are nothing new, of course. The Longitude Prize—a purse of up to £20,000—was offered by the British Parliament in 1714 for the discovery of a practical means for ships to determine their longitude. This was an enormous problem on the high seas, as the inability to work out longitude on the sailboats of the age often led to costly and deadly errors in navigation. The greatest minds of the British scientific academy wrestled with this problem but could not crack it. Sir Isaac Newton, for example, was convinced the answer lay in astronomy.

Happily, the Board of Longitude set up to administer the prize did not favor those with fancy credentials or, for that matter, those with British passports. This was a true global exercise in open innovation. And in the end, it was a self-educated English watchmaker, John Harrison, who found a down-to-earth solution. His invention, a marine chronometer, ultimately transformed ocean transport.

Nearly a century later, Napoleon offered a prize of 12,000 francs for an invention that would preserve food well so that his army could march on a happy stomach. He had found on his earlier campaigns abroad that locals often refused to sell his army food, or that there was simply not enough to feed his troops even if it was seized at the point of a gun. Nicolas Appert, the son of a vintner and a purveyor of bonbons, took the prize in 1809 with a disarmingly simple solution. He put food in champagne bottles, which he then sealed and threw into vats of boiling water. Though he could not explain why, it turned out that food trapped in airtight containers did not spoil if it had been heated. This insight led to related advances, such as using tin cans instead of bottles, which directly led to a surge in the amount of vegetables, meat, and fruits eaten by the growing urban masses of Europe—a huge boost to public health. It remains the basis of canned food today.

Perhaps the most dramatic such incentive prize in history was the Orteig Prize, which ushered in the age of long-distance air travel. Raymond Orteig, a flamboyant hotel magnate, sent a letter in 1919 to the head of the Aero Club of America, offering a $25,000 prize to "the first aviator who shall cross the Atlantic in a land or water aircraft (heavier than air) from Paris or the shores of France to New York, or from New York to Paris without a stop." Nobody even dared attempt such a flight in the five years Orteig stipulated, so he extended the deadline by another five years. As technology had advanced by then, numerous teams poured vast amounts of money into the effort.

All in all, nine aviators joined the fray and spent a combined total of $400,000. The winner was, of course, Charles Lindbergh, an airmail pilot and mechanic, who pulled off the feat of daring in May 1927. That prize demonstrates how incentive prizes can spur innovation in cost-effective ways. For one thing, the total investment far exceeded the actual value of the purse, offering a huge bang for the buck. Also, such prizes often turbocharge the tinkering process that leads to breakthrough innovations. Lindbergh, for example, started with a conventional plane but modified its fuselage, wings, cockpit, and various other features to withstand the journey. Another element of such prizes is that they attract enormous amounts of publicity to a given grand challenge. When Lindbergh's plane went on a national tour after his victory, it is claimed that one-quarter of the country came out to gaze in wonder at the *Spirit of St. Louis*. The Orteig prize and the resultant Atlantic crossing kick-started the aviation industry, argues Diamandis, and led directly to the development of today's $250 billion aviation business.

Alas, incentive prizes then fell out of favor in subsequent decades, especially among governments. There were still plenty of prizes around, but these—such as the Nobel—mostly rewarded accomplishments after the fact. The problem is that there is little evidence that such recognition prizes actually spark innovation. T. S. Eliot famously remarked after receiving his Nobel that it was like getting "a ticket to one's own funeral . . . no one has ever done anything after he has got it."

Prizes for All?

The big news is that incentive prizes are back in fashion. McKinsey did a thorough global review of prizes and awards and found that a big shift is under way from recognition prizes to incentive prizes in recent years. Its experts also catalogue a surge in prizes offered for science and engineering, climate change and space—a departure from the dominance of arts and literary prizes of the past.

There is now also evidence that such incentive prizes actually spur innovation. A study led by Liam Brunt of the Norwegian School of Economics scrutinized agricultural inventions in nineteenth-century Britain, and found a link between prizes and subsequent patents. The Royal Agricultural Society of England (RASE) awarded nearly two thousand prizes from 1839 to 1939, ranging from prestigious medals to purses worth £1 million in to-day's money. They found that not only were prize winners more likely to receive and renew patents (a useful if imperfect proxy for innovation) but even losing contestants went on to seek patents for more than thirteen thousand inventions.

Incentive prizes spark innovation in several important ways that go beyond mere money. The academics studying the agricultural prizes in Britain, for example, thought that the prestige involved with winning such a prize was a more powerful force than money. Many inventors, including one who founded a company that later became International Harvester, a well-known manufacturer of agricultural machinery, proudly advertised the fact that their inventions won RASE medals.

Another feature of well-designed incentive prizes is that they can attract enough investment and invention to create entirely new industries. The key lies in the power of a provocative prize to inspire by transforming what people believe is possible.

The Ansari X Prize, for example, attracted over $100 million in investment into the (previously nonexistent) private-sector space industry—and all that for a prize worth only $10 million. The technology developed for the winning spaceship is now being used by Virgin Galactic, part of Richard Branson's business group, in its new commercial space travel service. For a mere $200,000 or so, Virgin Galactic will soon whisk you into suborbital space from its spaceport in New Mexico. Many of the losing contestants have formed companies and are now profiting from the burgeoning sector.

The most striking benefit is the opening up of the innovation process. Firms increasingly turn to InnoCentive and its online rivals. After all, everyone has had an aha moment—but usually nothing comes of it. The democratic nature of online prize platforms may be making the world a smarter place by connecting grand challenges with hitherto untapped human potential.

A study co-authored by Karim Lakhani of Harvard Business School, which reviewed many thousands of problems solved on InnoCentive, confirms this. It found that outsiders not from the scientific or industry discipline in question were more likely than subject-matter experts to solve a challenge on that Web platform. Intriguingly, women were more likely than men to be successful solvers—which Lakhani thinks may indicate that brilliant women are often sidelined at their corporate or academic jobs, leaving them with the time and incentive to pursue outside prizes.

Companies are waking up to this notion that incentive prizes are a powerful way to attract clever outsiders to a thorny problem. Netflix, an American company that rents DVD or digital copies of movies to customers online, decided in 2006 that it wanted to improve the algorithms that help it match available movies with customer tastes. It offered a $1 million prize to anyone that could beat the model developed by its in-house experts by 10 percent. The firm was stunned to receive entries from more than 55,000 people in 186 countries. Not only did the contest tap open innovation, but it also benefited from online networking and collaboration. Astonishing as it may seem, the winning team's seven members all met together for the first time during the prize ceremony in 2009.

Inspired by such successes, governments are now growing keen on prizes. Britain and several other countries, in cooperation with the Gates Foundation, are funding the Advanced Market Commitment (AMC), a massive prize for development and diffusion of vaccines for neglected diseases of the developing world. The first such prize, at a cost of $1.5 billion, was offered to pharmaceutical firms to deliver vaccines for pneumococcal disease (a big killer of children in the poor world) at low prices. Merck and Pfizer are now shipping this vaccine.

Government agencies ranging from NASA to the city of Chicago are now using online prize platforms to offer prizes, and international governments are making inquiries too. Thanks to a big push by the Obama administration, Congress passed legislation at the end of 2010 that grants every federal agency the authority to run incentive prizes. This matters, because before the law passed, only NASA and the Department of Defense had clear legal authority to run such prizes.

Grand or Booby?

This all is very exciting, but there are some trade-offs and limitations. Nobody should care if a plutocrat tries to spend his fortune on fanciful prizes—as one Robert Bigelow, heir to an American budget-hotel fortune, did on an overly ambitious $50 million space prize that failed miserably. But government resources are scarce, and taxpayer money spent on prizes may come at the expense of other policies, such as grants to universities or tax credits for corporate investment in research. What is more, prizes used as public policy can be vulnerable to political manipulation. In one case, an American government prize for environmental performance saw the winning firm suppress its breakthrough when the losers lobbied Congress to relax the relevant regulations in their favor.

Thomas Kalil, a science advisor to Barack Obama and a longtime advocate for the use of incentive prizes by government, acknowledges the potential pitfalls. Still, he argues that the very process of dreaming up challenges will sharpen up the bureaucracy's approach to big problems: "I like prizes because they force agencies to think clearly about outcomes."

One success was NASA's Lunar Lander Prize, which delivered a much greater bang for the buck than the traditional procurement process. Robert Braun, the agency's chief technologist, points to the example of its recent prize for the design of a new astronaut's glove. The winning entry came not from an aerospace firm but from Peter Homer, an unemployed engineer and onetime sailmaker in Maine. He used the $200,000 in winnings and his well-deserved fame to launch a new firm in aerospace. Kalil insists that prizes make for good policy because they can generate a "diversity of ideas from experts in many different disciplines."

Fine, but not every problem can be solved with a prize. Where the objective is a technological breakthrough, clearly defined prizes work well. Other perils can also trip up prizes. Netflix tried to run a second prize after its wildly successful first but encountered a fierce public backlash over privacy rights: it turned out that the "anonymized" customer data given to contestants was not so anonymous after all. The firm was forced to scrap the effort. Reed Hastings, Netflix's chief executive, reports that his firm has not used this mechanism again: it's just one tool in the toolbox, he now says, albeit a highly effective one. Even in areas where other open innovation approaches seem promising, prizes may be inappropriate. And as governments drift toward using prizes for policy ideas rather than technical challenges, as Chicago recently did to increase use of its mass transit system, the results may get woolier and less useful.

Some politicians have even talked of setting up funds worth billions to spur drug development. Ah, but prizes may not be as useful for that purpose, warns Tachi Yamada of the Gates

Foundation. He has credibility in this area. Not only was he formerly the head of research and development at GlaxoSmithKline, one of the world's biggest pharmaceutical firms, but his current foundation is also a big believer in incentive prizes in other areas of development. It offers millions of dollars in small and big prizes to people coming up with radical new ideas to tackle various global grand challenges.

But developing a new drug and bringing it to market takes fifteen years or more, and Yamada thinks even the AMC's carrot of $1.5 billion may not be enough incentive. Observing that no purse can match the $20 billion or so a blockbuster pharmaceutical drug can earn in its lifetime, he cautions that oftentimes "market success is the real prize."

Never Invented Here

The upshot of this exciting move toward openness is that researchers can no longer ignore ideas that are "not invented here." Managers need to focus on extracting value from ideas, wherever they come from. After all, history shows that companies and countries that come up with new technologies are often not the ones that commercialize or popularize those inventions. Thomas Edison did not invent the lightbulb and Henry Ford did not invent the automobile, but the business models developed by those innovators helped them make fortunes commercializing those inventions.

That is a lesson that government officials and global technocrats at such organs as the United Nations would do well to learn too. That is because the world is getting to be a much riskier place, as the next chapter describes, and the new risks of the hyperconnected global economy demand bold new strategies for innovation that go beyond the traditional turf-bound, insular approaches. Richard Halkett, formerly executive director of policy and research at the National Endowment for Science, Technology, and the Arts (NESTA), a British research body devoted to innovation policy, jokes that the right policy for companies and governments obsessed with creating national innovation champions should really be "never invented here." He may be right.

6

Black Swan Kills Sitting Duck

Mankind is entering an age in which the danger posed by highly unlikely but devastating events can no longer be ignored. One sort of risk arises from catastrophes such as the BP oil spill in the Gulf of Mexico, the massive earthquakes in Japan and Haiti, and other recent deadly events. As society has advanced, the costs of such disasters have grown exponentially. But there is an even greater worry, as the subprime-mortgage-induced financial meltdown and Icelandic-volcano-induced global chaos demonstrate. The dramatic increase in the complexity of industrial, financial, and economic networks means that extremely rare localized crises can unexpectedly and rapidly cascade into systemic risks that expose the unknown fragilities of many wider, interdependent networks.

The challenge for innovators today is to confront this more dangerous world boldly, without abandoning risk taking, but also to do so wisely, by building resilience into supply chains, organizational culture, and society at large. Doing so will require rethinking how to trade off risks smartly, how to weigh

costs against benefits more efficiently, and how to experiment
and fail more often but more gracefully.

This chapter presents the evidence for thinking that the world
economy is indeed getting riskier, for individuals as much as
for firms and nations. This does not, however, need to lead to
a defensive crouch: innovators who are prepared for a riskier
world when rivals are not will find opportunity where others
encounter adversity.

The world is getting to be a more dangerous place. This creates both problems and opportunities for innovators. The previous two chapters have shown that innovation is getting faster and more open. This chapter argues that it is getting riskier too. It lays out the case for thinking that the global economy is entering riskier times, and explains how leaders can build resilient systems to predict, prevent, and prepare for such risks—and possibly even profit from them along the way.

Hang on a minute, though. The notion that the world is getting riskier might seem strange to some. After all, isn't the history of human progress one of improving living conditions and greater prosperity for most of mankind?

At one level, such skepticism is justified. Through most of history, the ordinary person's life was nasty, brutish, and short. The biggest explanation for this, of course, was that almost all of mankind lived in grinding poverty through almost all of history. But the last two centuries have seen a spectacular rise in per-capita income, starting with Europe and the United States, but spreading powerfully to China and other emerging economies in recent decades. Aside from poverty, two other hazards made life particularly risky in the past: physical violence and the all-too-common public health threats that led to misery and, often, premature death. On these important measures, there is no doubt that life today is much less risky than in the past.

Consider violence for a start. Steven Pinker, a renowned cognitive scientist and author, has scrutinized the number of bloody wars, murders, executions, cruel and unusual punishments, highway banditry, sword fights, and other sorts of violent acts inflicted by man upon man, and he concludes that humanity lives in the best of times. Of course, the notion of the noble savage was always a myth: archeologists have shown that even the supposedly peace-loving Maya of Mesoamerica were, in fact, quite violent at times. But what of the twentieth century, often said to be the bloodiest in history? (Cue film footage of the two world wars or Stalin's pogroms, each of which killed many millions of unfortunates.) Pinker points out that despite that undeniable and tragic death toll, when one takes into account the overall global population, the last century was actually much less violent in proportional terms than other epochs. And mankind is getting less and less violent as time goes on.

He believes a confluence of happy factors explains this, ranging from the spread of democracy and the rule of law to changing attitudes toward corporal punishment, warfare, and chivalry. Perhaps surprisingly, he adds globalization and the information revolution to the mix, arguing that these trends widen the "circle of empathy": a genocide in a remote corner of the world that surely would have gone ignored by uninformed outsiders now may, just possibly, prick the conscience of CNN viewers in powerful countries who push leaders to act. A good recent example is the decision by Western powers in early 2011 to intervene in the Libyan conflict between Muammar Gaddafi, the long-ruling tyrant, and rebels in the eastern provinces.

Another impressive advance has come in the shape of public health innovations, such as antibiotics and vaccines, that have extended lives, reduced misery, and otherwise improved the health of everyone on earth. A century ago, adult life expectancy was less than half of what is enjoyed by most people on earth today and infant mortality was tragically common. Through most of history, people were at constant risk of being struck down by plagues and pestilences of unknown origin. Today, scientists of course know that most were caused by bacterial or viral sources. A simple cut that now would be healed in days by the use of a bandage and antibiotics could, back then, result in an infection that left a person stone-cold dead.

Despite these advances in tackling everyday dangers, mankind is nevertheless entering more perilous times. That is because of the rapid rise of two very different and much more worrisome sorts of threats: costly catastrophic threats and global systemic risks.

Our Final Century?

More than half a century after the height of the Cold War, Martin Rees, a distinguished veteran of the antinuclear movement, believes that the world came closer—and more often—to the brink of thermonuclear destruction than most people realize. Could it happen again? More broadly, could mankind, even unwittingly, unleash a chain of events that destroys the natural environment, and ultimately humanity itself?

The debate over how to safeguard the world is not limited to disaster scenarios, of course. Conservationists, politicians, and scientists of every hue continue to hold forth on mankind's environmental depredations. For Rees, a respected Cambridge University astrophysicist and Britain's astronomer royal, the emphasis is on warning: he penned *Our Final Hour* a few years ago as a clarion call. For others it is the more difficult task of trying to devise prescriptions.

The specter of a terrorist attack or an accident involving bio-organisms or nanotechnology so concerns Rees that he is ready to wager anyone $1,000 that one million people will die as a result of a single horrendous act by 2020. In addition to threats from disgruntled misfits or religious radicals, he worries about the destruction of the natural environment that may result from broader policy choices made by society. And he is particularly concerned that the current pattern of global economic development might fuel climate change and biodiversity loss on such a scale as to lead to environmental disaster. One of the most brilliant scientists of the age estimates that mankind might have only a fifty-fifty chance of surviving this century.

Consider, for example, the mysterious decimation of the bee population in various parts of the world due to something called colony collapse disorder. This had been observed in Europe and the United States for several decades. But in 2011 the United Nations Environment Programme (UNEP) issued a warning confirming that this problem was a global one with potentially devastating consequences for humanity. That is because bees are nature's chief pollinators, and more than two-thirds of the world's food supply relies on them doing their mundane jobs. Achim Steiner, head of UNEP, put it bluntly: "Human beings have fabricated the illusion that in the twenty-first century they have the technological prowess to be independent of nature. Bees underline the reality that we are more, not less, dependent on nature's services in a world of close to seven billion people."

What's more, the evidence is quickly mounting that the world is being buffeted by catastrophic risks, which by definition are low-probability but high-impact events, much more often these days. The most obvious recent example would be the triple tragedy of earthquake, tsunami, and nuclear meltdown endured by Japan in 2011, but other examples include the costly BP oil spill in the Gulf of Mexico, the devastating earthquake in Haiti, and the floods that ravaged parts of Pakistan recently.

It is tempting to dismiss this string of accidents as mere anecdote. It would certainly be unscientific to claim that any single weather-related event was definitively caused by climate change. However, the economic evidence suggests that there is something more worrisome going on. The Inter-American Development Bank has analyzed four decades of disaster data for Latin America, and it finds that the cost imposed by catastrophic risks is now increasing at four times the rate of economic growth in the region. Troublingly, the experts estimate that foreign aid covers only about 8 percent of the direct cost of dealing with those disasters.

Swiss Re, a leading global reinsurance firm, follows disaster trends extremely closely (understandable, since reinsurers get stuck with the bill). Even before the Japanese crisis of 2011, the firm sounded alarm bells about the rising incidence and soaring cost of catastrophic events. The global annual cost of such disasters averaged, in inflation-adjusted terms, roughly $25 billion a year back in the 1980s; in the decade following 2000, that figure shot up to $130 billion per year. The year 2008 saw the toll rise to $270 billion (only $52 billion of which was insured) and the loss of life reach 240,000. Nouriel Roubini, a prominent economist at New York University's Stern School of Business who correctly predicted the financial crash of 2008, recently addressed a group of the world's leading risk managers and experts and made this startling statement: "Events which should happen once in fifty years are happening very often, and we don't know why."

There are a few clues. One is that thanks to urbanization and demographic shifts, far more people now live in cities and close to waterways. Because this clusters both people and economic activity, it magnifies the toll extracted by a given disaster if it happens to hit close to those cities. Climate change, and the associated disruptive weather patterns that it spawns, may also be contributing to the freakish storms seen of late. Another factor to consider is that the world is now much wealthier than it was in the past and therefore simply has more assets to lose in any given incident.

Although all of those circumstances play a role, each by itself feels unsatisfying as the sole explanation for the trend. Larry Brilliant, the head of the Skoll Urgent Threats Fund, believes there is a more powerful connection. His nongovernmental group monitors risks in such areas as climate change, water scarcity, pandemic diseases, and nuclear proliferation. Reflecting on the growing nature of these wicked problems, he remarks, "Globalization has accelerated them all . . . they all have worldwide impacts and no single country can tackle them alone."

The Paradox of Globalization

Brilliant's observation reflects a powerful and contrarian insight: the same globalization that has fueled global economic growth and the rise of the middle classes in emerging economies in recent decades has also made it much easier for catastrophic risks to become global rather than local calamities. That points to the second and even more worrying development: the increase in global interconnectedness is leading to a higher level of systemic risk. Catastrophic events such as the BP oil spill are bad enough, especially since they are getting costlier, but that event did not precipitate a systemic crisis. In contrast, the subprime mortgage meltdown in the United States sparked contagion that came perilously close to causing a genuine systemic meltdown in global financial markets. The worry is that the global economy now faces a rising level of risk because of the proliferation of incredibly complex and interlinked systems that extend well beyond high finance.

Every year, the World Economic Forum surveys hundreds of the world's leading academic risk experts, corporate risk managers, government disaster-planning officials, and others concerned about this topic in preparing its annual report on global risk. The group's track record is impressive. In its reports from 2006 onward, for example, the WEF consistently identified asset prices, indebtedness, and fiscal crises as top global risks—and, of course, it was proved right.

When the WEF put together its report for 2011, it had this to say: "The world is in no position to face major new shocks." And yet, the group lamented, "we face ever greater concerns regarding global risks and the prospect of rapid contagion through increasingly interconnected systems and the threat of disastrous impacts." At the very top of the list of those global threats was climate change. However, two other cross-cutting threats also made the top of the list. First, glaring gaps in global governance bothered the risk managers. They pointed, in particular, to the difficulties encountered by negotiators of the climate change accords under the UN's Kyoto Protocol and the World Trade Organization's Doha round of trade liberalization talks. The other top risk cited was growing economic disparity, seen both among and especially within countries. These risks, the experts warned, meant that the same globalization that has brought the world closer together may lead to a backlash that tears the world apart.

No Safety Net

Tying together the threads of globalization and interconnectedness, Herman "Dutch" Leonard of Harvard University points to
another factor that is making the world economy riskier today. He
observes that many of the systems that have developed to allow
the 24/7, open, and connected global economy are complex and
interlocked—but goes on to note that the buffers and shock absorbers in that system are insufficient and under great strain. A good
example of this can be seen in the global supply chain. Led by cost-
conscious and efficiency-minded multinationals such as Walmart,
firms everywhere have migrated to lean inventory management
techniques and just-in-time manufacturing.

This is great when times are good, but when disaster strikes
it can amplify the impact of any local disruption. The explosion
of Eyjafjallajökull, an Icelandic volcano, in 2010 and the Japanese
tsunami in 2011 both had much greater than expected ripple effects on the global supply chains of everything from food to cars
to iPads. Leonard observes that the eruption disrupted delicately
balanced systems and brought the global economy to within days
of a spiraling supply chain calamity. After the Japanese disasters,
Harley-Davidson had difficulties getting hold of radio components.
Sony ran short of displays and batteries. Toyota, GM, and other
automobile manufacturers were forced to cut production because
of parts shortages caused by the earthquake and tsunami. Apple
took extraordinary measures to make sure it got the parts it needed
in time for the much-anticipated launch of the iPad 2 in early 2011,
but it was still knocked sideways by the Japanese tragedy—not because of shortages at its primary suppliers but because of woes at

the suppliers to those suppliers. What all that shows, argues Leonard, is that "our buffers are drained."

The central arguments about systemic risks are put forward persuasively by Charles Perrow in *Normal Accidents*. A complex system is one that is made up of three or more subsystems. The subsystems are linked with each other, creating feedback loops that can self-reinforce or cross over and reinforce each other. Crucially, such systems are tightly coupled, meaning that there are no buffers or shock absorbers in the links between subsystems. This means that when something goes wrong in one subsystem, it automatically produces input errors in the subsystems it is connected to, which, when amplified by the feedback loops, leads to chaos. In fact, because errors will eventually occur in two subsystems simultaneously, pushing the system past its margin of safety, a failure of the whole system is on the cards virtually by design.

"A collapse, often sudden, of the whole system is not only possible but inevitable," insists Leonard. He points to the telling example of the South China snowstorm of 2008. This was a bad but not cataclysmic storm, but because of the failure of multiple subsystems it wreaked economic havoc and proved much deadlier than it should have. Multiple bits of essential infrastructure—rail, electricity, food supply—all collapsed at around the same time. The reason, Leonard argues, was because they all needed each other: the food moved on rail; the rail was electric; electricity production needed coal; coal arrived only by rail; the snowstorm killed the power.

This is a huge problem that will only get worse unless leaders in business and government come together to manage these risks more sensibly. Nassim Taleb, author of the bestseller *The Black Swan*, warns against complacency, given today's interconnected systems: "Globalization creates interlocking fragility, while reducing volatility and giving the appearance of stability."

In *Global Catastrophic Risks*, a thoughtful collection of essays, Richard Posner argues that the world is underinvesting in the mitigation of several global catastrophic risks of the sort that Rees worries about. In that same volume, Robin Hanson offers this compelling reason to pay attention: "The main reason to be careful when you walk up a flight of stairs is not that you might slip and have to retrace one step, but rather that the first slip might cause a second slip, and so on until you fall dozens of steps and break your neck. Similarly we are concerned about [catastrophes] not only because of their terrible direct effects, but also because they may induce an even more damaging collapse of our economic and social systems."

Prevent, Predict, Prepare . . . and Profit?

That is a frightening thought, but happily a vanguard of risk managers and governance experts is coming up with something resembling a manifesto for action. The group draws inspiration from successful responses to past natural disasters, though the lessons gleaned there apply much more widely. Whether one is dealing with financial meltdowns, pandemics, nuclear crises, or terrorism, the risk experts associated with the WEF argue that the principles arising from global experience with natural disasters "are unanimously deemed applicable."

One broad theme emerging from this work is the desperate need for integrated, cross-industry, pan-regional risk analysis—not the bureaucratic silos and navel-gazing approaches taken in the past. An example of what works is the Mekong River Commission

(MRC), which oversees resource planning and disaster management for that Southeast Asian river delta. Most such bodies in other regions are local or national at best and usually look only at specific issues such as flood management. In contrast, the MRC counts five regional governments as members, and it performs thoughtful cost-benefit analyses on issues ranging from energy and water to food—all of which, of course, are linked both to the river's health and to each other. And given the rapid contagion seen in the recent financial crisis, such cross-jurisdictional cooperation makes sense at the global level in tackling many big risks.

Cross-disciplinary thinking makes sense within countries too. That makes it desirable to appoint chief risk officers for countries, much as companies do today, so that they can scan the horizon for longer-term and interlinked threats that individual ministries may ignore. To its credit, Singapore already has an expert government body that does something like this. Larry Brilliant thinks it is just as important to educate those at the bottom about risk as those at the top. He wants schools to teach children what he calls "the four R's": reading, writing, arithmetic, and risk literacy.

Beyond that general philosophical shift, the specific recommendations now bubbling up fall into three broad categories: prevention, prediction, and preparation.

Some disasters will happen no matter what measures are taken in advance to prevent them, but the world can do much better on the prevention front. Both Chile and Haiti were struck by massive earthquakes around the same time in 2010, but the former was a minor crisis whereas the latter was a horrific, large-scale meltdown of the entire country. Why? One obvious reason is that Chile is wealthier than Haiti, which helps in many ways, but it is still a developing country with lots of poor people. What Chile did have, though, was much better building codes and safety regulations that were actually policed and enforced, so the housing stock and infrastructure in the earthquake zone were much better able to withstand the blow. That suggests one way countries can prevent some of the losses arising from inevitable disasters is to have proper regulatory precautions in place in advance.

A related point is the need to avoid policy distortions that encourage reckless behavior in the first place. One problem arises from externalities that are ignored by public policy. Consider the contribution to global warming made by burning carbon-intensive fuels such as coal: the energy user pays a market price for coal, but she gets off lightly by not paying for the damage done to the environment and human health by burning that filthy fuel. Policies that internalize that externality, such as carbon taxes imposed on fossil fuels, would help change behavior and possibly prevent future natural disasters.

Governments should also abolish perverse subsidies that lead to behavior that puts people needlessly at risk. A good example is the encouragement by governments—including that of the United States—to build in areas well known to be at risk from hurricanes and flooding. Policies such as subsidized flood insurance and development-friendly zoning regulations make it cheaper for people to move into such areas as the North Carolina and Florida coasts that are picturesque but hurricane prone. Such policies also give the implicit guarantee of rescue by taxpayer-financed first responders, search-and-rescue teams, and so on to people who get in trouble by putting themselves in harm's way.

Another good way to deal with big risks is to try to predict hazards using intelligent infrastructure. Embedding energy grids, buildings, and other bits of the built environment with smart sensors, alarms, sniffers, and other signaling devices can help risk minders keep their fingers on the pulse of emerging threats. This looks to become a multibillion-dollar industry. IBM was early in this game, promoting its vision for a "smarter planet" made up of digitally connected traffic systems, energy grids, and even entire cities. Hewlett Packard is working on a "central nervous system for the earth," while Cisco trumpets "smart and connected communities."

Smart systems can also help avoid problems like climate change and water scarcity in the first place by improving the efficiency with which resources are consumed. Much of the world's fresh water is wasted before it reaches thirsty mouths, for example, and centralized electricity grids are needlessly inefficient. The sector is attracting many young technology companies, a sign perhaps of innovations to come. One of them, Israel's TaKaDu, offers a Web-based service that uses sensors, data, and analytics to become the "eyes and ears" of water utilities.

A thoughtful exploration of future trends in resilience supports the argument that smart systems can help. The Rockefeller Foundation asked the Global Business Network (GBN) to put together likely scenarios for the evolution of technology and international development. After an extensive survey of the topic and interviews with scores of leading experts, GBN came up with four plausible scenarios that it plots along two axes: one axis shows the world's adaptive capacity, while the other gauges its political and economic alignment.

The best possible outcome would be a world that scores highly on both axes, a scenario called Clever Together: "a world in which highly coordinated and successful strategies emerge for addressing both urgent and entrenched worldwide issues." If alignment is strong but adaptive capacity weak, the experts predict Lock Step: "a world of tighter top-down government control and more authoritarian leadership, with limited innovation and growing citizen pushback." If adaptive capacity is high but political and economic alignment weak, they expect a Smart Scramble: "an economically depressed world in which individuals and communities develop localized, makeshift solutions to a growing set of problems." The real worry, though, is that both political coordination and adaptive capacity will collapse, leading to the Hack Attack: "an economically unstable and shock-prone world in which governments weaken, criminals thrive, and dangerous innovations emerge." The report concludes that while the four scenarios vary significantly from each other, one common theme emerges: new innovations and uses of technology will be a big part of the story going forward.

The move toward smart systems is exciting, but it does raise concerns too. Some, such as the threat posed to privacy by putative Big Brothers having access to so much data, can probably be managed. However, if the headlong rush toward intelligent infrastructure merely creates a gold-plated version of today's brittle, centralized systems, then it will only be setting the world up for an even harder fall in the future. All that data will be giving risk managers a false sense of security, argues Harvard's Dutch Leonard, because all centralized systems have the potential to fail—"and when they do, they break with a vengeance." His research suggests that people underestimate the risk of systemic breakdown and overestimate the robustness of such systems.

From Risk to Resilience

That points to the third way that the world can deal better with catastrophic risk: better preparation. That argues for decentralization and empowerment of localized decision making. Organizations typically have a response plan crafted at headquarters that

kicks in when a crisis hits. The snag arises when business is inter-
rupted not in the way the playbook anticipates but in some strange
and disconcerting new way. When a crisis hits in an unexpected
way—as Chicago experienced during a crippling snowstorm in the
winter of 2010–11 that shut down even this city of broad shoulders—
a previously determined centralized plan may have to give way to
intelligent improvisation. But in Chicago's case, the city's officials
were too wedded to their centralized evacuation plan to let go of
it, even after it became clear that it was failing.

A better way, says Leonard, is to "figure out how to make your
'edges' learn and respond quickly to unexpected risks." This is
not as outlandish as it may sound. Vivek Kundra served as Barack
Obama's first chief information officer at the White House, but
before that he was in charge of technology for the city government
of Washington, D.C. In thinking about crisis planning, he draws
inspiration from networked, distributed systems such as the Internet that he believes have no single point of failure. He ordered the
installation of global positioning technology on the district's snowplows and made the information available online so that people
would not have to go outside to find out which streets had not been
plowed or what the road conditions looked like. He beams with
pride when he describes how dealing with crippling snowstorms
got easier as ordinary citizens began to use the GPS data, assess
local conditions through firsthand experience, and suggest better
routes for the snowplows to follow.

Decentralized approaches offer an attractive way forward, but
depending on how they are carried out they can be a source of
strength or of inefficiency. Resilience is much more likely to feature in systems that are decentralized, intelligent, and well coordinated. Leonard argues that thus far what the world has mostly seen
are two undesirable alternatives: systems that are decentralized

and coordinated but sluggish, or ones that are decentralized and adaptive but uncoordinated. He adds an optimistic note: "While we underappreciate the risks of such systems, we also tend to underestimate the ingenuity and resilience of people when there are system-level issues."

Alas, trusting open systems and decentralization does not come easily to managers or government officials, who tend to shut down and adopt a bunker mentality during crises. Doing scenario-planning exercises, carrying out dry runs, and practicing improvisation can help. So too does letting employees know that they will not be punished after the fact for their decisions, as long as they did so with the best information available at the time and in a manner consistent with the organization's values.

But this is not a call for complete decentralization, which can also lead to bad outcomes in a crisis. Ushahidi, a dynamic nonprofit outfit that provides free software and Web tools for open and collaborative innovation, found that many people used its interactive mapping and communication tools in the aftermath of the Haiti earthquake to help with disaster relief. Unfortunately, the information posted grew chaotic and at times conflicting, leading to confusion and possibly hurting the aid effort. The firm has since launched Swift River, an initiative designed to verify and filter raw input so that the do-gooders do not get led down false trails in the wake of tragedy.

Another way risk managers can better prepare for inevitable disasters is the creative use of insurance products. When extremely damaging hurricanes or droughts hit, most poor countries scramble for money, and they rarely get enough from aid to rebuild and help the victims properly. Hoping to break that cycle, Mexico has agreed on an insurance policy with Swiss Re and the World Bank that would pay money to farmers automatically if hurricanes or several other specified types of natural disaster cross agreed thresholds of intensity. Vietnam has entered into a similar insurance deal that would pay out money to poor rice farmers if bad weather results in rice yields that fall below agreed levels. In effect, these countries are paying a small amount now to transfer part of the risk of future disasters onto capital markets, and in doing so providing their vulnerable populations with a valuable safety net.

The most controversial way to prepare better for a riskier world is to stockpile. This applies both to industrial corporations, which worry about physical stocks, and to financial institutions, which are concerned about capital adequacy ratios. This is a difficult pill for businesses and banks to swallow, as carrying more inventory or maintaining more capital and liquidity means higher costs. However, lean and just-in-time inventory management systems are simply not robust enough to handle the sorts of disruptions that today's unexpectedly interconnected supply chain produces. And being out of stock costs money too, as firms are discovering to their detriment. A study published a few years ago found that firms that suffered from significant supply chain disruptions saw their share returns drop by a third versus the benchmark for their industries. Similarly, taking outsized risks without sufficient capital and liquidity to cover them is a recipe for disaster in times of market stress. And the blow dealt to a firm could be fatal, as recent experiences have shown.

That is especially true if competitors prepare more robustly and are able to stay in the game. Consider what happened in the wake of the Icelandic volcano surprise that shut down air traffic in large parts of Europe in 2010. Many firms struggled to understand the systemic problem, which their standard disaster plans had not predicted, and then found their supply systems too rigid to deal with the shutdowns. Not customers of DHL, though: its managers quickly switched cargoes to southern European airports, which were not immediately affected by the volcano, and arranged trucks and ships to substitute for air cargo. Even though it slowed things down a bit, the managers insisted on full scanning of all packages on the new routes, which allowed customers to track their packages through the crisis. Transparency and nimble, decentralized systems saved the day.

In sum, what the world needs now is to invest in resilient systems that prevent, predict, and prepare for the costly catastrophes buffeting the world economy. The conventional notion of resilience smacks of passivity and invokes the unattractive image of a defensive crouch, but Nassim Taleb argues against this. Instead, resilience should be seen as a fount of competitive advantage for industries and countries, a source of innovation and experimentation for cities, and a spigot of future profits for companies.

The challenge of building resilient infrastructure is setting the worlds of architecture, design, and city planning alight. For example, developers in New York are now considering the use of advanced absorbent materials for sidewalks in low-lying areas at risk from sea-level rise: the clever concrete sucks in water as fast as it comes in, to avoid the worst damage from sudden floods, and releases it only slowly over time. City planners in Asia and the Middle East are building resilient eco-cities from scratch, hoping to leapfrog ahead of Western rivals (who are often stuck with legacy infrastructure of the vulnerable, nonresilient variety) in attracting the knowledge workers and creative companies of the twenty-first century.

Judith Rodin, head of the Rockefeller Foundation, offers this elegant motto for coping with this risky new world: "We must have the capacity to respond adaptively to both acute and chronic stresses—while flourishing." Rather than merely returning to the status quo after the shock ends, she argues, truly resilient systems adapt and change with the times. The global economy is moving faster, growing more open, and getting riskier—meaning innovators must also adapt and change if they are to flourish. And, argues Stewart Brand paradoxically, they must be bold enough to take more risks—albeit more carefully considered ones—if humanity is to overcome this generation's grand global challenges.

In some respects, Brand's green credentials are impeccable. His mentor was Paul Ehrlich, the author of *The Population Bomb*, published in 1968. That book, and the related Club of Rome movement of the 1970s, famously predicted that overpopulation would soon result in the world running out of food, oil, and other resources. Though it proved spectacularly wrong, its warning served as a clarion call for the modern environmental movement.

Brand made his name with a publication of his own, which also appeared in 1968, called *The Whole Earth Catalog*. It was a pathbreaking manual crammed with examples of small-scale technologies to enable individuals to reduce their environmental impact, and is best known for its cover, which featured a picture of the Earth from space (which Brand helped to persuade NASA to release). The book became a bestseller in anticorporate and environmental circles. In 1985 Brand cofounded the WELL, a pioneering online community that was a precursor of today's social-networking websites such as MySpace and Facebook.

Brand still has a following among the Birkenstock set, and he even lives on a houseboat in Sausalito, near San Francisco. But meet him in person and it becomes clear he is not exactly your typical crunchy-granola green. Sitting down to lunch at a posh beach resort on Coronado Island, off San Diego, he does not order a vegan special but a hearty Angus burger with bacon and cheese, french fries, and a side order of lobster bisque. "I'm genetically a contrarian," he says with a broad smile.

That is pretty evident from his recent proclamations, as the septuagenarian countercultural icon remains determined to rock the boat. But this time his target is the environmental movement itself. He has come up with a series of what he calls "environmental heresies," which he hopes will influence a new generation of pragmatic, problem-solving greens. Three things that most greens vehemently oppose—genetic engineering, urbanization, and nuclear power—should, he believes, be embraced on environmental grounds.

Start with genetic engineering. Many greens object to the idea, fearing a deluge of "Frankenfoods" and the contamination of pristine wild species. But Brand points to the work of the late Norman Borlaug, the Nobel Prize winner who proved the Club of Rome (and Brand) wrong with his "green revolution" in agricultural productivity. Brand now sees great promise in using genetic science to feed the world, and perhaps prevent future wars, by making crops that are more disease-resistant, drought-tolerant, and produce higher yields.

Similarly, he argues that urbanization can be good for the environment. Mankind has now become a primarily urban species for the first time in its history, and every serious forecast predicts a surge in the size and number of megacities. Most environmentalists are dismayed at this trend and worry about the implications of urbanization for air pollution, resource consumption, and so on. But Brand bluntly rebuts them, insisting that megacities "will increase the Earth's carrying capacity for humans."

That may seem an odd argument from a man who wrote a guide to natural living and going "off the grid," but it reflects another aspect of the maturation of his views. Cities are good for the planet, he argues, because they are engines of wealth creation, and greater prosperity makes promoting sustainability easier. When poor people move from bleak subsistence farming to the economic opportunities found in urban slums, he insists, they no longer need to chop down endangered trees or eat bush meat. "Nature grows back," says Brand. He also believes cities unleash innovation—pointing to the use of mobile phones in slums to send money—and reckons the next big trend will come "not from Japanese school-girls, but slum-dwellers in Africa."

Brand's critics accuse him of romanticizing the potential of megacities. But his support for the revival of nuclear power is even more controversial. For years, he held the orthodox environmental view that nukes were evil. He now confesses that this was merely "knee-jerk opposition," not a carefully considered opinion. His growing concern about global warming, which he calls "the single most important environmental threat facing mankind," explains his U-turn in favor of this low-carbon but hugely unpopular source of electricity.

The turning point came, he says, when he visited Yucca Mountain, a remote site in the Nevada desert where the Department of Energy had for years planned to bury the country's nuclear waste. He was visiting the site as part of his Long Now project, which aims to build a "clock" that will last ten thousand years or more in the hope of encouraging society to think about very long-term issues. While studying the deep hole in the ground at Yucca for tips on building his clock—the site, like the clock, is being designed to survive unscathed for thousands of years—he had an epiphany.

Although greens and other antinuclear activists oppose the Yucca Mountain project (opposition that led the Obama adminis-tration to try to kill it), Brand says he realized that "we are asking the wrong question" about nuclear power. Rather than asking how spent nuclear fuel can be kept safe for ten thousand to a hundred thousand years, he says, we should worry about keeping it safe for only a hundred years. Because nuclear waste still contains an enormous amount of energy, future generations may be able to harness it as an energy source through tomorrow's better technologies.

But what about the nuclear accidents in Japan that unfolded following the recent tsunami? Surely that is the clinching argument against this technology? That is certainly the lesson learned by Germans, who voted to kill off the country's big nuclear power sector in the wake of the Japanese accidents. Brand acknowledges the tragedy in Japan but insists on putting that experience in context. In the grander scheme of things, far fewer people have been hurt or killed by that episode (or by all nuclear plants through history, for that matter) than have been harmed or killed worldwide by the burning of coal—a point usually ignored by antinuclear activists. Carbon-free nuclear power remains a potent and scalable way to tackle climate change, he insists. The right way to see the Japanese disaster is as a learning experience: the nature of interconnected risks and the likely human responses have been put to the test and now can be improved for next time.

Shades of Green

Brand may well be wrong about nuclear power: the energy source that was once claimed to be "too cheap to meter" looks more likely to be remembered by history as too costly to matter. Even so, he gets one big thing right: his willingness to get his hands dirty and balance one risk against another, rather than clinging to ideologically pure positions when confronted with difficult choices, sets Brand apart from the many ideologues in the environmental movement.

Indeed, he proudly calls himself an "eco-pragmatist." He argues that two ideological camps have dominated the green movement for too long: "the scientists and the romantics." The former group has been stuck in the ivory tower, while the latter has held on to noble but impractical views that, he reckons, have often been contrary to rational scientific thinking. The grip that these two rival camps have had on environmentalism, he says, explains its malaise.

But growing public awareness of climate change and other green concerns promises to end this. "Environmental change changes everything," he insists, "and among the biggest change of all will be in environmentalism itself." As environmental issues have moved up the technological agenda, says Brand, there has been a large influx of engineers into the environmental movement. These "techies" had previously been deeply skeptical of the greens, but he now thinks they may save the cause even as they save the planet. Unlike the romantics and the airy scientists, he says, "engineers focus on solving problems."

Brand's own pragmatism can be seen in his willingness to own up to his mistakes and learn from them. When his alarmism over the Y2K computer bug turned out to be wrong, for example, it made him realize that his own personal computer was a poor proxy for the world at large, which is "modular, shockproof, and robust." And the key mistake made by the Club of Rome's forecasts (which he calls "self-defeating prophecies"), he now acknowledges, was to see the world as static and to place too little faith in the possibilities of technological progress. He firmly believes society can develop the resilience needed to survive and even flourish in the coming era of black swans.

His critics might argue that Brand now places too much faith in clever engineers and fancy technology to solve the world's environmental problems. But he can respond that his pragmatic approach goes back a long way and has deep roots. As he put it in the introduction to *The Whole Earth Catalog*, written four decades ago: "We are as gods and might as well get good at it."

So what should divine governments, companies, and individuals do if they aspire to flourish in this age of complex risks? The final section of the book explains how to harness innovation in the Age of Disruptive Innovation.

PART THREE

GREED:

How to Win in the Age of Disruptive Innovation

7

The Sputnik Fallacies

The need for innovation has never been greater, as the first section of the book explained. In addition, the very ways in which innovation happens—meta-innovation—are changing fast, as the second section of the book argued. That points to a pressing question: what to do about it? This final section of the book delves into the question of what governments, companies, and individuals can do to win in the age of disruptive innovation.

This chapter turns a critical eye to the arguments put forward by proponents of industrial policy. It is fashionable today to argue that the rise of China represents an existential economic threat to the West, one that can only be countered by a dramatic government effort akin to the Apollo moon shot.

It is right to say that developed countries need to fix various aspects of their innovation ecosystems. The United States, for example, must address flaws in its policies on immigration, education, and basic infrastructure. However, calls for an aggressive return to industrial policies of the sort seen in the 1970s and 1980s are wrongheaded and dangerous. Especially given the dramatic changes in how innovation is happening from the bottom up and the inside out, a return to the failed centralized approaches of the past would be folly.

Will China eclipse the United States as the world's innovation powerhouse? At the end of the Second World War, American spending on research and development made up half the world's total; today, it has dropped to one-third. South Korea, China, and India are pouring tens of billions of dollars into scientific fields that range from genomics to nanotechnology. They are producing staggering numbers of engineers and scientists, who in turn are publishing lots of papers and acquiring ever more patents.

The notion that Asian innovation is surpassing that of the West has led to much public anguish in the United States. In 2009, the Aspen Institute put on a major conference in Washington on the topic of the U.S. innovation crisis that attracted many chief executives, cabinet officials, congressional leaders, and experts on various aspects of the topic. To set the stage, the organizers revealed the results of a big poll sponsored by Intel that showed that Americans were tremendously insecure about their country's economic leadership: roughly the same numbers believed that the United States would remain in the global innovation lead as felt that China would pass the United States. *Newsweek* ran an article about all this at the time titled, "Is America Losing Its Mojo?"

The pessimistic drumbeat only grew louder in coming months. A commission of twenty eminent people organized by the National Academy of Sciences and the National Academy of Engineering, which included Nobel laureates and heads of leading companies, had produced an influential report back in 2007, called *Rising Above the Gathering Storm*, on the threat to America's leadership in the global economy. In 2010, at congressional urging, the commission released an update on that warning. Far from improving, declared the panel of grandees, the storm is now "rapidly approaching Category 5." The group demanded immediate government action.

This call to arms is echoed by many who see China's rise as a threat akin to the Soviet Union's Sputnik program, which sent the first manmade object into orbit back in 1957. That daring feat so shocked the United States that it led to a dramatic expansion of efforts in science, engineering, and space—a government-funded boom that kicked into high gear with John F. Kennedy's call in 1961 for the country to put a man on the moon by the end of that decade. Michael Mandelbaum, a foreign policy expert at Johns Hopkins University, has claimed that "our response to Sputnik made us better educated, more productive, more technologically advanced, and more ingenious."

On this view, the United States should seize on the new Red Menace to launch another bold, government-led "moon shot" that would boost innovation and put the country back on top. A growing chorus of business leaders, academic experts, and labor bosses is calling for a dramatic change in government policy to salvage the broken U.S. innovation system. Thomas Friedman has devoted various of his *New York Times* columns to this topic, one of his favorite themes, and they have served as rallying cries for the "new Sputnik" movement.

The Sun Also Sets

Hang on a minute, though. Look closely at the claims made by the chorus of doom, and it turns out there are three dangerous fallacies embedded in the Sputnik analogy. First, this approach assumes that the rise of the rest must come at the expense of the West. The second mistake is the assumption that China's innovation capacity is already on par with that of the United States. Finally, and perhaps most important, the moon shot mentality leads too easily to a top-down, government-dominated approach to innovation that is out of synch with the global trend toward the bottom-up, open innovation approaches that are essential to tackling the world's most difficult problems.

Consider the flaws in turn. For one thing, the Sputnik mindset approach assumes that innovation is a zero-sum game. If China is up, then the United States must be down. But that is not necessarily true: history shows that one company or country can benefit from the development and marketing of a clever invention, while the robust diffusion and adoption of such inventions can also benefit many others. This is a lesson that should have been made clear by the wave of hysteria in the West over Japan's rise in the 1980s. Back then, it was popular to decry the unstoppable rise of that Asian power as an economic force that would suck away American jobs and lead inexorably to the decline of the United States. Yale University's Paul Kennedy asked in his 1987 book *The Rise and Fall of Great Powers* (which posited that Japan would surpass the United States just as surely as the Yanks surpassed the Brits) just how powerful, economically, Japan would be in the early twenty-first century. His answer: *"much more powerful."* Lester Thurow, dean of MIT's Sloan School of Management during that period of American malaise, argued that "Japan would have to be considered the betting favorite to win the economic honors of owning the twenty-first century." Both experts fueled the insecurity of the day that America's market-oriented economy would decline as Japan's government-directed miracle economy soared.

In fact, Japan's peaceful rise did not come at the expense of the United States, and China's advance today does not have to come at the West's expense either. Just as a rising tide lifts all boats, the economic dynamism of the emerging giants today can open vast new markets and expand global trade, increase opportunities for specialization, enrich lives everywhere, and increase opportunities for competitive American firms. But the tide will not raise boats that have holes in them, which is to say it is still worthwhile for firms to remain fit and for governments to ensure that the preconditions for successful innovation are in place—including keeping out of the way when old industries and uncompetitive firms have to die to make way for vibrant new players.

To see why, consider what actually happened to Japan after those predictions made in the 1980s. After reaching the number two spot in the global economy, the country plunged into a lost decade of economic stagnation, consumer atrophy, and deep national anxiety. In fact, on some measures China has passed it to become the world's second-biggest economy. Part of the explanation for what went wrong lies on the demand side of the ledger. After Japan's real estate and stock market bubbles burst, the country was overburdened with bad debt. Rather than deal with the problem swiftly, as the United States did during its savings-and-loan crisis, Japanese policy makers chose the less controversial path of flooding the market with government love and money. It did not work. Consumers were unpersuaded of the country's prospects, and demand remained anemic.

The less understood part of the Japan story has to do with supply, however. The country's demography did not help, as it is one of the most rapidly aging societies and one with very low rates of fertility. It is also one of the developed world's most insular and anti-immigrant nations. That double bind means the supply of available workers is declining and the theoretical growth potential for the economy is taking a hit. Still, observes Harvard's Clay Christensen, Japan remains a wealthy, educated, and technologically sophisticated economy, so it should have been able to rebound by now if the government had gotten out of the way of the proper functioning of capital and labor markets.

Precisely because its firms had been so successful at disruptive innovation, Japan's once-ridiculed companies (it seems unimaginable now, but Hondas were once known for unreliability, not quality) had come to dominate global markets in cars, shipbuilding, steel, and semiconductors. They surpassed their American rivals—who had been complacently basking in the profits to be found at the technology frontier—to become top of the heap. Ah, but that rise to the technology frontier is what made those Japanese upstarts vulnerable to disruption from the next wave of disruptive innovation, argues Christensen. Japan could have gotten its economy out of the cellar if its business and political leaders had encouraged the redeployment of capital and labor from stagnant, overcapitalized industries of the past to new, emerging technologies and enterprises. Instead, they defended unviable jobs and bloated companies they considered national champions, and erected trade and other barriers to protect them. That allowed the robust and more open economies of Silicon Valley and Bangalore to grab the lead in software services, Internet technologies, and other related industries of the future. Thanks in large part to those misguided industrial policies on the supply side of the ledger, Japan's economy continues to stagnate—and its technology firms remain laggards in the Internet revolution.

The Red Menace, Reconsidered

Another fallacy embedded in the Sputnik conceit is that China has already matched America's innovation prowess and is set to surpass it. In fact, even conceding all the gains made by emerging markets around the world, the United States remains the heavyweight champion of innovation. Whether it is by traditional measures, such as spending on research and the number of patents registered, or less tangible but more important ones, such as the number of entrepreneurial start-ups, levels of venture capital funding, or the payback from new inventions, the United States is invariably near or at the very top of all relevant global rankings.

There is more competition at the top of those rankings these days, but there are many reasons to think that the U.S. economy will remain on top for quite some time yet. While it is true that Asia will probably surpass the United States in absolute research spending and sheer numbers of technical graduates, there are reasons to be skeptical about some of the foundations of Asian innovation. In *Advantage*, a well-researched book released in 2011, Adam Segal of the Council on Foreign Relations argues that America's "unipolar moment" in the global economy may be over, but that Asia's rise does not necessarily foreshadow the decline of the United States. He points to evidence that challenges the quality of the many patents, papers, and engineering degrees seen in India and China.

Research done by Vivek Wadhwa, an entrepreneur turned academic, has debunked various myths built up around Asian engineering prowess. In work done with colleagues at Duke University a few years ago, he showed the claims that China and India were graduating far more engineers than the United States were wildly overstated. More important, while some schools, such as the

Indian Institutes of Technology, produce world-class graduates, his research suggests that a number of the degrees issued from other Indian engineering schools are of poor quality. Proof of that comes from the unwillingness of multinationals and high-end local employers to accept graduates with those degrees. Also, many firms, such as the Indian software giant Infosys, are forced to spend fortunes retraining their incoming employees with local engineering degrees. When one considers the quality of engineering talent, argues Wadhwa, the United States remains on top.

Much has also been made out of China's dramatic rise in the league table of intellectual property rights. Not so long ago, the country was known more for counterfeit drugs, pirated CDs, and patent cheats than for original innovation. Yet consider this headline from a Thomson Reuters bulletin in late 2010: "China Poised to Become Global Innovation Leader." The publishing firm's researchers surveyed the patenting activity of a number of countries, from the developed world's giants to China and Korea, and concluded that the total volume of first-patent filings in China shot up at an annual growth rate of 26 percent from 2003 to 2009; the patenting rate of its nearest rival, the United States, grew at only 5.5 percent during that period. The outfit predicted that China will overtake Japan and the United States to be the global patenting leader soon. Sounds impressive, until one asks about the quality of those patents. Look closely and it turns out that about half of the patents filed by Chinese firms in 2009 were so-called utility model patents, which Thomson Reuters itself describes as "less-rigorous, more affordable forms of patents" that provide ten years of protection versus twenty years for invention patents. Again, that suggests that claims of America's imminent demise in this area are to be taken with a grain of salt.

That is not to say that China lacks ambition, resources, or seriousness in its quest to become an innovation powerhouse. Quite the contrary, in fact. The latest five-year plan from Beijing's technocracy puts "indigenous innovation," by which it means creating value through homegrown invention rather than merely copying or stealing, at the top of the country's economic priorities. This is a huge problem, and one that worries many foreign technology companies. Some are so keen to get access to the Chinese market that they agree, under intense pressure, to share their precious intellectual property with local partners. Many in the aerospace industry say GE caved in this way with a controversial avionics deal it struck with Chinese partners recently, but Jeff Immelt is adamant that such is not the case; in his view, the deal was worthwhile because it secures his firm a powerful position in the country's booming aviation industry. Intel does both manufacturing and research in China, but Justin Rattner, its chief technology officer, confirms that his firm forbids cutting-edge technology ("our crown jewels," he calls them) from entering that country.

The Chinese leadership is putting the squeeze on foreign technology firms precisely because it understands how far behind the West its technology firms are. That is not to dismiss the amazing contributions being made by its frugal innovators, of course, but by definition the frugalistas described earlier in this book start at the bottom of the value chain before working their way up to such elaborate technologies as the latest jet engines. That is why the Beijing government's goals include a desire to improve the economy's competitiveness by directing it toward technology ownership and upgrading the structure of exports from low-cost manufacturing goods to higher-value-added products and services. By building up the innovative capacity of local firms, the government hopes to reduce the dominant share of high-tech exports commanded by foreign-owned firms in favor of local ones.

All that is necessary because locals know that China still has a long way to go to match the innovation ecosystem of the United States. In fact, the same Intel poll that showed Americans to be so anxious about a rising China revealed that more than 80 percent of Chinese reached by pollsters believe that the United States is firmly in the global lead.

The OECD recently examined China's innovation policies and potential in great detail and concluded that while the country is already a major player in science and technology, its output still falls short of the levels in OECD countries with similar levels of R&D expenditure. This inefficiency, argue the agency's experts, points to broader deficiencies in the policies and governance system used to promote innovation as the country moves from a planned economy to something resembling a market-based one. While acknowledging the country's dramatic increases in research spending and levels of patenting, the experts observe that these have "yet to translate into a proportionate increase in innovation performance." That is in part because the ability of the business sector to make productive use of all that investment in R&D is constrained by lack of proper infrastructure, talent, and culture. That is in sharp contrast with the United States, which does much better in speeding inventions out of academic and government laboratories into the marketplace (though, it must be noted, it could do still better).

China's ambition of becoming the world's innovation super-power faces other obstacles too. R&D money is only one part of what it takes to kick-start a modern innovation economy. The country's norms on corporate governance, enforcement of intellectual property rights and antitrust laws, and financing of R&D are all not up to international standards yet. With small exceptions such as the nanotechnology sector, the country's basic research efforts are not yet well connected with its technology development juggernaut. The OECD also found that the country's industrial policies have created disconnected islands of innovation in various regions or subsectors, but too few interconnections between the various bits of this archipelago. That limits the spillovers beyond the borders of those islands and creates too great a physical separation between knowledge producers and potential users.

The upshot is that while China is clearly an ambitious rising power, there is little basis to think that it has even come close to surpassing America's innovation prowess. The OECD's most sensitive recommendation for China helps explain why. Though acknowledging that the country's government does need to play a role in improving such things as corporate governance, regional disparities, and environmental protection, which the markets will not tackle on their own, the experts insist that all-knowing central planners should actually do much less in many areas. China must adjust the role of the government, insists the agency, by "overcoming the legacy of the planned economy by encouraging changes in the attitudes and methods of work of government officials so as to allow market forces, competition, and the private sector to have a greater role."

That insight points to the third problem with the Sputnik analogy: it puts policy makers on the slippery slope to the failed interventionist approaches of the past, like the heavy-handed industrial policies adopted by many countries back in the 1970s. Keen to get America's innovation mojo back, Barack Obama used his State of the Union speech in 2011 to declare this a new Sputnik moment. But China's rise is that of a gradual and mutually beneficial tide, not a single aggressive act or specific blow to the United States. What's more, the moon shots were a costly and centralized technology push (the Apollo effort cost some $150 billion in today's money, on some estimates) that is entirely unsuited to twenty-first-century models of innovation. Robert Solow, the Nobel Prize–winning economist, acknowledges that the United States must improve the productivity of its economy. The way to do this best, he explains, is to "encourage innovation in sectors with large and growing markets, such as energy." The centralized Apollo approach worked for getting a man on the moon and back safely, costs be damned, but it is entirely inappropriate for the clean energy challenge. Ensuring that seven billion people across the globe get access to safe, clean, affordable, and convenient energy services requires the nimble interplay of policy, markets, technology, and consumers.

Yet most of the Asian countries hoping to challenge the innovation supremacy of the United States have strong, government-led innovation policies in place. As in the case of Singapore and Korea, these are often technocratically brilliant. However, innovation is not in its essence a top-down process, and so this will not be enough for sustained success. Many of these countries lack America's resilient, open, and risk-taking culture. China would do well to learn from the experience of state planners in Europe who also have tried to engineer innovation policies to compete with the United States. They have discovered that the American approach, for all its inadequacies, fares better than the brittle, centralized innovation policies that have largely failed across the Atlantic.

The Dangers of Dirigisme

The recent scene in Salzburg was one that Joseph Schumpeter and Peter Drucker surely would have approved of. Several dozen leading government officials and academics from around the world gathered at Schloss Leopoldskron, a spectacular rococo palace located on the shores of an idyllic lake. They came not for the fresh Alpine air, the hearty Austrian fare, or even the hills alive with the sound of music. It was for a conference organized by the Salzburg Global Seminar, a European think tank, to discuss what they could do to turn their economies into innovation powerhouses.

Holding such a meeting in the heart of Europe seemed only fitting—and not just because Schumpeter and Drucker, the two great theorists of innovation, both hailed from the region. After all, it was also a European, France's Georges Doriot, who invented venture capital during his time teaching at Harvard. And it was another Frenchman, Jean-Baptiste Say, who coined the word *entrepreneur* two centuries ago to describe the plucky upstart who "shifts economic resources out of an area of lower and into an area of higher productivity and greater yield."

Yet the star of the show was the United States. Everyone wanted to learn how Silicon Valley was created and how it has managed to keep its edge despite various booms and busts. Asia also made its mark, with innovation gurus from places such as Singapore bragging about how many billions of dollars they are spending on technology parks, tax breaks on foreign investment, and scholarships for their bright young things to go to MIT and Stanford.

So what about Europe? The blunt answer is that the old continent is something of an also-ran when it comes to innovation. That does not mean the region has no innovative companies—it certainly has a few in some areas, especially retail and financial services, with firms such as Zara, a Spanish fast-fashion chain, and Direct Line, a British online insurer. But these tend to be exceptions. It is not much of an exaggeration to say that, aside from mobile telephony, Europe has not come up with a globally disruptive innovation in decades—although Skype, an Internet telephony firm that is now part of Microsoft, once looked like it might qualify.

Europe's innovation malaise is the result of a complex mix of factors. Some places, such as Ireland, Finland, and parts of Scandinavia, are doing better than others (or at least, in Ireland's case, did so before the recent financial crash). And Cambridge, England, can reasonably claim to have created Europe's best innovation cluster, albeit one that falls far short of Silicon Valley. The main thing holding back continental Europe is that it is a lousy place to start a new company. It can cost a lot of money and it takes too long to set up a business. According to the World Bank's influential annual "Doing Business" report, government red tape means it takes nineteen days to open a business in Germany. That is certainly better than the twenty-three days it takes in Japan, but it is much more cumbersome than the six days it takes in the United States or the mere three it takes in Singapore.

In 2006, venture capitalists invested only about $9 billion in the European Union, while their American counterparts splashed out some $45 billion on new ventures. The link between venture capital and innovation is a strong one. Samuel Kortum and Josh Lerner, two American academics, have shown that "a dollar of venture capital could be up to ten times more effective in stimulating patenting than a dollar of traditional corporate R&D." They scrutinized twenty manufacturing industries between 1965 and 1992 and found that the amount of venture capital money in a sector dramatically increased according to the rate at which businesses in that sector took out patents. From 1982 to 1992, they calculated that venture capital funds amounted to just 3 percent of corporate R&D but 15 percent of all industrial innovations.

It is true that patents have become less important in many industries and so they are an imperfect proxy for all innovation. And in some cases venture capital funds will follow rather than create innovation. Nevertheless, patents are still widely used, and Kortum and Lerner successfully validated their results with other measurements too.

But surely innovation and entrepreneurship are not the same thing? Following the most useful definition—that innovation brings to the marketplace fresh thinking that creates value for a company, for its customers, and for society at large—someone who opens yet another corner café may be a successful entrepreneur but not much of an innovator. The ones worth paying attention to are a special type of innovative entrepreneur who embraces new ideas and has the ambition to scale them quickly. These are the people who are able to carry out the creative destruction that Schumpeter marveled at. In Europe they are still too thin on the ground: too many Europeans opt for comfortable jobs working for Siemens or Electricité de France rather than the risk and bother of starting speculative new companies.

This is worrying for Europe. National champions and incumbents are not disruptive innovators. Upstarts are. From 1980 to 2001, all of the net growth in American employment came from firms younger than five years old. Established firms lost many jobs over that period and dozens fell off the Fortune 500 list. In fact, big corporations have been dying off and disappearing from stock market indices. Most of the dynamism of the world economy comes from innovative entrepreneurs and a handful of multinationals (including GE, IBM, and P&G, all of whom have stayed on the Fortune 500 list for many decades) that constantly reinvent themselves.

Carl Schramm, president of the Kauffman Foundation, which studies entrepreneurship and innovation, says that "for the United States to survive and continue its economic and political leadership in the world, we must see entrepreneurship as our central comparative advantage. Nothing else can give us the necessary leverage to remain an economic superpower." A recent study funded by his think tank reviewed jobs data from the U.S. Census Bureau from 1977 to 2005 and found that during this period existing firms were net job destroyers, losing one million jobs net combined per year. In contrast, in their first year, new firms added an average of three million jobs. Because start-ups that get going without government help are almost the only real source of job growth in the United States, the foundation concludes that government industrial policies aimed at preserving jobs at big companies or luring larger, established firms into a particular region will inevitably fail. Such policies are "doomed not only because they are zero-sum, but because they are based in unrealistic employment growth models."

The U.S. economy is not a free market paragon, to be sure. The Internet and related industries have all benefited from the spillover effects from government funding of universities and from military spending. However, it is wrong to think those factors alone explain American dynamism. The Soviet Union spent lavishly on its military and space programs during the Cold War, but because its economic system was ossified, there were few spillover effects.

What is more, Europe itself spends a lot of money on higher education and has a number of top universities with leading academics and researchers who produce excellent papers and win Nobel Prizes. The problem is that their ideas tend to stay in their ivory towers. Part of the explanation is that innovation is still seen as being driven by government spending on R&D, when in fact most innovation now happens in services and business models. Studies have shown that companies that outperform their peers put a much bigger emphasis on business model innovation. Indeed, that is a mistake that even the great Clay Christensen originally made. When he first developed his groundbreaking theories on disruptive innovation, he focused on the specific technologies in question—such as inexpensive computer disk drives, for example, that ultimately drove out the expensive incumbent storage technology—that he believed to be key. But as he researched the topic further, he realized that it was not the gadget or gizmo but the combination of new technologies with radically different business models that added up to disruptive innovation.

That is a lesson that many officials in Europe have not fully absorbed. The European Union has an official target to raise government R&D spending, and there is much angst over patents—an obsession that Japanese planners share. A recent edition of *Science, Technology and Innovation in Europe*, an annual report by the statistical arm of the European Commission, reveals exactly what is wrong. It is chock full of figures, broken down by region and industry, of research spending, patents filed, scientists employed, and other important-sounding variables. The problem is that these are all inputs into the innovation process, not outputs. There is only a cursory discussion of venture capital and no attention paid at all to entrepreneurship—the most powerful way to turn ideas into valuable products and services.

The World Is Spiky

Another problem is that European officials, like government bureaucrats everywhere, are obsessed with creating geographic clusters like Silicon Valley. The French have poured billions into *pôles de compétitivité*, and many others are doing much the same. There are dozens of aspiring clusters worldwide, nicknamed Silicon Fen, Silicon Fjord, Silicon Alley, and Silicon Bog. Typically governments pick a politically influential part of their country, ideally one that has a big university nearby, and provide a pot of money that is meant to kick-start entrepreneurship under the guiding hand of benevolent bureaucrats.

It has been an abysmal failure. The high-tech cluster in and around Cambridge, England, is the most often-cited counter-example. Hermann Hauser of Amadeus Capital, a leading British venture capitalist (who, curiously, also hails from Austria), is an optimist: "Silicon Valley is still the lead cow, but Cambridge is the best in Europe." Perhaps, but that is faint praise. The main problem, argues Georges Haour of IMD, a Swiss business school, is that Cambridge suffers from the Peter Pan complex: "Inventors never want to grow up, they are happy with modest success." One veteran of the city's start-up scene even argues that its success came "in spite of, not because of," government and university support.

Experts at INSEAD looked at efforts by the German government to create biotechnology clusters on a par with those found in California and concluded that "Germany has essentially wasted $20 billion—and now Singapore is well on its way to doing the same." A World Bank assessment of Singapore's multibillion-dollar efforts to create a "biopolis" reckoned that it had only a fifty-fifty chance of success.

The real problem holding back innovation in many countries is too much government in the form of red tape and market barriers. Planning restrictions have prevented the expansion of Ahold and other highly efficient retailers in France. Closing hours in several EU countries also act as an inhibitor. Studies of Japan and South Korea suggest the heavy hand of government is even more stifling in those countries: outside a small, highly competitive group of export industries (cars, electronic goods, and steel), inefficient, coddled domestic sectors are slow to adopt new technologies or business practices.

In the end it is companies, not regions, that are competitive. So the question for government is how to attract many competitive firms. That should throw cold water on cluster-mad politicians. It also points to sensible prescriptions to promote innovation.

First of all, stop spreading money around in politicized fashion trying to clone lots of Silicon Valleys. Steven Koonin, an official in the U.S. Department of Energy who served previously as chief scientist at BP and as the provost of the California Institute of Technology, has said that European countries spread research funds too thinly anyway. Often this leads to money being divided up on a political basis, with funds going to institutions based on influence in Brussels and European capitals rather than on the promise and merit of a particular research effort. The United States has no problem with big awards, so innovators can achieve scale. That is precisely what BP has done, setting up a $500 million research alliance run by the University of California at Berkeley to look into advanced biofuels.

However, there is an even more important factor than money: culture. Nokia's success was not the result of farsighted planning or subsidy by the government of Finland. One Nokia executive confides: "The biggest boost to our firm was the deregulation that followed the second world war and the government's avoidance of protectionism." One of the most innovative things Nokia did was to spot that the handset could also be a fashion accessory. And coming from such a small and open market, it was forced to think globally.

Second, governments keen to promote innovation need to look out for market distortions and overregulation that can be stripped away. This is not to argue for no regulation: as the latter part of this chapter argues, there is actually a pressing need for a more muscular, but carefully circumscribed, role for government. The problem is that entrepreneurs can face an uphill battle legally, not just culturally, in many countries. The bankruptcy code in many places is excessively burdensome, even banning some failed entrepreneurs from running a company for years. Contrast that with America's Chapter 11 bankruptcy proceedings, which quickly redeploy both the bankrupt firm's physical assets and the creative energies of its leaders.

In India an overbearing system known as the Licence Raj choked the creativity out of most sectors of the economy for decades, through a mix of overregulation, petty corruption, and centralized planning. But the bureaucrats in Delhi did not understand computer software well enough to regulate it. And by the time they caught on, innovators in Bangalore and other corners of India had created a world-class industry. A similar story may be unfolding quietly in parts of China. Adam Segal has studied high-technology firms in Beijing, Shanghai, Guangzhou, and Xian. His research shows that smaller entrepreneurs in the private sector—sometimes called bamboo capitalists—are likely to be more innovative than bigger ones reliant on government largesse.

All across the developing world, where chaotic and corrupt rule can impede growth in myriad ways, extraordinary innovators are starting to flourish wherever they are not choked off by bureaucrats or fat cats. Freedom from "legacy," in the shape of stranded assets such as fixed-line telephony or centralized power grids, has liberated African entrepreneurs and allowed them to leapfrog with technology—from having no electricity to using solar cells, for instance. So where does that leave the present Goliath of innovation, the United States?

Patching the Holes in the American Vessel

John Kao is concerned about the United States losing its global lead and becoming "the fat, complacent Detroit of nations." In his book *Innovation Nation*, he points to warning signs, such as the United States' underinvestment in physical infrastructure, its slow start on broadband, its pitiful public schools, and its frostiness toward immigrants since September 11, 2001—even though immigrants have provided much of America's creativity. He even stoutly defends his description of the rise of Asia's innovators as a silent Sputnik. What the United States needs, he reckons, is a big push by federal government to promote innovation, akin to the Apollo space project that answered Kennedy's call and put a man on the moon.

Curt Carlson puts it in starker terms: "India and China are a tsunami about to overwhelm us." As head of California's Stanford Research Institute, which was founded in 1946 by the university to foster innovation and economic development in the region, Carlson knows the strengths of Silicon Valley from firsthand experience. Yet here he is insisting that American information technology, services, and medical devices industries are about to be lost. "I predict that millions of jobs will be destroyed in our country, like in the 1980s when American firms refused to adopt total quality management techniques while the Japanese surged ahead." The only way out, he insists, is "to learn the tools of innovation" and forge entirely new, knowledge-based industries in energy technology, biotechnology, and other science-based sectors.

These thoughtful gurus are right to sound the alarm bells, as there are signs that the United States' innovation ecosystem needs attention in areas such as education and basic infrastructure. However, given the dismal failure of industrial policies in the past, one should still remain skeptical of any calls for aggressive government intervention across the board. The Council on Competitiveness, an influential coalition of leading business interests, recently concluded in a report that, by and large, the outlook is bright for the United States. Yet the same council's innovation task force also gave warning that other countries are making heavy investments that threaten to erode the U.S. position. It called for a big push in four areas: improving science, engineering, and math education; welcoming skilled immigrants; beefing up government spending on basic research; and offering tax incentives to spur U.S.-based innovation.

These are mostly sensible recommendations because they focus on those framework conditions and bits of infrastructure that the market would not provide on its own. Still, governments should tread carefully even in these areas. Consider the call to beef up American technical education. This is sensible, but some go too far in dismissing the value of arts, design, and other creative parts of the curriculum. Bill Gates is firmly in the technologists' camp, exclaiming, "If we lose engineering, I don't know what's left!" Steve Jobs, in contrast, argued that the United States is flourishing because firms such as his, unlike Asian rivals, have the creativity and flair to integrate low-value components manufactured cheaply elsewhere into gorgeous and lucrative devices such as the iPad. The United States clearly needs to improve its education system, but the right way forward would provide holistic training that balances stronger technical and vocational education with more creative fields that encourage critical and integrative thinking.

Just as with education reform, the case for immigration reform is overwhelmingly strong in the United States. Many studies have shown that immigrants have played a central role in the country's economic vitality—especially well-educated engineers from India and China. Vivek Wadhwa estimates that from 1995 to 2005, 52 percent of Silicon Valley's technology and engineering companies were founded by immigrants. Most came to the United States to study and stayed on to work. That group also filed a quarter of the country's global patents.

The problem is that after 9/11, Americans turned frosty toward such folk, making it harder for them to stay on after studies to work. Gates points out the absurdity of subsidizing the computer science degrees granted to foreign graduate students at top state schools such as the University of California at Berkeley only to chuck those brilliant immigrants out of the country when they ask to work and pay taxes in the United States after graduation. This chill came just as the economies back home skyrocketed, making it much easier for the new generation of hungry young world-beaters from those emerging markets to skip America and seek their fortunes back home instead. Nativists and xenophobes may cheer, thinking this means more jobs for red-blooded Americans, but that is wrong. Wadhwa points out that this simply means "there will be fewer start-ups, that entrepreneurship will boom instead in countries like India and China, and that Silicon Valley will face unprecedented competition from American-educated and -trained talent" that is forced to go home. In other words, unless the United States reforms its immigration laws quickly, it is about to lose the extraordinarily valuable gift of the world's most talented and enterprising minds that its economy has benefited from these past decades.

The recommendation from the Council on Competitiveness that the United States should boost its investment in research and development is also sound, but again the devil is in the details. If such investment is structured as technology-neutral policies that do not favor one particular firm or technology over another—for example, via stable, long-term tax policies that encourage corporate spending on research—then they are a good idea. So too are reforms of the way new inventions, often funded with government money, make their way from academic laboratories to the market. At the moment, the law gives the technology-licensing offices at universities too much power over what ideas make it out of the lab and into the office (though a Supreme Court case in mid-2011 suggested big changes may be on the way that favor innovators over administrators). Giving faculty and employees of government laboratories greater discretion over commercialization would transform a sclerotic, centralized process into a vibrant marketplace where scientists will have every incentive to turn obscure inventions into world-changing innovations.

That points to a related area where government action could help shore up one of America's traditional strengths: encouraging innovative entrepreneurship. Robert Litan, a scholar affiliated with the Kauffman Foundation and the Brookings Institution, coauthored an influential book some years ago called *Good Capitalism, Bad Capitalism* that argued that the most innovative economies have a mix of nimble start-ups (which come up with breakthrough innovations) and dynamic big firms (which do incremental improvements and scale up those breakthroughs). In contrast, the least innovative economies tend to have few start-ups and lots of state interference in markets. But he believes that the advantages held by big firms are eroding fast just as globalization, Web-enabled services, crowd-sourced capital, and other powerful changes in the global economy are tilting the playing field in favor of entrepreneurs. While in the past most start-ups targeted local markets, Daniel Isenberg of Babson College argues persuasively that today's start-ups can become "micromultinationals" from day one thanks to the Internet and global supply chain management tools.

In his new book, *Better Capitalism*, Litan argues that the most dynamic and high-growth economies of the future will be those that encourage high-growth entrepreneurship. How, exactly? "I'm not a fan of clusters; state guidance usually gets new technologies wrong . . . governments should get the basic infrastructure right and let capitalism work," he says. Still, he believes America needs to stoke the start-up bonfires by opening up immigration, investing in science and technology education, liberating intellectual property from academia, and fixing the country's fiscal mess through a value-added tax on consumption that would ease the burden of taxes in other areas like capital gains.

That is a sensible set of recommendations. And the industry lobbies are also right to say that there are important things the U.S. government must do to improve the country's innovation framework and stay ahead of the global competition. Where the prescriptions from such groups tend to go awry is when they argue for specific subsidies or tax breaks for favored industries (such as supporting only U.S.-based innovation in today's world of global creative networks). After all, the forces of creative destruction must be allowed to work their magic.

The Secret of Silicon Valley

Resilience in the face of disruptive forces gave Silicon Valley the edge over its nearest high-tech rival, Boston's Route 128 technology corridor. Both clusters were riding high until the personal computer and distributed computing changed the market. Firms went through wrenching change, but those in northern California, such as Hewlett-Packard and Xerox, emerged stronger than those near Boston, such as Digital Equipment and Wang—which no longer exist. As AnnaLee Saxenian of the University of California at Berkeley has shown, Silicon Valley's champions were nimble and networked, but those on Route 128 were brittle, top-down bureaucracies.

Sergey Brin insists that "Silicon Valley doesn't have better ideas and isn't smarter than the rest of the world" but thinks it has the edge in filtering ideas and executing them. That magic still happens and attracts people from around the world who are "bold, ambitious, determined to scale up, and able to raise money here actually to do it." Brin points to Elon Musk, founder of Tesla and SpaceX, as an example.

Musk moved from South Africa and eventually settled in California to make his fortune. Musk says his equation for success is drive times opportunity times talent. Unlike many countries, he insists, America is never satisfied with the status quo. "There is a culture here that celebrates the achievements of individuals—and it is too often forgotten in history that it is individuals, not governments or economic systems, that are responsible for extraordinary breakthroughs," he says.

That explains why innovation policies should carefully circumscribe the role of government. Liberty is a powerful force. In the past, Brin notes, innovation was dominated by elites—the "wealthy gentlemen tinkerers" of Victorian England, for example—who had privileged access to information, money, and markets. But America was different. Harold Evans, the author of *They Made America*, observes that the essential enabler of U.S. innovation prowess was "political innovation . . . a free society." Britain actually invented many marvels of the modern age—radar, penicillin, and the jet engine, among many—but it was America that commercialized these inventions at scale and turned them into genuinely valuable innovations. Evans thinks a key factor was the United States' system of universal education, which developed a broad scientific and technological workforce. Britain, in contrast, had an elitist and limited educational system. And these days, of course, much innovation happens from the bottom up and the inside out. That suggests an important but radically different role for government going forward.

A Policy Manifesto for the Age of Democratic Innovation

It is clear that the need for innovation has never been greater. As the world economy struggles to recover from the global financial crisis, governments are casting about for strategies to revive growth. They are also struggling to come up with solutions to difficult global challenges ranging from climate change and the threat of pandemics to the demographic and health burdens (think costly chronic diseases such as diabetes and heart disease) imposed by older, fatter, and sicker populations.

Accelerating the pace of innovation would certainly help countries deal with both problems. Because most of the output of rich countries now comes from nonmanufacturing sectors, where brain trumps brawn, boosting innovation offers a promising way to increase productivity and spur future growth. And even in traditional asset- and legacy-heavy industries such as manufacturing, the next chapter shows, investing in the knowledge component of those businesses can lead to a renaissance. Breakthrough technologies and disruptive business models, such as the spread in Africa of banking and medicine via mobile telephony, can make it much easier to tackle those thorny challenges.

Governments everywhere are now coming up with innovation policies they claim will boost national competitiveness and tackle environmental and other social goals. The U.S. government has bailed out GM and Chrysler, for example, and is throwing money at batteries, electric vehicles, and other energy technologies. Various European governments are following the example of their French counterpart, which is now subsidizing such "strategic" industries as toy making. Yes, really.

As that example suggests, a lot of things done in the name of innovation are simply a sham. Many of the national innovation strategies implemented in the wake of the financial crisis merely subsidize favored technologies or prop up uncompetitive national champions. In the worst cases, they are thinly disguised attempts at protectionism. Though dressed up in pro-market language, they are mostly a throwback to the failed industrial policies of the 1970s and 1980s.

These policies are far likelier to retard innovation than to spur it. That is because innovation is at heart a bottom-up process—a Schumpeterian dance of risk, failure, resilience, and reward that is foreign to all-knowing bureaucrats but second nature to entrepreneurs. Greed not only is good but also can do great good—if, that is, there are clear incentives to tackle the wicked problems of society.

But first governments must step back a little. History shows that official attempts to pick technology winners, no matter how initially promising, usually end in tears. Three decades ago, the French government developed Minitel, a national communications network that allowed users to send messages, book train reservations, and so on. This was a popular invention, and for its time a clever one. The snag was that bureaucrats insisted on keeping this a closed system, even after it became clear to everyone else that the future belonged to open networks such as the Internet. Minitel inevitably proved a dead end, and France lost out in the global Internet race.

The United States has its embarrassments too. In the wake of the 1970s oil shocks, the Department of Energy decided to invest heavily in producing synthetic petroleum, to end the country's addiction to foreign oil. Predictably, the project proved a costly flight of fancy: billions of dollars and many years were spent on this technology dead end, but not a single barrel of "syn-crude" ever reached the market. The current version of that boondoggle is the enormously damaging subsidy given to corn ethanol. This pleases the politically powerful farm lobby, but this perverse policy has diverted corn from food markets (fueling food price hikes that have hurt the very poorest) while also harming the environment (since corn ethanol, unlike the virtuous Brazilian sugarcane variety, is not green).

These policies have failed because, despite the best intentions of central planners, top-down innovation does not work as well as the bottom-up variety. This is especially true in energy, according to a comprehensive review of energy innovation coauthored by Richard Newell, currently head of the U.S. Energy Information Administration. He points to the current boom in the shale gas industry, which is the most extraordinary development in American energy in decades, and notes that it was not predicted by government planners. Newell's study shows that energy innovation is driven not by short-term bursts of government support but chiefly by bottom-up efforts and market forces. Indeed, the key to the shale breakthrough was not government subsidies for new technology but the clever and diligent application by market actors of existing technologies to new situations.

The top-down approach was always misguided, but it is absurdly out of place given the speed at which innovation happens today. Thanks to globalization and the rise of the information economy, new ideas move to market faster than ever before. This is in large part due to the shift from top-down innovation (of the sort made famous by AT&T's Bell Laboratories and other secretive corporate silos) toward more open, networked, and user-driven models of innovation. Think, for example, of the iPod: the research behind it was done by firms the world over, but Apple has reaped huge rewards from its skills in design, marketing, and systems integration.

Innovation is truly a global enterprise today. Much of the value created by firms is in the form of intangibles such as knowledge networks and open business models. Yet most governments cling stubbornly to national industrial policies that offer perverse incentives for local firms to squander resources on parochial technologies and outmoded business models. That suggests that innovation works best when government does least.

However, that is not to say that governments should do nothing at all. On the contrary, there is an essential, but carefully circumscribed, role for the state in fostering innovation. Despite the recent downturn, governments must continue to invest in the handful of areas that fortify an economy's capacity to innovate—and therefore, to grow more robustly—in the future.

For a start, only governments can ensure that the framework for innovation is sound. America's success at maintaining the rule of law, encouraging risk capital, and applying pragmatic bankruptcy codes all played a role in the spectacular rise of Silicon Valley, for example. Governments should also encourage investment in what the OECD calls "knowledge-supporting infrastructure," which ranges from smart electricity grids and broadband Internet networks to basic research and university education. That principle argues against massive cuts in education and infrastructure, for example. It would be far better for cash-strapped governments to cut spending on entitlement programs than to slash vital investment in the enablers of long-term economic growth.

But investing in the innovation framework must not mean picking technology winners. A better approach is the use of externalities pricing for such problems as carbon pollution, as it sets a societal goal but allows market forces—and, yes, greed—to find the most efficient way to solve the problem. Another promising advance is the official use of incentive prizes. Aneesh Chopra, the White House's chief technology officer, argues that new technologies and a new mind-set are enabling innovation in government itself. One example involves initiatives to put much previously inaccessible public information up on the Internet, which is democratizing government data. Another way government can help, he argues, is by pushing for common standards and transparency in such areas as electronic health records. He also argues that government must act as a catalyst for greater research collaboration among academic and private sector actors at the precompetitive level.

These efforts get an endorsement from an unexpected quarter: Craig Newmark, one of the true pioneers of the Web. He founded Craigslist.org, which is the online bulletin board used by countless millions to exchange goods and services. The upstart used to throwing rocks at the establishment has, it turns out, been advising members of Congress and the Obama administration on openness, networking, and what bureaucrats like to call Government 2.0. Newmark believes Gov 2.0 can become a big deal: "By exposing data, by fixing a lot of business processes, by using the technologies of the private sector, a lot of things are being made to work in Washington, and no one is talking about it." He is convinced that the tools of social media can be applied to civics, to rebuild what he calls "the immune system of democracy." He believes these remarkably disruptive tools may even transform government and its relationship with civil society.

These efforts at openness are to be applauded. But, sad to say, most of what governments around the world do in the name of innovation does not resemble such efforts in the least. That is why the biggest boost governments can give to national competitiveness is to stop doing some things. The first thing is to end perverse policies that discourage collaboration outside one's own firm or country. The tax credit offered by the U.S. government for corporate research is appropriately generous for work done inside a firm's labs (and Congress should make this stop-and-go policy permanent) but stingy if that same work is done with, say, university researchers. In contrast, Canada's tax law does not punish collaboration in this way.

The second thing is to stop creeping protectionism. International coordination of technical protocols can be a good thing: Europe's embrace of the GSM standard helped its firms grab an early lead in mobile telephony, for example. However, there are worrying signs that some proposals for technology standards (for example, rules on smart grid protocols or electronic health records) are really covert attempts to produce rules favoring local technology firms. History shows that such efforts can lock local firms into dead-end technologies and leave them unable to compete globally.

The most important thing that countries must stop doing is closing their doors to immigration. Flexible labor markets are essential for a vibrant economy. Given the democratization and globalization of innovation seen in recent years, companies must be allowed to tap freely into the brainpower of billions of innovators-in-waiting worldwide if they are to remain competitive. Just as important, bright sparks from around the world must have the freedom to pursue their studies and professional ambitions, wherever in the world that may take them. Studies of innovation clusters in Israel, Taiwan, and South India have shown that the catalyst sparking the rise of those aspiring Silicon Valleys was the constant flow of talented researchers, entrepreneurs, and venture capitalists to and from the actual Silicon Valley (which owes its own success in part to immigration). Think brain circulation, not brain drain.

In sum, there are some useful things that government can do to boost innovation. Most center around the framework conditions that allow market forces to function properly so that the seeds sown by innovative entrepreneurs fall on fertile soil. The next chapter explores whether big companies can realign incentives so that they too can tap into such innovation within their own ranks. Given the dismal failure of past efforts at top-down innovation, though, governments should approach even these policies with humility. In the end, the best industrial policy is probably no industrial policy.

8

Can Dinosaurs Dance?

The rise of nimble Asian competitors and the accelerating pace of technological innovation are putting established companies in a double bind. For the storied multinational giants of the rich world, this is a battle for survival. Some of the dinosaurs of the old economy will fall by the wayside, but others may yet adapt and flourish. Some such firms are fighting the forces of change, but others making everything from consumer products and cars to colas are frantically figuring out the new tools and rules of global innovation.

The best of the breed are finding ways to turn the disruptive forces to their advantage. Some are experimenting with reverse innovation, through which Western firms bring innovations developed in emerging markets back to their home turf. Another weapon in their arsenal is the stealthy but sure spread of software, information technology, and related hardware into every nook and cranny of industries such as steel, cars, and energy. By becoming more like information businesses, which harness the Internet-fired explosion of customer data through advanced analytics and business intelligence strategies, traditionally stodgy companies hope to have a fighting chance.

Learning the tricks of frugal engineering now emerging from developing countries is essential for survival, but will Big Data really save Big Business? Actually, history shows that most companies die off over time—IBM, which celebrated its centenary in 2011, is a rare exception—and the pace of such creative destruction is accelerating. If big firms want to flourish, they need to combine scale with agility. To do so, they need to experiment and learn much faster than in the past, thereby speeding up the "knowledge turns" in their business.

That is because the digital revolution turns out to be a double-edged sword. The transformation of slow-moving, bricks-and-mortar industries into knowledge businesses does give them a renewed lease on life but it also exposes them to disruption from anywhere—meaning everyone must innovate faster today. This chapter highlights the successes achieved by nimble incumbents and plants red flags on the pitfalls that have befallen the insular and lethargic as dinosaurs learn how to dance to a new tune.

Vinod Khosla and Larry Page, two giants of the New Economy, are plotting to save the old economy. The two Silicon Valley stars were chatting one evening several years ago at the Googleplex. The crisis that Khosla was concerned about was caused by carmakers' addiction to oil and the implications of that for national security and the environment. "The energy and car industries have not been innovative in many years because they have faced no real crisis, no impetus for change," he insisted.

The two were plotting what they hoped would be the next great technological revolution: the convergence of software and smart electronics with the grease and grime of the oil and car industries. This was an audacious goal, given that the entrenched incumbents of asset-heavy industries such as the car business tend to move slowly indeed. Khosla was kicking around his plans for getting "chip guys" together with "engine guys" to develop the clean, software-rich car of the future. Such breakthroughs happen only when conventional wisdom is ignored and cross-fertilization encouraged—"managed conflict," in his words.

Page had earlier hosted a gathering of leading environmentalists, political thinkers, and energy experts to help shape an inducement to get things moving: the Progressive Automotive X Prize, unveiled in early 2008. The organizers offered $10 million to whoever came up with the most efficient, affordable, and sexy car to obtain very high fuel economy using any form of energy. The winner, announced in 2010 after an exciting global competition, was the Edison 2, an incredibly aerodynamic vehicle that got over 102 miles per gallon of gasoline-equivalent energy. The charitable arm of Page's firm even shamed the established carmakers into investing in electric cars by taking hybrid gasoline-electric vehicles, such as the Toyota Prius, and proving that they could easily be turned into safe and supergreen plug-in versions that can be topped up from an electric socket.

Such pushes were necessary, as the dinosaurs initially refused to budge. Khosla believes that clean cars, using advanced biofuels or other alternatives, will come about only through radical innovation of the sort that Big Oil and the Big Three automakers avoid. Risk and acceptance of failure are central to innovation, he argues, but these goliaths typically avoid both. "Big companies didn't invent the Internet or Google, and much of the big change in telecoms also came from outsiders," he adds.

But these men are from Silicon Valley, and Silicon Valley is not America. It is tempting to dismiss such breathless talk of revolution as just more hype from people who are seeing the world through Google goggles. After all, go beyond the rarefied air of northern California and the rules of gravity are no longer suspended. The well-established industries they mock still move at their usual but reliably glacial pace, right?

Well no, actually. Rapid and disruptive change is now happening across new and old businesses. Innovation is becoming both more accessible and more global. This is good news because its democratization releases the untapped ingenuity of people everywhere, and that could help solve some of the world's weightiest problems. This will force the dinosaurs to dance in order to survive—and, just maybe, provide a renewed lease on life for the ones that come up with world-changing new ideas.

The seditious scene from the Googleplex also captures the challenge this presents to established firms and developed economies. For ages innovation has been a technology-led affair, with most big breakthroughs coming out of giant and secretive research labs, such as Xerox PARC and AT&T's Bell Laboratories. It was an era when big corporations in developed countries accounted for most R&D spending.

North America still leads the world in research spending, but the big labs' advantage over their smaller rivals and the developing world is being eroded. And research has found that companies are getting diminishing returns on in-house corporate research. Above a minimum threshold determined by the particular industry in question, spending more on in-house research and development has no correlation with any metric of the firm's financial success. This suggests that for most companies in most industries, merely pouring pots of money into in-house research will not help in staving off disruptive innovations: they must open up and radically reinvent their innovation process.

However, for those companies with sufficient scale and long-term planning horizons, there may be an argument for doubling down on the traditional corporate research model. Bill Gates, ever the contrarian, remains a big believer in this traditional approach. He argues that open approaches are fine for incremental improvements, but that if a firm is aiming to develop breakthrough innovations such as the next generation of nuclear plants—something Terra Power, a nuclear energy firm in which he has a stake, is attempting—it needs serious in-house research, patience, and deep pockets.

Visit the storied Bell Labs, now owned by the telecom equipment manufacturer Alcatel, and you still find lots of scientists and well-equipped laboratories on its leafy campus in northern New Jersey—but these days they are mostly chasing ideas that will produce winners in the marketplace, not Nobel Prizes. GE has doubled its research and development spending over the past few years, despite the global economic downturn, and dramatically increased its spending on software. All this is aimed at preparing the firm for the coming convergence of the old economy and the New Economy.

That points to several of the big lessons emerging from the experiences of established companies trying to cope with today's Great Disruption. Large firms must find ways of retaining their ability to scale good ideas—Immelt likes to say his firm isn't the best at invention, but it is terrific at turning $50 million ideas into billion-dollar businesses—while becoming much more agile. That means bosses must push internal bureaucracies and hierarchies to experiment more readily, failing faster and learning from mistakes more gracefully. They must also be much more open to ideas, including ones that are threats to existing business lines, coming from unexpected quarters outside the firm.

What's more, it is not just stodgy industrial firms that must learn to dance to a new tune: even high-technology firms that just a few years ago were themselves disruptive innovators will soon find that their comfortable perch is threatened by new and hungry upstarts. A good example is Intuit, a California firm that shot to prominence with TurboTax, Quicken, and other easy-to-use financial software. Scott Cook, the firm's founder and current boss, saw the inefficiencies, high costs, and customer frustrations evident at traditional tax preparation businesses. By building a simple, affordable, self-service tax preparation package, he did for personal finance what Ray Kroc did for restaurants with McDonald's.

That propelled Intuit into the ranks of billion-dollar businesses, but Cook was not satisfied. In the mid-2000s, he decided he needed to accelerate the firm's organic growth and cast a wider net for new ideas lest his firm grow vulnerable to disruption. To do this, he decided to move toward an open innovation model of the sort long advocated by UC Berkeley's Henry Chesbrough. This is easier said than done, he has discovered. Early efforts at collaboration with outsiders hit snags because employees were fearful of sharing intellectual property (company lawyers had advised them that patent applications might get "polluted" if outsiders were involved). Some collaborators, for their part, thought Intuit was flirting with them as a prelude to an acquisition bid. The firm's internal R&D teams worried their jobs were about to be outsourced, and some managers adopted a "not invented here" attitude.

To the firm's great credit, observes Chesbrough, Intuit stuck with its efforts to open up its innovation process. When the effort started, the firm took months to develop new ideas; recently, it produced in a matter of weeks an Android app with Google for online payments. When several new employees grew frustrated a few years ago at the internal silos and lethargic pace of cross-functional communications, they used the "10 percent time" granted them by the company to pursue any project they want (3M and Google let their employees have 20 percent off for pet projects) to create their own online tool. Not only does the entire company now use Brainstorm, the resultant software, for collaboration and knowledge sharing, but Intuit also sells this serendipitous invention to such customers as GE, Netflix, and the Wharton Business School.

Reflecting on his firm's progress, Cook says the hardest part of teaching his dinosaur to dance was changing corporate culture: "It requires a change to the standard process of development, relying less on secrecy and IP protection and more on collaboration—and no longer retreating to the old ways." In short, even firms that were paragons of New Economy disruption a few short years ago (think Google today, Facebook tomorrow) will, like Intuit, confront the same forces that are now forcing wrenching changes at the icons of the old economy.

Into the Looking Glass

Two decades ago, David Gelernter saw the coming convergence of the old economy and the New Economy. In his visionary tome *Mirror Worlds,* he predicted that "you will look into a computer screen and see reality . . . some part of your world—the town you live in, the company you work for, your school system, the city hospital—will hang there in a sharp color image, abstract but recognizable, moving subtly in a thousand places." That sounded like something out of Orwell or the dystopian *Matrix* movies to some, which perhaps explains why the Unabomber tried to blow him up.

Thankfully, the neo-Luddite terrorist failed, and the curmudgeonly Yale professor continues to crank on. And Gelernter's forecast that the digital world would converge with the real world is fast coming true. The rise of intelligent infrastructure and smart systems, which embed sensors into everything and link up using wireless communications networks, is indeed creating a digital version of reality. This raises important questions about security and privacy, but it also means that stodgy, asset-based industries such as steel, cars, and shipbuilding are turning into information industries—and therefore companies in those fields must innovate much faster than in the past.

The embedding of intelligence into dumb systems is nothing new, of course. For several decades, logistics firms and retailers such as Walmart have been putting RFID tags and related technologies into many products. This has made it possible for them to track everything from the location of specific cargoes on the freeways to identifying which specific size and variety of Jif peanut butter has just gone out of stock in which aisle of your local supermarket. But now, argue technology experts at McKinsey, this trend is accelerating toward what has been called the "Internet of things." "Embedded with sensors, actuators, and communications capabilities, such objects will soon be able to absorb and transmit information on a massive scale and, in some cases, to adapt and react to changes in the environment automatically."

Why does this matter? Because, argue the McKinsey futurologists, the spread of smart software and sensors into every nook and cranny of traditional, unsexy industries will make processes more efficient, give products new capabilities, and spark novel business models. For example, heart patients using implanted or wearable sensors now have a real-time guardian angel monitoring them all day and night, reporting to doctors if there is any cause for concern or if a medication needs to be modified. Insurers in Europe are offering to install sensors in cars to monitor behavior, so they can offer rates based on actual performance rather than demographic guesstimates. And luxury carmakers are putting in elaborate sensors that will automatically take evasive action when the car senses danger if the driver is asleep or distracted.

Stepping on the Gas

"A BMW is now actually a network of computers," declares Ulrich Weinmann. That may seem like an exaggeration until you step into a sleek Hydrogen 7 BMW sedan. Push the pedal to the metal on the autobahn and the car responds as every BMW should, cylinders growling enthusiastically as the ultimate driving machine races past slower vehicles. But this car is not like any other made by BMW. Press a button on the steering wheel and it seamlessly switches from burning gasoline to consuming hydrogen.

The key to this advance, says Weinmann, an innovation expert at BMW, is smart software. Electronics have been in cars for decades, but those were isolated "dumb systems," he adds. Now cars are crammed full of networks of computers, with smart software controlling and monitoring things. New BMWs were among the first to synchronize seamlessly with Apple's iPhone and download maps and directions from Google while you drive.

As the knowledge component of industries continues to grow, it will lower even further the barriers to entry in many businesses. Yet the same democratization of innovation that empowers the new firms can be used to generate much greater and faster innovation from within established companies. Some multinationals are already doing this in Asia to keep up with their local competitors.

The effects of this have become increasingly clear in heavy engineering. Reinhold Achatz, of Siemens, claims the German giant has undergone a hidden electronics revolution. "We have more software developers than Oracle or SAP, but you don't see this because it is embedded in our trains, machine tools, and factory automation," he says. Achatz calculates that as much as 60 percent of his firm's sales now involve software. Some 90 percent of the development in machine tools is in electronics and related hardware, and the figure is similar for cars.

The steady conversion of engineering into yet another knowledge-based industry forces the pace of innovation for all industries. "We are a quite mature industry, but customers now expect change faster," adds Weinmann. The demand for change is fastest in Asia. Several hundred new mobile phones are launched every year in China, and customers there now expect their new BMWs to be able to synchronize perfectly with each new handset, he sighs.

New competitors are emerging from unexpected quarters, which makes things difficult for established firms. One of them is Elon Musk, who is challenging incumbents in not one but two old-time industries. Musk made his fortune during the Internet boom by selling PayPal, an online payments system, to eBay for $1.5 billion. He now heads Space Exploration Technologies, known as SpaceX. This is a start-up offering private space launches. In 2010, it fired a rocket successfully into space, the first to be designed, paid for, and launched entirely with private money. Later that year, it managed to send the company's Dragon reusable space capsule into orbit and back to the surface of the earth safely, heralding a new chapter in private-sector-led initiatives at NASA.

SpaceX is the vanguard. Many private-sector newcomers, fed up with the overbearing ways of NASA and the big defense contractors, are working furiously to commercialize space. The X Prize Foundation and Google decided to fuel the fire by announcing a $30 million prize for the first private sector team to land and operate an unmanned rover on the moon. Peter Diamandis, the foundation's chairman, believes the old guard is no longer able to innovate. "Real breakthroughs require risk and the ability to absorb failure, and large organizations are incapable of such risk taking," he insists.

Musk is not waiting to win any prizes. Besides SpaceX, he has also started Tesla Motors, which has devised an electric sports car capable of accelerating from zero to 60 mph in four seconds and has a top speed of over 130 mph. More impressively, thanks to its advanced lithium-ion batteries and lightweight carbon-composite construction, the Tesla Roadster has a range of perhaps 200 miles on an overnight charge, less if driven fast and furious. The cars cost a pricey $110,000 or so, and the global recession hit the start-up firm's finances hard, but Musk managed to take Tesla public in one of 2010's most successful IPOs.

Can established corporate giants hope to compete against such disruptive innovators? The dinosaurs certainly are not giving up without a fight. Visit Walmart's headquarters in Bentonville, Arkansas, and you will be greeted by a large plaque in the lobby that says: "Incrementalism is innovation's worst enemy! We don't want continuous improvement; we want radical change." These are the words of Sam Walton, the firm's founder. And to his credit, Walton did radically change the general store with his innovative approach to low-cost, high-volume supermarket retailing. But ask

Linda Dillman, a senior official at the firm, about innovation at Walmart today and she concedes that radical thinking was easier when the firm was young. Size and scale offer many advantages, but they also carry with them the seeds of the firm's own destruction: lethargy and legacy. The bigger you are, suggests corporate history, the harder you may fall.

Ideas at Double Speed

That explains why many executives feel that the heat is on and that they must innovate faster just to stand still. In part due to the spread of information technology in traditional industries, product cycles are undeniably getting shorter. Gil Cloyd, the former chief technology officer at P&G, studied the life cycle of consumer goods in America from 1992 to 2002 (way back before the Internet's full impact was felt) and found that it had already fallen by half. It has surely accelerated further with the arrival in full force of the Web. That, he concluded, means his firm now needs to innovate at least twice as fast.

The American company famous for inventing the Post-it sticky note, 3M, also believes the world is moving much faster. Andrew Ouderkirk, one of the firm's celebrated inventors, thinks that is in part because many things that his company used to do in-house are now done by outsiders. To keep up, 3M carries out "concurrent development," which involves talking to customers much earlier in the process to try to shorten development times.

Even the firm that laid down the first long-distance telegraph lines thinks today's innovation frenzy is unprecedented. Achatz, of Siemens, is adamant that innovation is happening much more quickly and that "access to information is so fast now that it allows much faster product development cycles." His firm is convinced that there will be an explosion of medical know-how thanks to the advance of information technology into medicine.

Perhaps managers at firms everywhere should be both far-sighted and paranoid in equal measure as they scan the horizon for unexpected competitive threats. Embracing the digital revolution, as Siemens and other industrial giants are doing, is one good way to prepare for a disruptive future. Another is to push into difficult emerging markets in hopes of disrupting one's own business model.

Role Reversal

That challenging technique is what Vijay Govindarajan, an innovation expert at Dartmouth's Tuck School of Business, calls reverse innovation. This, he explains, is the mechanism by which the gap between rich and poor drives innovation. One pillar of this theory, which echoes the arguments about disruptive innovation put forward by Clay Christensen, exploits the performance gap: firms need to learn how to come up with cheap and cheerful products that achieve 50 percent of the performance of their gold-plated offerings at 5 percent of the cost, just as Indian and Chinese rivals do. Another pillar relies on filling the infrastructure gap: because the developing world lacks the legacy infrastructure of the rich world, that is where most of the new roads, airports, and buildings are being built. Because this infrastructure is built with the latest technologies and energy-efficient designs, companies that compete successfully can leapfrog ahead of rich-world rivals that stay focused on stagnant domestic markets.

The sustainability gap in poor countries, where resource problems such as water scarcity are often much more immediate than in wealthy countries, also offers incentives for breakthrough innovations that can be profitably brought back home. A regulatory gap between rich and poor countries will also spur reverse innovation, argues Govindarajan: pharmaceutical companies will do more clinical trials in India, for example, and stem cell or gene therapies will take off sooner in South Korea and China.

The upshot is that by recruiting ingenious local engineers and designers in places such as Bangalore and Beijing, and by paying close attention to trends and practices in the market, forward-looking Western firms in some industries are coming up with products and services that can be sold in other parts of the world too. For example, Nokia's engineers are finding that many Chinese and Indians access the Internet mainly through their mobile handsets. Such customers' requirements for their handsets may therefore be quite different from those of Western users, many of whom have computers at home and at work.

Unilever has long had a strong distribution network in India, but it has expanded its efforts with a division called Shakti, which provides Indian women's self-help groups with business education and the chance to earn a living selling cheap sachets of Unilever products. The effort has proved so successful that Unilever introduced a high-tech element: the Shakti entrepreneurs now run kiosks with personal computers that villagers can rent to send e-mails and browse the Web for things that can make a big difference to their lives, such as market prices for various commodities. Google has taken Wenda, a question-and-answer "knowledge community" product developed by its division in China (before the firm's withdrawal from that market in 2009) to help overcome a lack of local content, and launched it in the Russian market.

A. G. Lafley, the former boss of P&G, says many Asian firms began imitating what foreign ones did but are now "very innovative, especially with business models." Lafley sees Indian firms shaking up the way foreign companies operate, and not only with back-office services where many began. Hours after he uttered those words, Wipro, an Indian pioneer of software services, said it would open a new development center in Atlanta that will report back to its headquarters in Bangalore.

This is forcing P&G to innovate in other ways too. Lafley uses the example of detergents in China, where the company is using a low-cost manufacturing method that he likens to Coca-Cola's syrup model, in which the company supplies a concentrate to local bottlers. P&G provides secret, high-value performance chemicals to Chinese partners, who add basic ingredients and packaging before distributing the products.

The notion of dinosaurs learning to dance to a new tune is not as ridiculous as it may first seem. When the personal computer first arrived on the scene some three decades ago, the computing world was dominated by big, bureaucratic firms peddling mainframes and other centralized solutions. IBM, Digital, Wang, and other giants of that era pooh-poohed the PC, considering it a toy—and they dismissed the unknown Taiwanese manufacturers building and assembling it too. "There is no reason for any individual to have a computer in his home," declared Ken Olsen, boss of Digital Equipment Corporation, back in 1977.

History shows how wrong they were, of course: not only did the personal computer transform business, but its arrival proved the calling card for the rise of flexible Asian manufacturing too. Unable to adapt to a world of networked and distributed computing, Digital and Wang went bust. However, IBM set up its own PC division as a hedge on its bet—and managed to come up with a

personal computer offering, bundled in with lucrative service con-
tracts, that corporate clients loved.

And when this business model itself was at risk of being disrupted by the software-as-a-service approach pioneered by Sales-
force.com, IBM moved itself to a service-based approach and spun
off its PC unit altogether. To whom did Big Blue sell its unwanted
Lenovo division? Chinese investors, of course. That may seem
ironic, but it was ever thus in the computer business, as the history
of Intel reveals.

Lessons from a Master

Not too long ago, Andy Grove taught a class at Stanford Business
School. As a living legend in Silicon Valley and a former boss of
Intel, the world's leading maker of computer chips, Grove could
have simply used the opportunity to blow his own horn. Instead,
he started by displaying a headline from the *Wall Street Journal*
heralding the takeover of General Motors by the Obama administration as the start of "a new era." He gave a condensed history of
his own industry's spectacular rise, pointing out that plenty of ven-
erable firms—with names such as Digital, Wang, and IBM—were
nearly or completely wiped out along the way.

Then, to put a sting in his tale, he displayed a fabricated headline from that same newspaper, this one supposedly drawn from
a couple of decades ago: "Presidential Action Saves Computer Industry." A fake article beneath it describes government intervention to prop up the ailing mainframe industry. It sounds ridiculous,
of course. Computer firms come and go all the time; such is the
pace of innovation in the industry. Yet for some reason this healthy

attitude toward creative destruction is not shared by other industries. This is just one of the ways in which Grove believes that his business can teach other industries a thing or two. He thinks fields such as energy and health care could be transformed if they were run more like the computer industry, made greater use of its products, and dramatically accelerated the pace of innovation.

Though Grove's scientific credentials are solid, he will probably be best remembered as a daring and successful businessman. Richard Tedlow, a historian at Harvard Business School, calls him "one of the master managers in the history of American business." One reason is market success: under Grove's tenure, Intel came to dominate the microprocessor industry and its market capitalization rocketed up (making it, at one point, the world's most valuable company). A bigger reason lies in how exactly he managed to steer Intel to such spectacular success—a tale that shows how the fine American traditions of entrepreneurship, ambition, and sheer chutzpah can revive innovation at companies and countries alike.

One particularly risky decision he took is revealing. In *Only the Paranoid Survive*, Grove's bestselling book, he argues that every company will face a confluence of internal and external forces, often unanticipated, that will conspire to make an existing business strategy unviable. In Intel's case, such a strategic inflection point arose because its memory chip business came under heavy assault from new Japanese rivals willing to undercut any price Intel offered.

What could he do? The firm's roots and most of its profits lay in making memory chips; Intel's microprocessor group was just a small niche. The firm's two founders and much of its engineering staff were too emotionally wedded to its past successes to make a break. But Grove decided to bet the future of the company on microprocessors, a move that saved his company and transformed the industry. He argues now that it is not only companies that face such an inflection point; so too do societies and countries. That echoes a central premise of this book: the world is at a strategic inflection point, and the policy and investment decisions this generation makes in the next decade will cast a long shadow over future generations.

At the time, the microchip business was producing such unreliable products that customers insisted that companies such as Intel always license new products to a secondary supplier in order to ensure reliability of supply. Grove's efforts to tighten up quality control led to a commercial coup. When his firm introduced its widely anticipated 386 processor, he stunned the industry by declaring that Intel would not license any secondary manufacturers. This was a huge risk for computer makers, but such was their appetite for the new chip that they bought it anyway. Intel's ability to deliver good enough chips in large numbers meant profits no longer had to be shared with secondary manufacturers.

With his reputation for ruthlessness in the marketplace and rigorous discipline inside his firm, Grove has much in common with another American business leader: Lee Raymond, the formidable former chairman of ExxonMobil. Both men were feared not just by rivals but also by many of their employees. Grove once even spearheaded a sales campaign against a superior chip made by Motorola in an effort dubbed Operation Crush. When asked about such bully-boy tactics, Grove remains unrepentant. He even likes the comparison with the unloved oilman: "I never knew Lee Raymond, but he did take Exxon to the top of the Fortune 500—and that's OK with me."

Personal admiration aside, however, Grove is convinced that Exxon and its Big Oil brethren are in a sunset industry. He has written and lectured widely on energy and environmental topics in recent years, arguing that oil and cars are heading for a divorce. He regards electricity as the most promising replacement fuel, and thinks battery technology has the potential to produce an Intel-like giant as the industry develops.

Another business he believes to be ripe for disruption is health care. He complains that the industry seems to innovate much too slowly. The lack of proper electronic medical records and smart clinical decision systems bothers him, as does the slow-moving, bureaucratic nature of clinical trials. He thinks pharmaceutical firms should study the fast "knowledge turns" achieved by chipmakers, so that the cycles of learning and innovation are accelerated. A knowledge turn, a term coined by Grove, is the time it takes for an experiment to proceed from hypothesis to results and then to a new hypothesis—around eighteen months in chip making, but ten to twenty years in medicine.

Given the coming perfect storm of global challenges confronting the world economy, Grove is surely right in calling for a dramatic acceleration in the pace of global innovation. But can companies in slow-moving industries such as health care and energy (two sectors that GE's boss, Jeff Immelt, also thinks are the keys to his firm's and America's future) really respond to his call? The surprising answer is yes, as the experiences of Kaiser Permanente demonstrate.

How the Health Care Industry Can Save Itself

On a trip to America in early 2010, Nicolas Sarkozy, France's president, could not resist the temptation to needle his hosts. Just before the visit, his American counterpart, Barack Obama, had secured congressional approval of a controversial but ambitious plan (dubbed "Obamacare" by its critics) to expand the country's health insurance market dramatically. Observing that America is the only wealthy country to lack universal health coverage, Sarkozy sniffed: "Welcome to the club of states who don't turn their back on the sick and the poor."

Europeans have long thumbed their noses at the bloated U.S. health care system. It is true that parts of it are convoluted, cruel, and much too costly. But Richard Feachem, a health care expert and the former boss of the Global Fund to Fight AIDS, Tuberculosis and Malaria, argues that such a view ignores "nuggets of good practice." The best such nugget, he reckons, is Kaiser Permanente (Kaiser), a not-for-profit health insurer and hospital chain that in 2009 took in $2 billion more than the $40 billion it spent.

Though there are plenty of dedicated doctors and nurses, the American health care system is dominated by cream-skimming health insurers and the myriad fee-for-service providers they do business with, which drive up costs by charging high prices for piecework. Kaiser's business model integrates fixed-price health insurance with treatment at its own hospitals and clinics. This has led to big efficiency gains, making Kaiser one of the cheapest health care providers in most of the regional markets in which it competes. Thanks to Obama's reforms, more than thirty million Americans will enter the health insurance market over the next few years—and Kaiser's low prices should make it a big beneficiary.

Moreover, Kaiser's medical results are as good as its financial ones. By many objective clinical measurements, it is the best-performing health care outfit in the regions it covers. The firm's success obviously holds lessons for its American rivals, but given that Kaiser serves some 8.6 million patients—more than the population of Austria—and has come up with some world-beating innovations, Feachem believes that there is much that Europe can learn too.

At Kaiser's Oakland Medical Center in northern California, Christina Ahlstrand, a lifelong customer, has come to see her doctor, Jennifer Slovis. Ahlstrand had been experiencing "very low energy," so she e-mailed to see if she should get any blood tests done. After reviewing her electronic medical records (which include all her lab tests, prescriptions, e-mail exchanges, and notes from visits to all specialists), Slovis e-mailed her back saying she needed to see her in person.

Many health systems, including Britain's National Health Service (NHS), have tried unsuccessfully to implement comprehensive computer systems; patients and doctors often hate them. But studies published in the journal *Health Affairs* and elsewhere show that Kaiser's embrace of technology (its doctors conducted nearly nine million electronic consultations in 2010) has resulted in fewer frivolous visits, better medical outcomes, and soaring patient satisfaction. Patients can even send doctors photos of worrisome moles or slow-healing wounds by e-mail for remote diagnosis. In other words, Kaiser has managed to craft a learning system that meets Grove's call for faster knowledge turns.

Ahlstrand, like many Kaiser patients, loves this system. She also likes Kaiser's personal-health website, which gives her tips and points her toward classes on healthy living. Slovis, for her part, is pleased that her work is "nearly paperless" and that she can easily track the specialists treating her patients, "so I know exactly what's going on."

The ease with which Slovis tracks Ahlstrand's interactions with specialists and any resultant test results is indicative of the sort of integration that is missing in most health systems. George Halvorson, Kaiser's boss, argues that such coordination is all the more essential because of the dramatic rise of such lasting and expensive afflictions as metabolic syndrome, diabetes, and heart disease.

Kaiser also aligns incentives both to promote parsimony and to improve the quality, rather than merely the quantity, of the care it gives. Patients such as Ahlstrand use e-mail because it is free and convenient, whereas a personal visit can involve hassle and an out-of-pocket payment. Slovis and other Kaiser doctors are on fixed salaries, unlike America's many self-employed physicians, so they have every incentive to share information with other specialists and no financial motive to order unnecessary procedures.

Kaiser's third big advantage is that its integrated approach and incentive structure encourage investment in forms of long-term care such as the wellness classes that Ahlstrand enjoys. The firm is in the midst of a ten-year, $30 billion capital investment plan. It has now completed the rollout of its computer system—the biggest one in the world for private health care.

Many other insurers and health systems avoid making such investments because of "churn": patients switch insurers frequently, so any spending on preventive medicine, aimed in particular at avoiding expensive hospital visits in the future, ends up benefiting a rival company. Kaiser says its churn rate is well below that of its rivals, so it can invest for the long haul. It even funds an innovation center located in California that perfected the telemedicine systems its doctors are now using for remote dermatology consultations, for example.

Clay Christensen applauds the firm's culture of innovation. He notes that Kaiser's dentists routinely apply a coating to children's teeth that helps prevent cavities, a procedure that many other American dentists tend not to use. Why not? In an integrated system with incentives aligned properly, he argues, preventing future cavities saves the company money. In contrast, in a fee-for-service system, "future cavities represent future revenue."

If Kaiser's approach is so successful, why is it not more widely copied? A number of health systems from around the world, including Britain's NHS, have sent emissaries to California to study its approach, but efforts to replicate it have met with only limited success. Within the United States, a handful of outfits such as the Mayo Clinic independently evolved into integrated systems, but the rest of the industry remains a fragmented mess.

The prevailing culture of health care in the country is difficult to overcome. Some American patients, used to having all the scans and consultations with exotic specialists they want, costs be damned, do not like Kaiser's frugal ways. By the same token, some freewheeling American doctors do not like its rigid systems or fixed (albeit generous) salaries. Much the same applies in other countries: whether in politicized state-run systems or profiteering private ones, the incentives for doctors and patients are seldom as soundly aligned as they are at Kaiser. "Most of its success is explained by culture," says Alain Enthoven, a health economist at Stanford University, "and that is simply not easy to replicate."

If an American health care giant can learn to be so nimble, surely there is hope for many other big businesses now confronted with the threat of disruptive innovation. Reverse innovation will help steal the thunder of potential rivals from overseas, while investing in smart technologies and systems will help accelerate knowledge turns at home. The key lies in cultivating a culture that embraces change, experimentation, failure, and rapid learning.

If companies do that, they have a good shot at surviving, and perhaps even conquering entirely new markets. That is especially true because capitalists now have a powerful new ally in their quest for sustainable profits, as the next chapter explains: dynamic social entrepreneurs who want to harness market forces to save the world.

9

Greed for Good

A big problem for the future of capitalism and the earth is that corporate balance sheets and national accounts do not generally take account of natural capital, such as the value of ecosystem services provided by the Earth, or of the many intangible forms of human capital that matter in the Ideas Economy. Only when capitalism stops flying blind can mankind hope to start flying in the right direction. In fits and starts, governments and companies are moving toward cradle-to-cradle analysis of the true costs of goods and services.

Advocates of market-based solutions to grand global problems suggest that business can shift from being part of the problem to being at the heart the solution if capitalists take a longer-term and more honest view of the impact of business on society. On this argument, as governments embrace proper metrics and measurement of wellness and sustainability indicators and adopt laws that force companies to take account of such externalities as carbon emissions, incentives will shift. Greed can be harnessed as a force for good. But the key to this transformation is the powerful role individuals can play as innovative entrepreneurs.

Leading the charge toward hybrid business models of the future is a new breed of capitalist. Social entrepreneurs are motivated by the desire to bring about social change and to tackle the world's wicked problems, but they are hardly bleeding hearts. They see the profit motive and market discipline as important tools in designing socially responsible enterprises that are sustainable in the long term. And unlike some nongovernmental organizations of the past, they are generally willing to work with traditional corporations to advance their social agenda.

In time, goes the argument, the greater reward will go not to those who grab the quick and dirty buck but to those who earn the sustainable and sound billion. Financial experts see the beginnings of a new trillion-dollar asset class, akin to the earlier rise of emerging markets and hedge funds, in the growing band of "impact investors." Some even claim that these are the foundation stones for a new kind of socially aware capitalism that could prove the hallmark of the twenty-first-century global economy.

This does not mean that it will always be profitable for all businesses to solve all social problems. Alas, the rules of economics, just like the rules of gravity, still apply. Even so, the rise of social entrepreneurs is a powerful trend. Both big business and government need to pay attention, for the disruptive ideas and business models bubbling up from the bottom of the citizen sector have the potential to change the world.

Back in 1981, Jack Welch gave a speech at New York's Pierre Hotel that captured the zeitgeist of the age every bit as well as "greed is good," Gordon Gekko's catchphrase from the movie *Wall*

Street. Welch shot to business superstardom when he took over an ailing GE and started firing thousands of employees. His approach to downsizing was so tough-minded that he came to be known as "Neutron Jack"—after the neutron bomb, which is thought to kill people but leave buildings intact.

In that seminal speech, entitled "Growing Fast in a Slow-Growth Economy," made shortly after he took over the top job at GE, he spelled out his philosophy of cutting fat, selling off under-performing units, and aggressively driving up short-term profits at a pace that outdid national or global economic growth. He vowed that GE "will be the locomotive pulling the GNP, not the caboose following it." That call to arms, followed by a twenty-year tenure in which he relentlessly and successfully pursued quarterly profits, made him the poster boy for a certain brand of capitalism known as the shareholder value approach.

That approach has it strengths, to be sure. Managers have clear accountability and cannot easily loot their companies or pad their pockets. Shareholders are able to benefit directly from their invest-ments through quarterly returns. Unlike confused conglomerates or murky family-run companies, public corporations with manage-ments that must regularly report to shareholders on a quarterly basis are usually held to account. The result should be proper stew-ardship of precious assets. Welch certainly inspired many, and he was lionized as one of the heroes of American capitalism when he retired in 2001.

Yet in the wake of the global financial crisis it seemed he was offering something of a mea culpa for his advocacy of shareholder capitalism. In an interview with the *Financial Times* in 2009, he declared that the emphasis placed by companies on quarterly prof-its and share price targets had gotten out of hand. "On the face of it, shareholder value is the dumbest idea in the world," he declared.

"Shareholder value is a result, not a strategy . . . your main constitu-
encies are your employees, your customers, and your products."

Those are remarkable words coming from Neutron Jack, but
perhaps the shift is understandable. After all, the excesses of the
age of Enron and Lehman Brothers have shaken capitalism to its
core. Roger Martin of the Rotman Business School at the University of Toronto argues that just as Welch's first speech marked the
era of short-term capitalism, his second speech now ushers in a
new era. Martin believes the coming form of capitalism will focus
much more on community, and so will need rules and regulation to
protect that community. The watchword, he thinks, will be trust—
especially institutionalized trust.

How exactly are companies supposed to build such trust in
an age when many bosses seem rapaciously self-serving and out
of touch with the concerns of society or the need to tackle pressing global challenges? And what should the roles of government
and the nonprofit sector be? These dilemmas are leading to much
soul-searching, and lots of big questions are being raised today.
One way forward is through a reinvention of business models to
embrace transparency, honest accounting, and patient capitalism.
The deceptively small example of the Acumen Fund, a for-profit
but socially conscious investment outfit in New York, shows that
this can be done.

The Patient Capitalist

For the most part, champions of market forces are a glum lot these
days. But not Jacqueline Novogratz, a market-minded development
expert. The current crisis in capitalism, she believes, strengthens

her call for a sweeping change in how the world thinks about poverty, economic development, and global challenges. "The financial system is broken, yes, but so too is the aid system," she observes. In her view, "a moment of great innovation" could be at hand.

In *The Blue Sweater*, her autobiography, she describes her past frustrations working in such pillars of finance and development as Chase Manhattan Bank, the African Development Bank, and the Rockefeller Foundation. She found them bureaucratic, distant, and condescending to those they sought to help. So in 2001 she set up the Acumen Fund, a "social venture capital" outfit, to promote what she calls patient capitalism.

Acumen is an odd mix of charity and traditional investment fund. It takes donations from philanthropists in the usual fashion but then invests them in a businesslike way, by lending to or taking stakes in firms. The recipients—private ventures aiming for profits—must serve the poor in a way that brings broader social benefits. Acumen goes to great lengths to measure those benefits, and thus the efficiency of its work.

Acumen's charges are a diverse bunch. In India, Drishtee runs a network of Internet kiosks in rural areas, while LifeSpring runs low-cost maternity hospitals. A to Z Textile Mills, a manufacturer of antimalarial bed nets, has grown to become one of Tanzania's largest employers. Some ventures, including a Pakistani mortgage provider and an Indian pharmacy chain, have flopped. But many others manage to repay their loans (granted at below-market rates) or generate dividends. Acumen reinvests its profits in other companies, thus stretching the initial donations further.

The notion of applying business methods to philanthropy is attractive, but does it really work in practice? Acumen accepts that the use of performance indicators can provide a false sense of precision. After all, how can one prove beyond doubt that a water filter prevented a child from falling sick? But it is possible to use the results achieved by charities in the same field as a benchmark. Thus Acumen insists that A to Z's bed nets must cost less than the $10 that Malaria No More, a big traditional American charity, says it spends delivering each one it gives away.

Novogratz thinks such measures help guard against the inefficiency and corruption that often afflict traditional aid efforts. On one of her first assignments abroad, she spent countless days poring over the books of a struggling Kenyan microfinance firm. When her findings pointed to mismanagement and cronyism, her detailed handwritten report mysteriously vanished and she was sent packing. She explains that Acumen uses measures, however imperfect, that "take the pulse of the patient" so that necessary strategic changes can be made on the fly rather than waiting for "a thorough autopsy" when a venture fails.

Such pragmatism is typical of Novogratz. "We're not fundamentalist about anything," she says. But it also points to another critique of Acumen: its improvised approaches, sniff theorists, cannot be scaled up and are therefore not up to the task of tackling global poverty. At first blush there is something to this argument. After all, the fund has barely $40 million in investments, a trivial sum compared with the billions of dollars spent by governments or big charities such as the Gates Foundation.

Look more closely, though, and there is reason to think that Acumen is punching above its weight. For one thing, its novel approach is fostering a proper debate among development experts about the role of market forces and accountability. Acumen has its admirers at big development agencies. Novogratz was recently even invited to address UNICEF, one of the biggest. Her firm runs highly coveted fellowship and mentoring schemes, and its alumni are spreading its ideas throughout the development field.

The firm's influence in poor countries is also bigger than it first appears. By leveraging Acumen's funds to obtain other financing, recipients are able to magnify their impact. Even more important, perhaps, is the firm's catalytic role in sparking entrepreneurship in developing countries. Acumen devotes much time and money to training local managers, rotating experts from the developed world through its recipient firms, and disseminating successful ideas.

Novogratz hopes all this will help overcome cultural barriers that have held back business in some societies. She recalls how she advised a group of very poor women running a small, unprofitable bakery in Rwanda some years ago. She had to grapple with local social norms, such as the reluctance of its saleswomen to speak to strangers, but she ultimately succeeded in turning the business around.

When Novogratz returned to Rwanda years later, she discovered that the bakery had been wiped out by the country's civil strife. Some of the seemingly inhibited women who had worked there had subsequently taken up machetes in the country's genocide. Such unvarnished experiences of poverty point to the best reason to think Novogratz may yet succeed: unlike many in the development world, she does not romanticize poverty or patronize the poor.

She puts a strong emphasis on listening to those she seeks to help. Her advocacy of market-based approaches is inspired not by ideology but by the firm conviction that markets are the best "listening device" to ascertain the real needs and wants of poor consumers. This lesson is borne out by other social entrepreneurs serving the bottom of the pyramid. Traditional for-profit businesses hoping to conquer global markets would do well to pay attention.

That is because the Acumen story points to two powerful forces with the potential to upend the global economy's incumbents. The first trend is the dramatic transformation of the nonprofit world from sleepy, underresourced, and inefficient to market-minded, well-funded, and eager to change the world. The second trend, driven in part by the first, is the emergence of hybrid business models and coalitions that blend both for-profit and nonprofit aims. If these two trends alone materialize, they would do much to help the world tackle many of the difficult social and global problems that governments and businesses have failed to solve.

But some people go beyond this, building on these trends to make two further eye-catching claims. Some visionaries now argue that mankind has evolved to a point where the pursuit of purpose matters more to people than the pursuit of profit. On this view, mankind is progressing toward a genuinely empathetic era. Other pundits look at these two trends and conclude that capitalism itself is evolving into a higher form. Companies that want to flourish in the future must, on this argument, look beyond such familiar concerns as making profits and must instead strive to create shared value that will benefit all of society by finding solutions to difficult social problems.

Leave aside for the moment those extraordinary claims, which will be examined carefully later in this chapter. After all, just the first two trends by themselves are a big deal. The rise of a dynamic "citizen sector"—as Bill Drayton of Ashoka calls nongovernmental organizations—promises to drive much growth and innovation in the global economy in coming years, and to disrupt plenty of established business models along the way. Drayton believes it is also ushering in "a sea change in the way society's problems are solved." His forecasts are not to be dismissed lightly. Drayton is perhaps the most respected figure in this fledgling field, and Ashoka the oldest and most successful cultivator of social entrepreneurs worldwide. Bill Clinton, writing in his book *Giving*, described the soft-spoken

Drayton this way: "He is not well known . . . but to those who be-lieve in the power of private citizens to improve society, Bill Dray-ton is a hero."

Sipping tea at a quiet corner table in the Harvard Club of New York, dressed in a conservative suit and tie, the bespectacled Dray-ton hardly seems like a troublemaker. Yet his eyes light up and his voice grows passionate as he lays out his sweeping arguments for the rise of the citizen sector. Through almost all of mankind's time on earth, he observes, a very tiny elite controlled almost all wealth and power. Systems, be they government or church, were top-down. Ordinary people lived in grinding poverty, deprived of basic necessities, or at best did mindlessly repetitive and arduous jobs. Around 1700, though, something happened. Thanks to the industrial revolution, new institutions such as the limited liability corporation, and the strengthening rule of law, competitive and entrepreneurial businesses grew. The rise of a dynamic business sector led to extraordinary improvements in quality of life, he points out, yet the nongovernmental sector stagnated throughout that period.

Only about thirty years ago, he argues, did the charitable and social sector begin to grow more productive. There were, of course, individual social entrepreneurs such as Florence Nightingale who long ago made a difference—Drayton is himself a veteran of the American civil rights movement—but he believes they did not have a systemic impact on the productivity of the noncorporate, non-governmental sector. As governments began to step back around the world—be that because of ideology in Thatcher's Britain and Reagan's United States or because of the collapse of dictatorships and military regimes in the Soviet Union and Latin America—ordinary people filled the void. In India, he believes, the coming of age of the first postcolonial generation was the driving force, as dynamic young people decided that crony capitalists and incompetent officials of the Licence Raj were not doing enough to tackle the country's social ills. Given the dissatisfaction with bureaucracies seen around the world, as well as the fiscal woes of governments in many places, it seems unlikely that this trend will reverse anytime soon. The number of citizen sector groups, and the number of jobs created by those groups, has indeed shot up around the world at a faster pace than other sectors. The scope and scale of those social enterprises are also growing impressively.

Drayton vehemently insists that the productivity of this sector is also growing dramatically, accomplishing in a few decades what it took for-profit enterprises several centuries to accomplish. Lots of anecdotal evidence supports this thesis, but one expects a former McKinsey consultant such as he to have hard data and PowerPoint slides at the ready. Alas, it turns out there is insufficient quantitative evidence to back up this claim—in part, as discussed below, because this sector has yet to agree on the proper metrics for measuring social impact. Brushing aside that objection, he argues such leapfrogging is happening because the social sector can learn by analogy, copying what works in the corporate sector, thereby avoiding having to reinvent the wheel (for example, by simply buying computerized accounting systems off the shelf rather than starting with an abacus). He observes that many more people are educated today than back in 1700, which helps his efforts. It also helps that the sector is now attracting world-class talent—especially from the younger generations—which was not always the case for nonprofits in the past.

Another big reason to believe that the productivity of this sector is improving is the useful role that market-minded donors—dubbed "philanthrocapitalists" by Matthew Bishop (the *Economist*'s U.S. business editor) and Michael Green in an influential recent book—are playing. As they put it, such folk "see the world full of big problems that they, and only they, can and must put right." In short, a generation of billionaires who made their money the old-fashioned way are now trying to save the world in a newfangled way. By pushing the social sector to harness the profit motive to achieve social goals, the new generation of wealth wants to motivate greed for good.

Pierre Omidyar and Jeff Skoll, the men behind eBay, are among the most aggressive and influential of this breed. Omidyar was a key backer of Ashoka, and Skoll has set up a well-endowed center at Oxford University's Said Business School to study and promote social entrepreneurship. Some, such as Acumen, are making sure those that get their money have viable businesses in addition to social goals. Others, such as the Gates Foundation, are pushing recipients to be much more rigorous about analyzing impacts than nongovernmental organizations used to be in the past. Some are forging entirely new business models. When Google set up its charitable arm, Google.org, it decided not to set it up as a not-for-profit entity under American law. The firm saw that there were areas of social need where its internal innovation efforts may well be boosted if its breakthroughs (smart electricity meters and self-drive cars are two examples the firm has come up with) are allowed to get to market and make a profit.

Odd Bedfellows

Ashoka's founder, Drayton, believes the upshot of all this is that the social side of the world economy is becoming as entrepreneurial as the business side. As it does, big business can no longer ignore the social sector, dismissing it as small and unproductive. On the contrary, a growing number of forward-looking businesspeople are now joining hands with social entrepreneurs to create hybrid business models that aim to serve the long-neglected bottom of the pyramid—say, in ways that for-profit companies typically have not in the past (though some nimble dinosaurs now are trying).

A big obstacle to reaching such customers is that they are often in remote areas or slums not easily reached by traditional sales forces. Citizen sector organizations can act as demand aggregators, marketers, and even validators for a company seeking to persuade a reluctant community to embrace its offerings. For example, P&G is working with social entrepreneurs in a hybrid venture that is rolling out E-Health Points in Punjab, India. This start-up is establishing for-profit centers in underserved rural areas to provide health services as well as clean water. Its health workers roam the local area with backpacks carrying diagnostic equipment; a mobile phone captures and interprets the data, which can then be used for paid telemedicine consultations.

If you doubt that hybrid business models will succeed in very poor areas, consider this question: will seamstresses in Guatemala or poor farmers in India pay $3 for a pair of reading glasses? It seems unlikely. Such people are among the three billion or so who earn only a dollar or two a day, so $3 is a fortune to them. And yet VisionSpring, an American optical firm, is betting that they will pay that princely sum for its spectacles.

The notion that only subsidies or handouts can provide the world's poorest with essential services such as health care is wrong, says Jordan Kassalow, the firm's cofounder and a public health expert. Years of treating river blindness and other developing-world diseases as part of charity campaigns convinced him that such programs often falter when the money or political will dries up. He believes the bottom of the pyramid would be better served by campaigns that involve some payment, so that costs are covered and the schemes are financially self-sustaining.

Those public health campaigns also alerted him to the damage done by a common yet largely overlooked complaint known as presbyopia (which causes blurry close-up vision). "For every person that I treated for a serious eye condition," he says, "there were fifty that needed simple, nonprescription reading glasses." A pair of reading glasses, readily available in rich countries at pharmacies and corner shops, can solve the problem. But the rural poor have no such option.

"This is a failure of both government and the marketplace," says Kassalow. Government health clinics are understandably preoccupied with life-threatening maladies, and urban optical shops in poor countries typically shun simple reading glasses in favor of costly, high-margin prescription glasses. But this neglect takes a dramatic toll even on illiterates: farmers can no longer identify pests and choose the proper pesticides, craftsmen cannot manage fine handiwork, seamstresses cannot sew. As their sight fades, so does their income.

Precisely because that extra income means so much to the poorest, Kassalow thought, they might be willing to pay for a product that restores their vision and earning potential. His firm, which already makes fashionable and expensive reading glasses for the developed world (they are sold at fancy optical shops on Manhattan's Upper East Side, for example), has set up a philanthropic arm to sell glasses to people in the developing world. Using VisionSpring's existing design, marketing, and manufacturing facilities, it is now operating in India, Bangladesh, Mexico, and Guatemala.

The key to the business is a concept Kassalow calls microfranchising. "We deliver a 'business-in-a-box' to local entrepreneurs, train them, and enable them to make money helping people see better," he

says. Each pair of glasses that VisionSpring provides to these entrepreneurs costs the firm about $1 to make and deliver. The franchisee
pays it $2 or so and sells for about $3. Because every step of the value
chain is profitable, the business model is sustainable. Profits are rein-
vested to expand the program. The company is on track to sell more
than a million pairs by 2012 and five million by 2016.

To do so, it has forged partnerships with outfits that have strong
retail distribution in rural South Asia (where it is making its first
big push). Drishtee, an Indian firm with Internet kiosks in many
villages, is now selling reading glasses, as is BRAC, a community-
lending organization in Bangladesh. The firm has big plans for
African expansion too. Perhaps the most intriguing of VisionSpring's
partners are marketing giants with ubiquitous reach, including Unilever and ITC, an Indian tobacco conglomerate. "People clearly have
enough money to buy cigarettes and chewing gum," says Kassalow,
"so why not get them to spend that instead on health?"

As the real-world examples of the Acumen Fund and VisionSpring
show, greed (read: market forces and capitalism) can be a force
for good. In fact, harnessing greed wisely is a necessary precondition for kick-starting the innovation revolution needed to tackle today's grand global challenges. But does this really mean that profits
matter less than purpose or that capitalism itself is about to enter a
kinder, gentler era? Don't bet your pension on it.

The Invisible Hand Meets the Velvet Glove

The rise of social entrepreneurs, philanthrocapitalists, and hybrid
business models is surely to be applauded, but there are several
possible snags that could yet keep this movement from becoming

the transcendent force its boosters think it to be. One is the potential for muddled incentives that arises from lumping together profit and purpose breathlessly into one business model, without first developing meaningful measures and metrics for social impact. Another is the underdeveloped state of institutions, regulations, and other norms in the hybrid sector, which makes it ripe for exploitation and unintended consequences—growing pains that have already fueled a backlash in the field of microfinance. The biggest potential barrier, however, may be that of unrealistic expectations. Just consider the burden now being placed on the backs of those trying to improve the world: this movement, claim some management gurus and company bosses, adds up to a new and higher form of capitalism.

First, to purpose. There is no question that traditional business models that assumed everyone was motivated strictly by economic incentive are incomplete. As Dan Pink has argued in *Drive*, profit is a good motivation for some things but not for others. When people feel they do not have enough money for decent housing, food, and education, they obsess over it. However, behavioral studies suggest that unless people are working on rote mechanical tasks, simply paying more money will not yield more productivity. Since much of the world now lives in the Ideas Economy, employers clearly need to consider other ways of motivating talented workers. Pink puts the answer pithily: autonomy, mastery, and purpose. As most readers would readily agree, knowledge workers crave independence from bosses and relish being very good at their chosen jobs.

The more surprising finding for ardent believers in capitalism is that purpose can motivate people as powerfully as profit. You can see this in the willingness of many people with day jobs to spend their precious leisure time working on projects for free. Just consider the many millions of hours of work that people around the world have given away for free to build Wikipedia, Linux, and other open-source, collaborative ventures. Clearly having a social purpose can motivate people, and business models built on that insight can attract much-needed talent and capital to the citizen sector. "We are purpose maximizers, not just profit maximizers," says Pink, "and that can make our world just a little bit better."

Ah, but via that warm and fuzzy aspiration enters the muddle. In profit-maximizing capitalism, the goal for companies is crystal clear: maximize profits. This is not just a matter of greed. Peter Drucker argued that the greatest good a company can do for society is to excel at making the good or service it produces. It is true that even in strictly for-profit firms, incentives can get misaligned (over short-term profit versus long-term goals, say, or over conflicts between the interests of bosses versus those of employees). Still, profit is a pretty clear metric for measuring a firm's success at its core mission. Drucker in his later years came to be a great champion of the citizen sector, but he remained clear about the importance of businesses focusing on profit: "Profit is not the explanation, cause, or rationale of business behavior and business decisions, but rather the test of their validity. If archangels instead of businessmen sat in directors' chairs, they would still have to be concerned with profitability, despite their total lack of personal interest in making profits . . . a company can make a social contribution only if it is highly profitable."

So one difficulty arising from hybrid business models is the question of how to tell if a social business is being well run. How can investors tell if a firm making a bit of profit and delivering some social value (say, selling antimalarial bed nets) is actually a wonderfully run and efficient hybrid business or a mismanaged and underperforming firm that will soon hit the rocks? Richard Lyons, dean of the Haas School of Business at the University of California at Berkeley, acknowledges that this is a significant problem that the social enterprise movement—which he strongly supports—faces today: "We really need metrics."

The good news is that there are some people now trying to get the philanthrocapitalist world to agree on the importance of metrics, and to move toward common standards for measuring social impact (probably the best analog for profit in the nonprofit world). Brian Trelstad, the chief investment officer of Acumen, is one such courageous soul. He has scrutinized the various efforts that now exist to quantify the social impact of hybrid enterprises and concludes that these "tell a story" but "do not capture and generate data that can allow for an independent assessment of social innovation opportunities or their social impact." He laments that the field has yet to develop independent measurement tools, standardized criteria, or even common definitions of terms. Even seemingly quantitative methodologies such as sustainable return on investment (SROI), "blended value," and double/triple bottom-line accounting, he insists, "still fall short of providing reliable, rigorous, and objective quantification of social and environmental value."

His team at Acumen is developing a set of metrics, methods, and measures that it hopes will win wider acceptance. However, he is not holding his breath. Despite the blindingly obvious need to develop some sensible, common measures of performance, he finds that social businesses are generally not interested. More shocking, he has found that donors—whom one might think would welcome metrics that help them gauge if their money is being well spent—are generally uninterested in metrics too.

Part of the explanation for this apathy is understandable: the state of impact measurement is so poor today that embracing it would probably lead to false precision. Just measuring the output per dollar spent by a charity helping homeless people in Toronto get jobs as bike messengers, for example, may measure efficiency—but the better test of effectiveness would be a broader measure of impact (say, how many people got off welfare and took on taxpaying jobs as a result of the program). Asked if it is now regular practice among philanthrocapitalists to fund randomized control trials, which are the gold standard among economists for proving that a given approach works, to see if such schemes are actually having the impact claimed, he pauses and sighs. With a heavy heart, he reports that donors often do not want to spend the money required to acquire such evidence: "They're mostly interested in stories, not data."

There is now a fiery debate going on in the citizen sector about the role of metrics and measurement. This should be of great interest to those who want the citizen sector and hybrid business models to succeed. The right response to imperfect metrics is surely to invest in standardizing and improving them, not to abandon them altogether. As for the argument that precious donor money should go straight to charitable work, not on running expensive trials to measure impact, that sounds like the kinder, more charitable thing to do—but it is not. One philanthrocapitalist cites a real-world example of donors funding a new social business aiming at both profit and purpose, to the tune of $150,000 a year. Running proper trials to measure real-world impact would cost $100,000 in that case. The donors refused, insisting that the money should go instead straight to helping people through programmatic work, not measurement and metrics. Again, that sounds compassionate, even reasonable. But here is why that is a dangerously unhelpful stance to take. If that new social business was actually harming the people it sought to help, or even if it was just ineptly crowding out other social entrepreneurs or government agencies that could have done better, it does not deserve years and years of funding.

In short, the investment of $100,000 today would have prevented those donors from misdirecting millions in future years to that incompetent if well-intentioned social business. Richard Lyons agrees with this logic and thinks donors must invest in proper metrics and measurement if this sector is to grow—and deserves to grow. He cautions that measurement in this messy world of hybrid business models will "almost surely never be as tidy and clear as with for-profit ventures." Even so, he proposes what he calls the "running downhill" test. Many nonprofits live hand to mouth, begging for money and "running uphill" till they fail. And some nonprofits—Transparency International, say, which tracks levels of corruption in various countries—should never pursue profit. But many other sorts of charitable endeavors will be suited to the new hybrid model. Holding such businesses to the standard of making "nonzero financial returns" means they will be financially viable and not living off subsidies forever. With proper impact measurements in place, he reckons the test of ensuring that these ventures are running downhill will move the citizen sector a bit closer to the crisp performance metric that Peter Drucker wanted.

Microfinance, Megacontroversy

Is it immoral to profit from the poor? In *Philanthrocapitalism*, Bishop and Green include an anecdote that sheds light on this controversy. On this account, a heated debate broke out on this topic some years ago at the home of John Doerr, one of Silicon Valley's most successful venture capitalists. He had been captivated by the success of Grameen Bank, a pathbreaking Bangladeshi charity that has managed to make millions of tiny loans to very poor people—a concept known as microfinance. Among the invitees were Muhammad Yunus, who went on to win the Nobel Peace Prize for pioneering this innovation, and leading businessmen and philanthropists from the region. Doerr hoped all present would contribute money, and many did.

One who refused was Pierre Omidyar. After listening to all of the arguments, he was convinced that the not-for-profit model was the wrong way to go with microfinance. The need for microloans is so great, he reasoned, that donor money alone will never meet the need: a mixture of for-profit and nonprofit models was necessary to achieve scale rapidly. Yunus later recalled that dinner in an article in the *New Yorker*: "He says people should make money. I say let them make money—but why do you want to make money off the poor people? . . . when they have enough flesh and blood in their bodies, go and suck them, no problem. Until then, no."

That row anticipated another of the problems that could yet trip up the citizen-power revolution now getting under way: go beyond the stirring rhetoric, and it turns out that purpose and profit do not always mix well. In particular, people from the nonprofit and development world are often suspicious of the true motives of those who advocate using for-profit approaches to helping the poor. This issue came to a head in the microfinance world as for-profit microfinance institutions (MFIs) began to go public, earning huge payouts for their managers and investors. Compartamos, a Mexican MFI, was the first Latin American for-profit to go public back in 2007. SKS Microfinance, an Indian firm, went public in 2010 for $358 million in the largest such listing in that country's history. Deals such as these have poured salt into the wounds, as evidence has surfaced of how extremely poor people have endured high rates of interest at the hands of these firms. In some cases in India, farmers have even committed suicide rather than face the shame of not being able to repay their loans.

All this has provoked understandable revulsion and sparked a political backlash against for-profit microlenders. Yunus himself fueled the flames of this. Under attack for entirely unrelated reasons by politicians in Bangladesh (who ultimately succeeded in removing him from the top of Grameen Bank in 2011), he tried to direct attention back to those profiteering scoundrels. In an opinion piece run by the *New York Times* not long before his ouster, he declared that "commercialization has been a terrible wrong turn for microfinance." Branding his for-profit competitors as loan sharks, he insisted that the sector be reined in with heavy regulations. Lenders must take deposits, he said, as did Grameen. Regulators should also impose a rate cap of 15 percent above costs on all lenders, he insisted.

Reasonable and philanthropically minded people differ on whether microfinance—the poster child for the rise of the citizen sector—should have only nonprofit business models or a mix of for-profit and nonprofit. Yunus's position is certainly clear and uncompromising. Many leading figures from the world of philanthropy have voiced support for his position. Given his credentials, even those who may favor market forces may be tempted to agree with him. One influential voice who does not is Vinod Khosla, the venture capitalist. He invested several million dollars in SKS early on and stoutly defends its business model today. He is convinced it has done far more good than harm, despite the chorus of denunciations: "Millions of people now have access to financial services . . . that's more social than any nonprofit thing I could have done. And guess what? In the process, I made $100 million."

Matthew Bishop, who served as an advisor to the United Nations on microfinance before writing *Philanthrocapitalism*, stoutly defends Yunus against the politicized attacks on his reputation but still strongly disagrees with his position. In line with Khosla and Omidyar, Bishop argues that for microfinance to scale and help all those who desperately need help, private capital is a must. He observes that the not-for-profit version of MFIs have had thirty years since Grameen arrived on the scene to work out the kinks and scale properly. Yet barely 15 percent of people earning less than $1 a day have access to microcredit. The number of unserved soars dramatically if one raises the bar to include those making less than $2 or $3 a day—wretchedly poor people who are also surely deserving of loans. He also points out the unfairness of calling private sector MFIs loan sharks.

It is true that Compartamos charged very high rates—above 100 percent a year, a study concluded after the fact—when it could have charged lower rates and still made a profit. But it did so explicitly, in part, to attract more investors into a then-lonely and highly risky market—and succeeded in doing precisely that. Besides, loan sharks (the only real alternative many indigent people have) can charge far more than that in real life—and break people's legs if they do not pay. Not only did Compartamos not do any such thing, but its loans were clearly a better alternative for ordinary people—who managed a repayment rate upward of 98 percent, suggesting that this was not an impossible hardship.

What is the way forward for MFIs? The pendulum may be swinging toward the Yunus position, with several countries starting to impose arbitrary rate caps on lenders. That is probably a mistake: plenty of economic theory and history suggests that rate caps are likely to produce shortfalls in supply. In this case, the poor may have to endure a flight of private capital from microfinance because returns will be suppressed.

The real lesson here is not that profit making per se is wrong, but that unfettered markets are. The excesses seen at private MFIs should have been checked by proper regulation. Stiff antitrust laws and regulatory scrutiny by competent regulators will go far in modernizing and humanizing this sector without killing the goose that lays the golden egg. So too would demands for greater up-front transparency—especially on the true cost of loans, including any hidden fees—and the development of credit bureaus and other institutions that come with the broadening and deepening of new markets. As for Yunus's notion that all lenders must also be deposit banks, it turns out that this is not permitted in many countries. Regulations can be modified so that microlenders must also take in deposits, but again, forcing them to do this may well limit the number of investors interested in getting into microfinance.

The profit motive has been blamed for this crisis of faith in microfinance, but a failure of government is at least as much to blame. Regulators must be alert and keep both hands on the wheel, not fall asleep on the job, as has happened thus far. That insight explains why the citizen revolution has some way to go to achieve its aims. The mutual mistrust that business and nongovernmental organizations have long had has softened but is not completely gone, so the leaders of any alliances or hybrid value chains must always be on guard to nip such crises in the bud.

With luck, today's rows could prove merely the teething pains of a novel experiment in improving the lives of the world's poorest—an experiment that yields many lessons on how to build markets at the bottom of the pyramid. If that happens, could the world really enter a new, more empathic, and enlightened phase of capitalism?

Beyond CSR

Few management experts are as influential as Michael Porter. The brilliant Harvard Business School professor has shaped the thinking of a generation of leading corporate managers with his books on strategy, value chains, clusters, and competitive advantage. He is as courageous as he is forward-looking. A few years ago he even ventured into hostile terrain with his book *Redefining Health Care*, coauthored with Elizabeth Olmsted Teisberg, which stirred a hornet's nest by arguing that the fundamental incentive structure in the bloated U.S. health industry is distorted. What the industry needs to do is shift from its current model of fee-for-service, or piecework, he rightly argued, to "value-based competition" that rewards better patient outcomes.

The great hero of capitalist managers now has another really big idea: he believes it is time for a radical rethink of capitalism itself. In a much-discussed cover story published by the *Harvard Business Review* in early 2011, coauthored with Mark Kramer, he put forward a provocative thesis he calls "creating shared value," which represents "the next evolution of capitalism." He believes that the traditional business approach to social issues— spending money on corporate social responsibility (CSR)—is wrongheaded because it puts these vital issues into a ghetto apart from the core strategy of the business. Porter even praises the late Milton Friedman in passing, pointing approvingly to the conservative economist's opposition to CSR. Porter observes that so many companies are using such tactics as public relations exercises that there has been a backlash: "The more business has begun to embrace social responsibility, the more it has been blamed for society's failures."

Instead, he argues, companies must put society's great needs front and center when developing their strategies. Doing so will require managers to look beyond the quarterly returns and other short-term metrics, he insists, as these lead managers to ignore important customer needs. He also pooh-poohs the "presumed trade-offs between economic efficiency and social progress." In downplaying trade-offs, a notion held sacred by economists, he claims that there is "growing consensus that major improvements in environmental performance can often be achieved with better technology at nominal incremental cost and can even yield net cost savings." By vigorously pursuing strategies that create shared value, not just profit per se, he insists, the business world will "drive the next wave of innovation and productivity growth in the global economy."

In the brave new world of shared-value capitalism, the grand challenges facing the world today will best be solved by self-interested and profit-minded corporations: "Businesses acting as businesses, not as charitable donors, are the most powerful force for addressing the pressing issues we face." That may sound a bit like the famous notion put forward by Friedman that "the business of business is business," but in fact it is exactly the opposite. Friedman believed that it was reckless and inappropriate for the managers of a company, who have a fiduciary responsibility to maximize returns on behalf of a firm's owners (who are, of course, its shareholders), to spend company money on favored social causes or pet charities. Managers should instead return money to the owners, who are then free to give as generously to philanthropic causes as they want. Porter says capitalism can and must do better than this.

He also has little time for the conventional explanation of why market forces do not always solve problems such as environmental pollution, which involve externalities (say, the health impacts on people living downwind of a coal-fired power plant) that are not priced into the product in question (say, coal-fired electricity). Environmental economists have long argued that if governments want markets to deal with such externalities, they should introduce government policies (such as carbon taxes or cap-and-trade regulations, in the case of global warming) that internalize them by way of the price mechanism. Surprisingly, Porter is critical of externalities policies.

The idea of creating shared value is a breathtaking vision—but does it really add up? This question matters, because it points to the third big concern that could yet trip up the revolution launched by Drayton and the army of social entrepreneurs: the weight of unrealistic expectations. To be fair, Porter gets some big things right. For example, he is surely right that managers must take a long-term view of shareholder returns. If they do so, they will often find that it makes business sense to invest a bit more now on social "extras"—for example, in investing a bit now to improve energy efficiency or making sure the suppliers of its suppliers treat workers fairly—than a fly-by-night capitalist might.

Beyond the call for managers to think long-term, does this Big Idea really add up to a big idea? Opinion is divided. Many experts agree that there is a crisis of confidence in capitalism, and Porter is certainly right to look for creative ways corporations can win back the public's trust. A number of leading chief executives have warmed up to his theme. Nestlé's chairman, Peter Brabeck-Letmathe, and Pepsi's boss, Indra Nooyi, are two leading corporate voices that have embraced the shared-value vision. But not everyone is persuaded by this thesis.

Vijay Govindarajan of Dartmouth's Tuck School of Business says "shared value" is a nice phrase but asks, "What's new here? . . . Isn't this what business does at its best anyway?" He bristles at the notion that capitalism has to evolve to a higher plane to tackle society's problems. He points to the example of Henry Ford, whose radical and hugely profitable business model (aside from implementing the production line, he also paid above-market wages so his workers could afford his cars) created enormous shared value for his employees, for their communities, and for the country in general. Robert Stavins of Harvard's Kennedy School of Government, a leading environmental economist, disagrees about externalities-based policies. Several decades of successful experiments with such policies, starting with "eco-taxation" reforms in northern Europe and extending to many environmental regulations in the United States, show that they do work very well.

The *Economist's* "Schumpeter" column was deeply unimpressed: "It is not clear that Mr. Porter has come up with any tangible improvement on the current way of doing business. Is it true that shared value will 'drive the next wave of innovation and productivity growth in the global economy,' or merely a pious hope? For all we know the next such wave may come from energy-hungry, socially divisive businesses, given the paucity of evidence Mr. Porter offers to support his thesis."

That is probably too harsh a judgment. Even if he gets some things wrong—such as his dim view of externalities policies—he certainly gets the big picture right. The great opportunity lies in going from "greed is good" to "greed *for* good." Incentives matter, purpose matters, and enlightened corporations that take a long-term view will find taking on some of the world's difficult global problems to be profitable. This is not to say that all firms will find all societal problems to be profitable always. And it does not mean that the role for government or the individual is diminished. Porter himself says, quite rightly, that companies can't solve all of society's problems. And he gets the most important thing right, according to GE's chairman Jeff Immelt: "I agree with Michael Porter that the era of free capitalism without consequences is over."

That sentiment sums up the challenge and the opportunity facing business leaders, government officials, and aspiring innovators today. The rise of the citizen sector is very real. Aspiring innovators will need to overcome various obstacles that are difficult but not impossible to surmount—not least the burden of unrealistic expectations. But as social entrepreneurs and agile corporations experiment with new business models that take account of society's greatest needs, creative capitalism seems likely to make a big impact in coming years. And the difference between success and failure will often be determined by how powerfully motivated entrepreneurs are to bring about change.

If at First You Don't Fail, Try, Try Again

Jessica Jackley has already helped to make the world a better place. She cofounded Kiva, a path-breaking Internet outfit that lets people anywhere lend small amounts of money at affordable rates to aspiring entrepreneurs in the developing world. Kiva's partners are established microfinance outfits around the world (though hearing Mohammad Yunus inspired her to drop everything and pursue microfinance, Jackley thinks he is wrong about for-profit MFIs; she insists that both business models should be allowed to compete in the sector). Those local MFIs post profiles of poor local people with a business need—say, a new goat or a sewing machine—that requires some money. Ordinary people in distant parts of the developed world, sitting comfortably at their laptop computers, have been granting microloans in such small amounts as $25 to the entrepreneurs they wish to support. The firm has already channeled $200 million or so to the poor this way and has a repayment rate above 98 percent to boot. But the key to Kiva's success, she insists, is not impressive scale or even the stellar repayment rate but the personal connections that lead to empathy.

Not content with the success of one transformative firm, Jackley—who is still in her thirties—is busy building another. With a former classmate from Stanford Business School, she has launched ProFounder, a Web platform to help entrepreneurs in the United States "crowdfund" more efficiently. Most start-ups get most of their early money not from venture capitalists and certainly not from banks, which are too risk averse to back upstarts; instead, they get it from a circle of intimates known affectionately as "friends, family, and fools." Jackley knew from personal experience that this is an extremely stressful process made more so by the informal and awkward nature of these early contributions. (Did Uncle Frank really promise you $5,000 for your start-up at Thanksgiving, or was that the wine talking?) There are complex regulations governing such investments that vary from state to state, making life more difficult. Her for-profit outfit has done all the donkey work, so aspiring entrepreneurs need only tap their networks for money via her platform; the firm's automated systems deal with most of the paperwork.

Ask Jackley what it means to be an innovative entrepreneur, and she offers three answers that cut to the heart of this book's arguments about the democratization of innovation. First, she defines innovators as those who see possibility in the world and believe improvement is possible. But she warns that ideas, while great, do not add up to much, as innovation needs entrepreneurship to catalyze change: "As an entrepreneur, you must act every day on execution."

Most important is the collective vision a founder must instill in her team. Shared purpose leads to inspiration just as surely as the fear of letting down comrades leads to the perspiration needed to overcome inevitable obstacles. Everyone has the talent to be an entrepreneur, she thinks, but not everyone will like the lifestyle.

Reflecting on the decision to leave Kiva, which appears poised for spectacular growth and innovation (it could evolve into the first credit bureau for the world's poor, for example), to start ProFounder, she confesses that she is absolutely petrified of failure. "The first time you can get lucky, but the second time you have to be smart . . . and that's a high bar!" So why leave the comfort and success of Kiva? "I wanted to apply Kiva's lessons to another big, but similar, problem," she says. "I wanted to build something again." The drive to leave behind comfort and security to create a disruptive new organization even when confronted by powerful obstacles and a high chance of failure is the true mark of an entrepreneur. And by radically simplifying the early funding process for other entrepreneurs, she is contributing to meta-innovation—the ongoing innovation in how the world innovates.

Jackley's final insight is the most incisive. In her public speeches, she likes to invoke Thomas Kuhn's arguments about the nature of scientific revolutions and the importance of paradigm shifts. Asked to explain, she says today is an incredible time for innovations in how to reach out and help the poor. The key, though, lies in a change in mind-set. For ages, most of society—including her, she admits—thought what the poor needed was more charity and donor aid. But meeting countless inspiring but cash-strapped entrepreneurs in Africa and elsewhere convinced her that the old way was doing more harm than good, and that "the world's poor are also entrepreneurs and innovators with tremendous human potential."

The democratization of innovation promises to be an extraordinarily powerful force shaping the Ideas Economy. In the future, the difference between success and failure will often be determined not by lack of access to capital, markets, talent, or other conventional obstacles. In the age of disruptive innovation, resourcefulness will matter more than resources—and success or failure will be determined inside the mind of the innovator. Are you ready for the revolution?

CONCLUSION

We Are All Innovators Now

Now, more than ever, innovation matters. There is an urgent need for solutions to the novel problems of the twenty-first century. Innovators from unexpected corners with unfamiliar pedigrees are disrupting established business models and upending entire industries at breakneck speed. But if entrepreneurs, who are the vital carriers of innovation, are rewarded for solving socially important problems, greed can indeed do much good. Innovation could then turn these wicked global crises into unprecedented economic opportunities.

However, just because the world needs innovation and innovation is becoming more democratic, it does not mean the future is inevitably bright for all. A more likely outcome is that the world economy is entering a period in which we will see much more turbulence, which may produce unexpected winners and losers. Leading economies will be challenged by upstarts. Established companies in many sectors will be blindsided by unanticipated threats. Workers, even well-educated professionals in the middle classes, will find themselves increasingly unable to compete in a world evolving rapidly beyond their recognition. Governments, companies, and individuals alike will feel like they are running just to stand still.

So how to win in this coming age of disruptive innovation? Elon Musk put his finger on something important in describing his own path to success forging not one but three disruptive start-up firms—PayPal, Tesla Motors, and SpaceX. The right formula for success as an innovative entrepreneur, he says, is drive times opportunity times talent. That points nicely to a manifesto for flourishing in the new world economy.

Start with drive. Jessica Jackley is surely right to insist that idea generation gets you nowhere unless it is coupled with the hard slog of execution. Wonderful ideas for improving products, communities, or the world at large have long been around, but the innovation process was simply too elitist and closed off in the past to pick up on many of those ideas. As it opens up, though, bright sparks anywhere in the world, regardless of status or corporate affiliation, have the chance to make their mark and maybe make their fortunes too. What is more, as political and economic obstacles have faded and information and talent flows have accelerated, plucky upstarts are creating global micromultinationals—such as Jeff Denby's socially responsible underwear firm PACT—from day one.

Joseph Schumpeter hailed the entrepreneur as "the innovator who implements change within markets through the carrying out of new combinations." We need to do much more to encourage such entrepreneurial drive, as it may be humanity's best hope for increasing productivity growth, speeding the diffusion and adoption of worthwhile innovations, and tackling the world's grand challenges. That is because the leading countries of the world, especially the United States, may be entering a period of what has been called frontier economics. As older, easier sources of growth have started to dry up, knowledge-age economies are relying ever more on innovation to save the day. That requires start-ups to push the boundaries of technologies, business models, and social norms.

Jack Hidary is one of those provocateurs who is always pushing the boundaries of what is possible. He made his fortune with two technology start-ups, EarthWeb and Dice.com, but he has been spending most of his money and time trying to kick-start a clean energy revolution. He joined the board of the X Prize Foundation and cofounded the Progressive Automotive X Prize, which sought to develop vehicles that broke the 100-mpg barrier. He worked with several partners to develop the Cash for Clunkers program, which swapped more than 700,000 cars across the country in two months for an average gain in fuel efficiency of 62 percent.

In addition to incentive prizes and policy catalysts, he argues that a new kind of entrepreneurship is required to take on such big, complicated problems as the move to clean energy. The old model—he calls it Newtonian—saw a linear path in which entrepreneurs would start off alone with nothing, stumble on an idea, lock in their intellectual property, seek out seed funding, go to alpha and beta testing, and so predictably on. "It was all very cause and effect, slow to scale, and most ideas got stuck in the technology valley of death," he says.

In the new quantum approach he advocates, innovative entrepreneurship happens as a superposition of many simultaneous possibilities rather than a straight line, and propels multiple approaches involving entire ecosystems of players forward at the same time until a shakeout leaves just one set of winners standing. This is analogous to the wave function in quantum mechanics, which forces one pathway forward from a wide range of possibilities.

One of his main goals in clean tech has been to make electric vehicles accessible to the masses without consumers worrying about charging and infrastructure. Recognizing that the arrival of the always-on Internet-supported network enables a new generation of charging stations and vehicles, Hidary set out to build a consortium that could make this vision a reality. But instead of starting a new company, as he had in the past, he decided to catalyze a new set of consortiums and business models to push the technology forward. The key barrier to adoption of these vehicles, he reckoned, was the need for consumers and businesses to buy the car.

By a clever mix of cajoling, cooing, confronting, and cooperating with a variety of companies that make up the ecosystem of car, recharger, and power supplier, he has managed to forge a breakthrough that allows those firms to push the technology forward while advancing their own business differentiation. In mid-2011, Hertz announced that it would carry a large number of electric vehicles for rent in prominent locations in several countries, and GE came on board to supply the recharging infrastructure with other partners in tow. Parking garages, corporate campuses, utilities, and others joined in to roll out the infrastructure in distributed fashion. To tackle the world's most wicked problems, he argues, we need a range of tools in the toolbox—government policy, incentive prizes, industry coalitions, and so on—and the challenge for the new generation of entrepreneurs will be how to coordinate all this.

That example shows why companies and countries—not to mention friends, families, and fools—that remove obstacles from the path of trailblazing, innovative entrepreneurs such as Hidary will do better than those who do not. And if you are a person with a great idea but no business plan, you no longer have an excuse for sitting on the fence. Thanks to such advances as Web-based crowdfunding, even very poor people in hardscrabble parts of the world are now changing the world. So why are you still an innovator-in-waiting?

If the answer is that you do not know where to look for opportunity, consider the advice given by the OECD: the greatest potential driver of innovation and source of future productivity gains may well be intangible capital. It is easy enough to spot the tangible capital in an economy, whether capital equipment and machinery or buildings and infrastructure. But in the Ideas Economy, much of the value of firms is not captured on the balance sheet: it walks out the door at the end of the workday, trapped in the minds of the best employees. In today's open innovation ecosystems, one form of intangible capital is the knowledge networks that link decentralized nodes of open innovation. Of all the forms of intangible capital that look likely to drive future growth, the agency thinks the most promising are advanced software, Big Data, analytics, and design.

Those seem a bit prosaic at first. So to get a sense of the hidden opportunity here to change the world, take a closer look at design thinking. Tim Brown, the boss of IDEO, a consultancy that helped shape Apple's first mouse, does not have solutions to daunting global problems such as climate change, epidemics, and persistent poverty. But he believes he knows how to find them: with design thinking, by which he means the open-minded, no-holds-barred approach that designers bring to their work, rather than the narrow, technical view of innovation traditionally taught at many business and engineering schools. Firms that think like designers, which means embracing experimentation via rapid prototyping and fast failure, stand to win huge new markets and profits. The concept may sound pat and wooly, encompassing everything from savvier marketing to radical technological leaps. Yet design thinking is winning many converts in both industry and philanthropy.

A holistic approach to tackling problems produces more breakthroughs than does the MBA's traditional urge to make incremental improvements to existing products or processes. The traditional uncompromising focus on predictability and quality control exemplified by Six Sigma, a form of statistical analysis popular with manufacturers, can lead to "analysis paralysis" by discouraging sweeping changes that may cause disruptions in the short term but yield big benefits in the long run. GE is perhaps the company most closely associated with Six Sigma, but Jeff Immelt nevertheless thinks there is something to the argument for stepping out of silos. He is convinced that taking on such complex challenges as health care and energy, sectors on which he is betting GE's future, will require systems thinking that weaves together policy, economics, strategy, and technology in entirely new ways.

The key is to focus on the needs of people without losing sight of the big picture. George Kembel, the head of Stanford University's Institute of Design, points to Embrace, a fledgling health care firm created by a group of his former students. The problem they set out to fix was the appalling lack of proper medical care for premature babies in poor countries. One reason for this is that sophisticated incubators can cost $20,000 or more; even if a country receives the machines from donors, the lack of proper training and money for maintenance undermines their effectiveness.

Many attempts had been made to reduce the cost of such incubators, but the Stanford team took a different approach, by talking to locals in rural areas. In the process, it dawned on them that most babies in the developing world are not born in hospitals and so are unlikely to benefit from incubators even if the devices are working properly. The team designed a cheap and cheerful proxy: a tiny sleeping bag made of material that, when dipped in boiling water, retains heat for hours. The drive of these social entrepreneurs has met clear market opportunity, and they hope to start selling this $25 "incubator" soon.

Another example of how design can drive innovation and create opportunity is the democratization of manufacturing that is under way today. In the past, because the essential tools of the trade—such as lathes, injection-molding machines, and computer-aided design systems—were so expensive and large, only companies with deep pockets could aspire to design and manufacture new products for the global market. No longer. The rise of cloud computing and powerful design software, the miniaturization of essential hardware, and the rapid advance of 3-D printing are fomenting a manufacturing revolution. At the forefront of this movement is Autodesk, a California software firm that has for decades produced expensive 3-D software design tools for high-end applications (including designing Boeing aircraft and creating Hollywood films such as *Avatar*).

Without the knowledge of Carl Bass, Autodesk's boss, several younger employees developed cheap and cheerful design applications for the iPhone and iPad that have become runaway bestsellers. Bass confesses that if he had been asked, he would have crushed the project out of fear that it might weaken the firm's high-end brand. In fact, millions of new users are now familiar with his brand and existing customers are asking for more such applications. Bass says, "This was a wake-up call for us that the world is changing. It took twenty-seven years for us to get to 12 million units in sales, and now in eighteen months we've done it again." He argues that the spread of affordable design software, inexpensive digital fabrication labs, and outfits such as California's Tech Shop (which aim to do for manufacturing and design equipment what Kinko's did for photocopiers) means that everyone can join the "maker revolution." Bass goes so far as to say that there will be a renaissance in manufacturing in America—"as long as we redefine what manufacturing means."

And what about talent? Elites have long sniffed that when it comes to talent, either you've got it or you don't—but that view no longer holds in a world of democratic innovation. Every one of us has had an aha moment, after all, and the right sort of education and training can develop intangible skills and unleash the innovator trapped inside. At the level of many national economies, there is a massive talent crunch coming due to demographic trends that will produce a shock not seen since the Middle Ages. Experts at the World Economic Forum and the Boston Consulting Group have calculated that the working-age populations of many developed economies will start to shrink shortly, and they predict that "numerous organizations will be unable to find enough employees in their home markets to sustain profitability and growth." By 2050, the global population of those over sixty is predicted to exceed those under fifteen for the first time in history.

There is no easy answer, so countries need to try out a mix of policies to deal with the problem. Part of the solution is to encourage more skilled migration, as increased talent mobility is part of the solution. Again, think brain circulation, not brain drain. Those countries that do not, because of xenophobia or other factors, will risk losing out. Anticipating future skills shortages and encouraging public-private partnerships to retrain workers will help, as will tax incentives for businesses to invest more in training workers. Companies will also have to redouble efforts to diversify their workforces, scouring previously neglected demographics (the disabled everywhere, the elderly in developed countries, or women in emerging markets, for example) to find and develop talent.

However, the key to the development of talent lies in the hands of the individual. On this front, there is bad news and good. The bad news is that in many countries, official school systems and universities will not prepare you for the twenty-first-century innovation economy. In America, many public schools have notoriously been falling further behind international benchmarks for quality. But there is also cause for concern in Asian countries that celebrate "tiger moms" and produce high-scoring students, because much of the education in such systems emphasizes rote learning; critical thinking, a willingness to challenge conventional assumptions, and creativity often lose out.

The good news is that thanks to the new tools of the information age, it is now easier than ever to take charge of your own education. If the local school system does not provide strong science education, go online and contract with an inexpensive tutor from Kerala. If your child's math skills are falling behind those of her peers, improve them using the Khan Academy's excellent free lectures on the Internet—as over one million students already do. If it is more advanced skills you wish to top up, check out the many free courses that universities such as MIT now place online. If ideas and argument are more your cup of tea, follow the provocative series of free TED talks online and in real life at the thousands of TEDx events now popping up around the world.

In the age of disruptive innovation, the competitive edge may well go not to the smartest or wealthiest but to those who best learn how to keep on learning throughout their lifetimes. This will not be easy, because while the top-down system of mass-produced education that suited the industrial revolution has become obsolete, no coherent and clear system has risen to take its place. A fancy degree from Harvard Business School may not mean the same anymore, argues Christensen, observing that even business professors such as he are becoming obsolete thanks to online offerings. Reflecting for a moment on the prospect of the very same sort of disruptive innovation he has championed for a lifetime putting him out of business, he smiles broadly. That would be a fitting tribute to a man who, along with the late Peter Drucker, has done more than anyone to advance thinking on innovation.

Decades ago, at a time when many thought innovation was mostly a fringe activity to be relegated to the long-haired creative types, Drucker saw "innovation and entrepreneurship as purposeful tasks that can be organized—are in need of being organized." Though it may never become a quantifiable science, innovation is indeed evolving rapidly from a dark art to something resembling a mainstream practice. As the shroud of mystery fades, the process is becoming more accessible and a useful set of tools and rules is emerging. In that spirit, here are a handful of the most important new rules for the age of disruptive innovation.

The Disruptive Dozen:
The New Rules of Global Innovation

The very way in which we innovate is being reinvented, with wonderful but often unexpected consequences. If you want to prosper rather than perish in this coming age of disruptive change, you need to master the new rules of global innovation:

1. *Innovation is not a zero-sum game.* China's rise does not mean America's decline—but the rising tide will lift your boat only if you patch the holes in it first.

2. *Think locally, act globally.* Many of this century's thorniest problems—food and water scarcity, health scares—seem like local problems. In fact, they often arise from failures in national and global governance. Creative coalitions, regional approaches, and systems thinking are the way forward.

3. *Turn risk into reward through resilience.* Leaders must realign incentives for the private sector to build resilience into future infrastructure and supply chains. The

key is to shift from brittle, top-down systems to modular, flexible approaches that are more future-proof.

4. *Open up and say . . . aha!* Ivory towers are so yesterday. Open and networked innovation recognizes that the smartest people in your business no longer work inside your firm.

5. *Be the dinosaur that dances.* It may be unsexy to be the incumbent firm in an industry undergoing disruption by nimble upstarts, but that is no reason to stand still. Leverage your legacy assets, and ditch outdated business models even if they are profitable today but do not have a future.

6. *Elegant frugality trumps conspicuous consumption.* The fallout from the great recession is clear. Consumers in developed countries, not just poor folk in emerging markets, want products and services that offer better value.

7. *If at first you don't succeed, fail, fail again.* Transform your attitude toward risk so that you celebrate fast failure. It is not easy to fail elegantly.

8. *Forget Father—it's the user who knows best.* Bottom-up innovation works much better than the top-down kind. When customers help you create your products and services, the resultant ecosystem gives your firm the edge.

9. *Go whole hog.* As the life cycle costs and externalities involved with economic activity get priced into goods and services, systems thinking will beat silos.

10. *The path from stagnation to rejuvenation runs through innovation.* Easing the middle-class squeeze seen in many developed economies will mean improving productivity and boosting economic growth. The best way to do this is to invest in the long-term drivers of innovation such as education, research and development, and smart infrastructure.

11. *Put purpose on par with profits.* In the Ideas Economy, money will no longer be a sufficient motivator of talent. Look to emerging business models of social entrepreneurship and hybrid value chains for inspiration.

12. *Keep relearning* how *to learn.* Each of us has an innovator trapped inside, and today's innovation revolution promises to be much more democratic than the past—but you cannot rely only on traditional schools, fancy diplomas, and employers any longer. You must constantly work to figure out how innovation is evolving so that you can participate and prosper.

The democratization of innovation, once the preserve of technocratic elites in ivory towers, offers hope that the grand challenges of this new century can indeed be tackled. Ever deeper waves of innovation could, in time, even transform a world of scarcity and conflict into one of abundance and prosperity. That is because as the potential of seven billion innovators-in-waiting is unleashed, mankind will at last be tapping fully the one natural resource that we have in infinite quantity: human ingenuity.

ACKNOWLEDGMENTS

A great number of people have contributed to the making of this book, and I am grateful to all of them.

First, I thank John Micklethwait, the editor-in-chief of *The Economist*, for giving me time to write this book and for giving me permission to use articles that I have written for the magazine. I also thank Daniel Franklin and other editors and colleagues for their encouragement of this project.

Many of the themes, characters, and arguments found in this book were inspired by real-life conversations and debates that took place on the Ideas Economy stage (www.ideas.economist.com). This is a path-breaking series of innovation conferences and multi-media events started a few years ago by *The Economist*. I have had the privilege of chairing this series, and the pleasure of working closely with the sparky people curating the content. Justin Hendrix, Sean McManus, and the entire Ideas Economy team deserve tremendous praise for their efforts.

I have also been fortunate to have sharp people outside *The Economist* supporting my efforts. I am grateful to Andrew Wylie, my agent, for fighting in my corner; I also thank Scott Moyers for his invaluable early support. I had a hunch when I first spoke with

Hollis Heimbouch about innovation that she would be the perfect editor for this book—and her wise and graceful edits certainly proved me right. I thank her and the entire team at HarperCollins for their fine work.

Finally, I am grateful to my wife, Michelle, for both her unflagging support and her keen editorial judgment. In addition to insightful comments on impenetrable draft chapters, she also offered a timely and incisive critique of the book's structure that led to a vital mid-course correction. All that, even as she had her hands full with much more important matters.

To Michelle, to all my long-suffering friends and family, I say thank you from the bottom of my heart.

NOTES

Please note that the Web links below were functional when this book went to press, but of course such links often change. Where possible I have tried to give relevant details (such as time and place of a speech, etc.) associated with a link so that the determined reader can Google her way to the desired information even if the link no longer works.

Introduction

16   **the world's wicked problems:** This term of art has a long and rich history. For more, see Horst Rittel and Melvin Webber, "Dilemmas in a General Theory of Planning," *Policy Sciences* 4 (1973); and more recently, John Kao's "What Is Large Scale Innovation," 2009, www.johnkao.com/Large%20Scale%20Innovation.pdf.

Chapter 1: Wicked Problems, Wiki Solutions

22   **Can you change the world:** Jeff Denby gave a lively presentation of his business strategy at this Ideas Economy event in March 2010: http://ideas.economist.com/presentation/sustainable-underwear.

26   **Geoffrey West:** West presents his arguments on the role that scaling plays in driving innovation at this Ideas Economy event on Intelligent Infrastructure in September 2010. Careful listeners will catch his off-color description of the

Singularity concept (described in Chapter 4), which he thinks is complete bunk: http://ideas.economist.com/presentation/urban-physics.

26 More amazingly, the rise of those economies: For a good overview of the prospects for ending absolute poverty in this century, see Jeffrey Sachs, *The End of Poverty: Economic Possibilities for Our Time* (New York: Penguin, 2005). Note I mean absolute poverty, as measured by such objective standards as the UNDP's human development metrics, not relative poverty. In that sense, the Good Book is right, as income inequality will always be with us.

27 The World Economic Forum has dubbed this: The World Economic Forum's work on this topic includes a thoughtful report highlighting the interlinkages: "Water Security: The Water-Energy-Food-Climate Nexus" (2011), www .weforum.org/reports/water-security-water-energy-food-climate-nexus.

28 William Baumol: For a masterly analysis of entrepreneurship through human history, see David S. Landes, Joel Mokyr, and William J. Baumol, eds., *The Invention of Enterprise: Entrepreneurship from Ancient Mesopotamia to Modern Times* (Princeton: Princeton University Press, 2010). See also this entertaining romp through the history of innovation with two grand masters, Baumol and Harold Evans, at this Ideas Economy event in March 2011: http:// ideas.economist.com/video/masters-innovation.

30 Larry Brilliant: For an overview of the grand global challenges of the twenty-first century, see "Sustaining Humanity," a lecture he gave at the University of Michigan on March 16, 2011: http://lecb.physics.lsa.umich.edu/ CWIS/browser.php?ResourceId=4021.

33 Jung is a cofounder: Many in Silicon Valley maintain that Edward Jung and his more famous cofounder, Nathan Myhrvold (the former chief technology officer of Microsoft), are opportunistic patent trolls. Intellectual Ventures has in the past fiercely rejected this label. Pressed on this point during an interview in May 2011, the amiable Jung insisted his firm was chiefly about long-term investments—but he acknowledged that it was something of a patent troll as well.

36 Beware the Superbug: The parts of Chapter 1 dealing with bacterial superbugs draw on analysis done for an Economist briefing on the same topic. I thank my colleagues and collaborators in that effort, Natasha Loder and Geoffrey Carr.

Chapter 2: Cheap and Cheerful

56   This so-called localized modularization approach: The arguments put forward by John Seely Brown and John Hagel on Chinese innovation are found in their "Globalization and Innovation: Some Contrarian Perspectives," a paper prepared for the annual meeting of the World Economic Forum, Davos, Switzerland, January 25–30, 2006, www.johnseelybrown.com/davos.pdf.

57   Aravind, a pioneering Indian eye hospital chain: Though C. K. Prahalad first brought the Aravind story to global attention, a number of independent studies, including by leading business schools, have validated Aravind's model. A good recent analysis is found in Suchitra Shenoy and Pavithra Mehta, *Infinite Vision: How Aravind Became the World's Greatest Business Case for Compassion* (San Francisco: Berrett-Koehler, 2011).

63   For example, says Christopher Wasden: The PWC Innovation Scorecard for the global medical devices sector, published in January 2011, is found here: http://pwchealth.com/cgi-local/hregister.cgi?link=reg/innovation-scorecard.pdf.

Chapter 3: Of Stagnation and Rejuvenation

69   the transformative power of mobile telephony: For more on how cell phones and related technologies have impacted the lives of the bottom billion, see Vital Wave Consulting, *mHealth for Development: The Opportunity of Mobile Technology for Healthcare in the Developing World* (Washington, DC: UN Foundation–Vodafone Foundation Partnership, 2009), www .globalproblems-globalsolutions-files.org/unf_website/assets/publications/ technology/mhealth/mHealth_for_Development_full.pdf, and Isaac Mbiti and David N. Weil, "Mobile Banking: The Impact of M-Pesa in Kenya," National Bureau of Economic Research, NBER Working Paper No. 17129, June 2011, www.nber.org/papers/w17129.pdf.

71   Though some dismiss any talk of a middle-class squeeze: Barack Obama has often commented on the middle-class squeeze, for example, during his State of the Union speech of 2010. Ronald Haskins made his observation during "America's Endangered Middle Class: Exploring Progressive and Conservative Remedies," an event organized in February 2011 by the Brookings Institution in Washington.

72   Consider the evidence: The best data sets for working out the Gini coefficient and other metrics relevant to income inequality in America are maintained by the Internal Revenue Service and the U.S. Commerce Department.

72   Alan Greenspan: He made similar comments at various times, but most notable was during congressional testimony given in June 2005. See Peter Grier, "Rich-Poor Gap Gaining Attention," *Christian Science Monitor,* June 14, 2005, www.csmonitor.com/2005/0614/p01s03-usec.html.

74   Indefensible as these are: For a thoughtful take on the broader implications of tax breaks for employer-provided health insurance, see Len Nichols and Sarah Axeen, "Employer Health Care Costs in a Global Economy: A Competitive Disadvantage for U.S. Firms," New America Foundation policy paper, May 2008, www.newamerica.net/publications/policy/employer_health_costs_global_economy, and Jonathan Gruber, "The Tax Exclusion for Employer-Sponsored Health Insurance," National Bureau of Economic Research, NBER Working Paper No. 15766, February 2010, http://econ-www.mit.edu/files/6404.

77   What should one make of this: The McKinsey Global Institute has done quite a bit of work on productivity growth versus stagnation. The consultancy's website ran a debate between Tyler Cowen and two MIT experts, Andrew McAfee and Erik Brynjolfsson: "The Debate Zone: Has the U.S. Passed Peak Productivity Growth?" http://whatmatters.mckinseydigital.com/the_debate_zone/has-the-us-passed-peak-productivity-growth.

79   Angus Maddison: Much of Maddison's work can be found on his website, www.ggdc.net/MADDISON/oriindex.htm. Since his passing, a group of dedicated scholars has maintained another site, which publishes work done in the same spirit: www.ggdc.net/maddison.

80   For example, health care gobbles up: See, for example, the OECD's ongoing work on health indicators across the developed world at their website, OECD.StatExtracts: http://stats.oecd.org/index.aspx.

84   In early 2011, Ben Bernanke: His speech, "Promoting Research and Development: The Government's Role," given at the conference "New Building Blocks for Jobs and Economic Growth," Washington, DC, May 16 2011, can be found at www.federalreserve.gov/newsevents/speech/bernanke20110516a.htm.

86   The great Victorian age of invention: For more on this topic, see Vaclav Smil's scholarly *Transforming the Twentieth Century: Technical Innovations and Their Consequences* (New York: Oxford University Press, 2005), and my colleague Tom Standage's delightful book on the age of the telegraph, *The Victorian Internet* (New York: Walker, 2007), http://tomstandage.wordpress.com/books/the-victorian-internet.

87   The American financial industry: A provocative report on this topic is Paul Kedrosky and Dane Stangler, "Financialization and Its Entrepreneurial Consequences," Kauffman Foundation Research Series: Firm Formation and

Economic Growth, March 2011, www.kauffman.org/uploadedFiles/financial
ization_report_3-23-11.pdf.

Chapter 4: The Singularity and Its Discontents

93 *Time* **even put the Singularity on its cover:** Lev Grossman, "2045: The
Year Man Becomes Immortal," *Time*, February 19, 2011, www.time.com/time/
health/article/0,8599,2048138-1,00.html. Singularitarians often check out
Kurzweil's website at www.kurzweilai.net.

94 **One man who was not at all surprised:** Vivek Kundra, who served as the
Obama White House's chief information officer until mid-2011, is a believer in
the Singularity. See "An Interview with Vivek Kundra," http://ideas.economist.
com/presentation/interview-vivek-kundra.

96 **Even in the heart of Silicon Valley:** The skeptical gathering was one
of the many spontaneously organized "unconference" sessions at the annual
SciFoo conference, a marvelous event organized by Google and O'Reilly
Media. Several hundred of the world's very sharpest scientists and technology
experts, Google's founders Larry Page and Sergey Brin, and a few lucky journalists come together for a weekend of provocation and prognostication. There
is no prearranged agenda whatsoever, merely a set of large white boards, empty
meeting rooms, and lots of good food and wine.

98 **His magazine ran a damning critique:** Mark Anderson, "Never Mind the
Singularity, Here's the Science," *Wired*, April 2008, www.wired.com/medtech/
drugs/magazine/16-04/ff_kurzweil_sb.

98 **"Forget the Singularity":** Juan Enriquez's essay was published by the Technology, Entertainment and Design (TED) conference's publishing arm in 2011. A
detailed book building on the essay is forthcoming, but this talk covers the key points
of his argument: www.ted.com/talks/juan_enriquez_shares_mindboggling_new_
science.html.

99 **There is reason to think all of this talk:** See "The OECD at 50: Science
and Technology, 2010."

100 **William Nordhaus:** See William D. Nordhaus, "Two Centuries of Productivity Growth in Computing," *Journal of Economic History* 67, 1 (March 2007).

100 **For example, the 2030 Water Resources Group:** Not to be confused with
the Water Resources Group, a for-profit firm, the 2030 Water Resources Group
is a collection of leading experts and public figures concerned about the global
water problem. See its "Charting Our Water Future: Economic Frameworks to

Inform Decision-Making," 2009, www.2030waterresourcesgroup.com/water_full/Charting_Our_Water_Future_Final.pdf.

105 Paul Saffo: Saffo makes the argument that the Singularity will come, but "we won't even notice." Views of the future of innovation put forth by Google's Hal Varian and Paul Saffo, offered at the start of an Ideas Economy conference in March 2011, are found here: http://bit.ly/gbQY8a.

Chapter 5: So Long, Silo

109 The only way forward, the firm decided: The *Harvard Business Review* published "Connect and Develop: Inside Procter & Gamble's New Model for Innovation" in March 2006; it ran a story reviewing that program's progress, "How P&G Tripled Its Innovation Success Rate," in March 2011.

114 Big-company bosses have figured out the bottom line: The source for these R&D figures is Henry Chesbrough.

117 Studies have shown that how people relate to the products they use: See, for example, work by NYU's Sinan Aral.

121 What's more, at times hardly 1 percent: See, for example, work by the Wharton School's Peter Fader.

123 as typically happens in incentive prizes: For an academic investigation of prizes, see Brian Wright, "The Economics of Invention Incentives," *American Economic Review*, September 1983. See also V. V. Chari, Mikhail Golosov, and Aleh Tsyvinski, "Prizes and Patents: Using Market Signals to Provide Incentives for Innovations," Working Paper 673, Federal Reserve Bank of Minneapolis, Research Department, August 2009.

127 Happily, the Board of Longitude: See Dava Sobel's lively history of this prize, *Longitude: The True Story of a Lone Genius Who Solved the Greatest Scientific Problem of His Time* (New York: Walker, 1995).

128 When Lindbergh's plane went on a national tour: The estimate of the number of people who saw the plane comes from Peter Diamandis.

129 McKinsey did a thorough global review: McKinsey & Company, "And the Winner Is . . . : Capturing the Promise of Philanthropic Prizes," 2009, www.mckinsey.com/app_media/reports/sso/and_the_winner_is.pdf.

129 A study led by Liam Brunt: Liam Brunt, Josh Lerner, and Tom Nicholas, "Inducement Prizes and Innovation," Centre for Economic Policy Research,

CEPR Discussion Paper No. DP6917, July 2008; an abstract is at http://papers
.ssrn.com/sol3/papers.cfm?abstract_id=1307507##.

131   A study co-authored by Karim Lakhani: See Karim R. Lakhani, Lars Bo
Jeppesen, Peter A. Lohse, and Jill A. Panetta, "The Value of Openness in Scien-
tific Problem Solving," Harvard Business School, HBS Working Paper 07-050,
January 2007, www.hbs.edu/research/pdf/07-050.pdf.

132   Thomas Kalil: Before he joined the White House as a science advisor,
Thomas Kalil was an advocate of government embracing incentive prizes. See
"Prizes for Technological Innovation," Brookings Institution, Hamilton Project
Discussion Paper 2006-08, December 2006, www.brookings.edu/~/media/
Files/rc/papers/2006/12healthcare_kalil/200612kalil.pdf.

Chapter 6: Black Swan Kills Sitting Duck

138   Consider violence: Steven Pinker lays out his arguments on violence
at this Ideas Economy event in September 2010: http://ideas.economist.com/
presentation/history-violence.

139   More than half a century after the height of the Cold War: So how
does Martin Rees justify his suggestion that mankind might have only a 50-50
chance of surviving the twenty-first century—our final hour, to use the alarmist
title of his book? Rees took my review copy of *Our Final Century* (as the British
edition of his work was called) and penciled in a question mark after the title.
He said his British publishers had ruled the question mark out. He insisted that
the American publisher, Basic Books, even changed the title from *Our Final
Century* to *Our Final Hour* upon publication in 2003. Reese is clever enough to
know that the end is not nigh, but he put up with the chicanery in order to gain
a wider audience. A small sin, perhaps, in such an important book.

140   Consider, for example, the mysterious decimation: For more on the trouble with the bees, see "UN Report Warns Bees Now Disappearing Worldwide,"
The Extinction Protocol, March 22, 2011, http://theextinctionprotocol.word
press.com/2011/03/22/un-report-warns-bees-now-disappearing-worldwide.

143   Every year, the World Economic Forum: For more on the WEF's ongoing work and analysis of risk issues, including its new initiative to create a
global risk response network that could serve as an early warning system for
systemic risks, see the page on "Global Risks" on the WEF's website, www.we
forum.org/issues/global-risks. Please note: I serve as an advisor on sustainability issues to the WEF's Global Agenda Council network, but I played absolutely

no role in developing the WEF's correct predictions of global financial troubles. Also, on the rising cost of disasters, see the analysis done by Swiss Re's experts at www.swissre.com/sigma.

146 *Global Catastrophic Risks:* Nick Bostrom and Milan Cirkovic, eds., *Global Catastrophic Risks* (New York: Oxford University Press, 2008), www .global-catastrophic-risks.com/docs/global-catastrophic-risks.pdf.

149 The Rockefeller Foundation asked: Rockefeller Foundation and Global Business Network, "Scenarios for the Future of Technology and International Development," May 2010, www.rockefellerfoundation.org/uploads/files/ bba493f7-cc97-4da3-add6-3deb007cc719.pdf.

156 great promise in using genetic science to feed the world: For more on how the global spread of genetically modified crops has taken place safely and to the great benefit of farmers in the developing world, see the annual reports put out by ISAAA at www.isaaa.org. I do believe that activists have a legitimate point in arguing for prudent regulations and for keeping a watchful eye on possible health, safety, and environmental issues—but two decades of experience across the world proves their wilder claims wrong and their obstructionist approach in Europe misguided. The concerns expressed by some that rapacious multinational corporations would use GMOs to trap small farmers into a new cycle of poverty are also important to note. On this score, the embrace by China and other emerging markets of this technology offers hope: even the chief technology officer of Monsanto acknowledges that a lot of the innovation in GMOs is shifting rapidly away from the developed world toward the research laboratories of such countries.

Chapter 7: The Sputnik Fallacies

164 *the Gathering Storm:* This report can be found at the National Academies Press website, www.nap.edu.

166 If China is up, then the United States must be down: Much of the concern about America's loss of competitiveness centers around the decline in manufacturing employment—remember Ross Perot's warnings about the "sucking sound" of jobs moving to Mexico because of NAFTA? New research into the matter, done by the Boston Consulting Group, suggests that manufacturing and other jobs are, in fact, coming back to the United States ("Made in the USA, Again: Manufacturing Is Expected to Return to America as China's Rising Labor Costs Erase Most Savings from Offshoring," Boston Consulting Group press release, May 5, 2011, www.bcg.com/media/PressReleaseDetails.

aspx?id=tcm:12-75973). One reason for this is that the wage gap with India and China is, due to rising wages in those countries, much smaller than it was twenty years ago. Another reason, says GE's boss Jeff Immelt, is that it is harder and more expensive to get educated and motivated employees in those countries now that they have plenty of other opportunities. His firm is currently moving call centers back from India to the United States, and he claims the wages are only about 10 percent more expensive in America for comparable workers. He predicts firms will keep manufacturing jobs relevant to servicing emerging markets in those markets, but bring back jobs that involve making stuff for Americans—a move that has pleasing side benefits in reducing supply chain risk.

169   Research done by Vivek Wadhwa: See, for example, Gary Gereffi, Vivek Wadhwa, Ben Rissing, and Ryan Ong, "Getting the Numbers Right: International Engineering Education in the United States, China, and India," *Journal of Engineering Education* 97, 1 (2008): 13–25. For his forceful and, in my view, correct arguments for reforming America's immigration laws, see Vivek Wadhwa, "Our Best Imports: Keeping Immigrant Innovators Here," *Democracy Journal* 21 (Summer 2011).

171   The latest five-year plan from Beijing's technocracy: For more on China's innovation ambitions, see China's 12th Five-Year Plan (2011–2015), www.gov.cn/english/2011-03/05/content_1816822.htm; "Hearing on China's Five-Year Plan, Indigenous Innovation and Technology Transfers, and Outsourcing," June 15, 2011, U.S.-China Economic and Security Review Commission, www.uscc.gov/hearings/2011hearings/written_testimonies/hr11_06_15.php; also see Dieter Ernst's work at the East-West Center.

172   The OECD recently examined China's innovation policies: *OECD Reviews of Innovation Policy: China* (Paris: OECD, 2008), www.OECD.org/sti/innovation/reviews/china.

175   Schloss Leopoldskron: The cognoscenti will have recognized this as the setting for *The Sound of Music.*

176   Samuel Kortum and Josh Lerner: Samuel Kortum and Josh Lerner, "Assessing the Contribution of Venture Capital to Innovation," *RAND Journal of Economics* 31, 4 (Winter 2000): 674–92, http://home.uchicago.edu/kortum/papers/rje_2000.pdf.

184   The Council on Competitiveness: The papers referenced here, as well as much other research of relevance to national competitiveness, can be found at www.compete.org.

186   Giving faculty and employees of government laboratories: See the provocative arguments made on this topic by Robert Litan and the Kauffman

Foundation. On the striking Supreme Court decision on academic innovators, contrast the *New York Times* editorial denouncing it with Vivek Wadhwa's take on the matter: "Innovation's Golden Opportunity," *Washington Post*, June 10, 2011, www.washingtonpost.com/national/on-innovations/innovations-golden-opportunity/2011/06/09/AGWrnJOH_story.html.

186   encouraging innovative entrepreneurship: The topic of entrepreneurship was explored in some detail with leading academic experts (among them UC Berkeley's Henry Chesbrough and Babson's Daniel Isenberg), government figures (Aneesh Chopra, the White House's chief technology officer) and cutting-edge entrepreneurs (among them SpaceX's Elon Musk and Twitter's Jack Dorsey) at the Ideas Economy event held in March 2011. The full two-day event can be viewed on www.foratv.com for a fee, or tantalizing tidbits can be viewed for free at www.ideas.economist.com. Look in particular for the explanation from TrueCar's Scott Painter (a remarkable serial entrepreneur who has raised over $1 billion for several dozen firms he has started) of why he refuses to hire any entrepreneurs at his firms.

186   While in the past most start-ups targeted local markets: Daniel Isenberg has written much about entrepreneurship that is worth reading. See, for example, his "The Global Entrepreneur," *Harvard Business Review*, December 2008, http://hbr.org/2008/12/the-global-entrepreneur/ar/1.

188   AnnaLee Saxenian: The comparison of Silicon Valley and Route 128 was made in an earlier work of hers, *Regional Advantage: Culture and Competition in Silicon Valley and Route 128* (Cambridge, MA: Harvard University Press, 1994). Her more recent and equally worthwhile book, *The New Argonauts: Regional Advantage in a Global Economy* (Cambridge, MA: Harvard University Press, 2006), shows exactly why immigrant networks connecting Silicon Valley with hot spots of global innovation like Israel, Taiwan, and southern India should be viewed as brain circulation rather than brain drain.

190   Yes, really: The French government's sovereign wealth fund, Fonds Stratégique d'Investissement, put $3.1 million into Meccano, a local toy manufacturer. Why making those toys in France, as opposed to making them anywhere else, is of "strategic" import was not disclosed, perhaps for national security reasons.

191   This is especially true in energy: See Richard Newell discuss the fine book on energy innovation edited by him and Harvard's Rebecca Henderson (*Accelerating Energy Innovation* [Chicago: University of Chicago Press, 2011]) at an Ideas Economy event held in September 2010: http://ideas.economist.com/presentation/interview-richard-g-newell; Henderson's comments on this and related topics are found here: http://ideas.economist.com/presentation/capitalism-and-climate-change.

194 In contrast, Canada's tax law: See the OECD's comparative analysis of national innovation policies for more on this point.

194 However, there are worrying signs: I think there is a real danger that efforts at developing smart grids or electronic health records, done in the name of enhancing national competitiveness, will be co-opted by the technology firms that are most favored by politicians in Beijing and Seoul or who have the best lobbyists in Washington and Brussels. One proposal now making the rounds that would address this problem of elite capture is for the creation of a Sustainable Energy Free Trade Agreement, or SEFTA (see www.youtube.com/watch?v=l8_wIZ3oFZ0). Such an accord would differ from the WTO's frustrated efforts at a new global trade pact in that it would be only for a coalition of the willing: those countries that want to go further than global norms on standards harmonization, market access, subsidy withdrawal, and so on are free to do so—and laggards are welcome to join later. There is a precedent for this in the information technology free-trade accord reached during the Clinton administration, which has proved to be GATT and WTO compatible. Please note: My role here is merely as an advocate of this idea. Credit for it goes to the entire sustainable energy Global Agenda Council that I chaired for the World Economic Forum, especially to Michael Liebreich, Peter Brun, and Busba Wongnapapisan.

195 the best industrial policy is probably no industrial policy: See Clay Christensen's observations on why government intervention often stifles innovation here: http://ideas.economist.com/video/innovation-and-government-intervention-0.

Chapter 8: Can Dinosaurs Dance?

200 That points to several of the big lessons: For a useful take on how managers at incumbent firms, who face the unenviable task of delivering short-term profits even as they invest in the innovations that drive long-term results, can cope, see Vijay Govindarajan and Chris Trimble, "Stop the Innovation Wars," *Harvard Business Review*, July-August 2010.

200 experiment more readily, failing faster: There is no shortage of books and articles on the importance of experimentation and failure in the innovation process. My favorite site is the courageous one maintained by Bessemer Venture Partners, arguably the oldest extant VC firm in America, that tracks the firm's biggest failures over the years (www.bvp.com/portfolio/antiportfolio.aspx). Fascinating work is being done at the Stanford Institute of Design on novel approaches to innovation that incorporate design, rapid prototyping, and fast failure. See also Tim Harford, *Adapt: Why Success Always Starts with Failure* (New York: Farrar, Straus and Giroux, 2011). A number of leading thinkers, ranging from John Sexton and Shirley Tilghman, who are respectively heads of NYU and Princeton, to Steven Pinker and Clay Shirky, give their insights on failure at "The Ideas Economy, Failure, and Innovation," PopTech, http://poptech.org/the_ideas_economy.

201   Intuit, a California firm: Intuit's progress in opening up its innovation process is reviewed in Roger L. Martin, "The Innovation Catalysts," *Harvard Business Review*, June 2011, http://hbr.org/2011/06/the-innovation-catalysts/ar/1. You can hear Scott Cook present various ideas of his at Ideas Economy events (www.ideas.economist.com).

202   Two decades ago: David Gelernter, "Surviving the Unabomber," Big Think, April 27, 2010, http://bigthink.com/ideas/19763. He spoke about the prospects for, and perils arising from, intelligent infrastructure at this Ideas Economy event in September 2010: http://ideas.economist.com/presentation/human-network.

203   McKinsey futurologists: See Jacques Bughin, Michael Chui, and James Manyika, "Clouds, Big Data and Smart Assets," *McKinsey Quarterly*, August 2010. See also recent in-depth reports by the firm on Big Data and productivity.

204   "A BMW is now actually a network": While the hydrogen-powered roadster is a sexy and potentially über-green idea (if the hydrogen is made from renewable sources), it is one that is ahead of its time. BMW developed the Hydrogen 7 to the point where it was ready for full commercialization, but because the market for hydrogen and fuel cells (a related technology) never materialized, the German firm never put this model into production.

208   reverse innovation: For more on reverse innovation, including how it compares with the notion of disruptive innovation, see Vijay Govindarajan's articles in *Harvard Business Review* and his postings on his blog: www.vijay govindarajan.com.

211   Andy Grove: For more on Andy Grove, see both his books and the authorized biography by Richard Tedlow, *Andy Grove: The Life and Times of an American* (New York: Portfolio, 2006).

215   The best such nugget . . . is Kaiser Permanente: For more on Kaiser Permanente's success in using electronic medical records to improve patient outcomes, see various articles in *Health Affairs*, including Catherine Chen et al., "The Kaiser Permanente Electronic Health Record: Transforming and Streamlining Modalities of Care," *Health Affairs* 28, 2 (March-April 2009): 323–33, http://content.healthaffairs.org/content/28/2/323.abstract, and Yi Yvonne Zhou et al., "Improved Quality at Kaiser Permanente Through E-Mail Between

Physicians and Patients," *Health Affairs* 29, 7 (July 2010): 1370–75, http://content.healthaffairs.org/content/29/7/1370.short.

Chapter 9: Greed for Good

219 A big problem for the future of capitalism: For more on proper accounting of natural capital, see works by Amory Lovins of the Rocky Mountain Institute, including *Natural Capitalism: The Next Industrial Revolution* (Great Barrington, MA: E. F. Schumacher Society, 2003). On cradle to cradle analysis, see Bill McDonough's writings and the work of his Cradle to Cradle Products Innovation Institute (www.c2ccertified.org).

220 Financial experts see the beginnings: In December 2010 J. P. Morgan released a report done in collaboration with the Rockefeller Foundation, "Impact Investments: An Emerging Asset Class," that argued that impact investing could become an asset class with value in the range of $400 million to $1 trillion. To investigate the underlying assumptions, see the full report here: www.rockefeller foundation.org/what-we-do/current-work/harnessing-power-impact-investing/publications.

220 Jack Welch: On Welch's apparent U-turn (some still claim he has not changed his position at all), compare his comments made in 1981 with this interview given to the *Financial Times* in March 2009: www.ft.com/intl/cms/s/0/294ff1f2-0f27-11de-ba10-0000779fd2ac.html#axzz1Re1HSmap.

222 Roger Martin: Martin spells out his views on the evolution of capitalism in "The Age of Customer Capitalism," *Harvard Business Review*, January–February 2010.

226 Bill Drayton: Drayton summarizes his worldview in "Tipping the World: The Power of Collaborative Entrepreneurship," *What Matters*, McKinsey Publishing, April 8, 2010, http://whatmatters.mckinseydigital.com/social_en trepreneurs/tipping-the-world-the-power-of-collaborative-entrepreneurship. David Bornstein, *How to Change the World: Social Entrepreneurs and the Power of New Ideas* (New York: Oxford University Press, 2007) traces Drayton's history and profiles Ashoka's "change makers" in depth.

230 A big obstacle to reaching such customers: For a well-grounded, skeptical take on what multinationals can and cannot do at the bottom of the pyramid, see Ashish Karamchandani, Mike Kubzansky, and Nishant Lalwani, "Is the Bottom of the Pyramid Really for You?" *Harvard Business Review*, March–April 2011.

233 Dan Pink: For a brilliant cartoon rendering of Pink's ideas, see this video produced by the RSA: www.youtube.com/watch?v=u6XAPnuFjJc. Also, for more on using purpose as a motivator for social good, check out Purpose, a nonprofit started by Jeremy Heimans and David Madden. Heimans makes the case for the "movement entrepreneur" here: http://ideas.economist.com/presentation/movement-entrepreneur.

235 Brian Trelstad: On Trelstad's concerns about metrics, see "Simple Measures for Social Enterprise," *Innovations*, Summer 2008.

238 a concept known as microfinance: On the debate among economists on the true impact of microfinance and the importance of randomized control trials, see Dean Karlan, *More than Good Intentions: How a New Economics Is Helping to Solve Global Poverty* (New York: Dutton, 2011) and the feisty panel discussion "Promise and Peril of Microfinance Impact Evaluations" during the Microfinance USA Conference, New York, May 23–24, 2011: www.microfinanceusaconference.org/videos-2011/session-01-promise-and-peril.php. On related topics, also see Abhijit Banerjee and Esther Duflo, *Poor Economics: A Radical Rethinking of the Way to Fight Global Poverty* (New York: Public Affairs, 2011). A pointer to recent economic studies on the impact of microfinance is "Microfinance's Elusive Quest: Finding an Accurate Measure of Social Impact," Knowledge@Wharton, http://knowledge.wharton.upenn.edu/article.cfm?articleid=2391.

241 The profit motive: For a lively debate on this matter, see Matthew Bishop's video encounter with Felix Salmon, complete with color commentary by the thoughtful David Roodman: http://blogs.cgdev.org/open_book/2011/02/felix-salmon-and-matthew-bishop-head-to-head.php. All three have excellent blogs that are worth a look.

243 companies must put society's great needs front and center: On the question of whether taking the long view will really lead businesses to solve big social problems profitably, see this intriguing paper: Daniel Altman and Jonathan Berman, "The Single Bottom Line," June 13, 2011, http://dalberg.com/sites/dalberg.com/files/sblfinal.pdf.

Conclusion: We Are All Innovators Now

252 what has been called frontier economics: The arguments about frontier economics are put forth well in Brink Lindsey, "Frontier Economics: Why Entrepreneurial Capitalism Is Needed Now More than Ever," Kauffman Foundation Research Series on Dynamics of Economic Growth, April 2011, www.kauffman.org/uploadedFiles/frontier_economics_4_06.pdf.

253 Jack Hidary: For more on Jack Hidary's role and vision for electric cars and ride-sharing, see www.youtube.com/watch?v=RmOL1fN_jpQ.

255 most promising are advanced software, Big Data: On the transformative power of Big Data, see "Big Data: The Next Frontier for Innovation, Competition, and Productivity," McKinsey's Global Institute, May 2011, www.mckinsey.com/mgi/publications/big_data/index.asp. Also see some very cool data visualizations, as well as discussions about the future of Big Data, at an Ideas Economy event in June 2011 (on www.fora.tv for a fee, free snippets at http://ideas.economist.com/video/power-big-data).

255 Apple's first mouse: A typically Gladwellian take on the development of the computer mouse by Xerox PARC, IDEO, and others is found in Malcolm Gladwell, "Creation Myth: Xerox PARC, Apple, and the Truth About Innovation," *New Yorker*, May 16, 2011, www.newyorker.com/reporting/2011/05/16/110516fa_fact_gladwell.

255 The traditional uncompromising focus: Design thinking has failed to achieve its promise and it is time to move onto the next management fashion, argues Bruce Nussbaum, one of design thinking's greatest proponents over the past decade, in "Design Thinking Is a Failed Experiment. So What's Next?" Fast Company's Co.Design, www.fastcodesign.com/1663558/design-thinking-is-a-failed-experiment-so-whats-next. For more on the tension between Six Sigma and design thinking, see Tim Brown, "Six Sigma and Design Thinking," *Design Thinking: Thoughts by Tim Brown*, September 10, 2009, http://designthinking.ideo.com/?p=387, and a related article by Sara Beckman, "Welcoming the Old, Improving the New," *New York Times*, September 5, 2009, www.nytimes.com/2009/09/06/business/06proto.html?_r=1.

256 The key is to focus on the needs of people: The nifty Embrace concept and product are explained at the Embrace website, http://embraceglobal.org, and on the website of the Stanford University Institute of Design, http://extreme.stanford.edu/projects/embrace.html.

257 everyone can join the "maker revolution": See Chris Anderson's fine cover stories on the topic in *Wired* (for example "In the Next Industrial Revolution, Atoms Are the New Bits," *Wired*, February 2010, www.wired.com/magazine/2010/01/ff_newrevolution/all/1), and his interview with Carl Bass in June 2011, www.youtube.com/watch?v=yXBGNggO3hI.

257 And what about talent: The WEF/ BCG report on global talent mobility, published in March 2010, can be found here (www.weforum.org/reports/stimulating-economies-through-fostering-talent-mobility?fo=1).

258 Companies will also have to redouble efforts: Pepsi has a stellar record in employing the disabled, which is worth further study and emulation. The Council on Competitiveness has done studies showing that it is older entrepreneurs, not two college dropouts working out of a garage, that are responsible for many of the start-ups in America. The group argues for rethinking the opportunities made available to older workers. See also Sylvia Ann Hewlett et al., "The Battle for Female Talent in Emerging Markets," Center for Work-Life Policy, 2010.

INDEX

ABOUT THE AUTHOR

VIJAY V. VAITHEESWARAN is an award-winning correspondent for *The Economist*. He joined the editorial staff in 1992 as its London-based Latin America correspondent, and opened the magazine's first regional bureau in Mexico City in 1994. From 1998 to 2006, he covered the politics, economics, business, and technology of energy and the environment. From 2007 to 2011 his portfolio encompassed innovation, global health, pharmaceuticals, and biotechnology. He is currently the magazine's China Business & Finance editor.

He is a life member at the Council on Foreign Relations, and an advisor on sustainability issues to the World Economic Forum. He teaches at NYU's Stern School of Business, and his commentaries have appeared in such outlets as NPR, the *Wall Street Journal*, and the *New York Times*. On the topic of innovation, he has addressed groups ranging from the US National Governors' Association and the UN General Assembly to the TED, AAAS, and Aspen Ideas conferences. He also serves as chairman of the *Economist*'s pathbreaking series of conferences and multimedia debates on innovation, the Ideas Economy (www.ideas.economist.com).

His last book, *Zoom*, co-authored with Iain Carson, was named a Book of the Year by *The Financial Times*. His first book, *Power to the People*, was reviewed by *Scientific American* as "by far the most helpful, entertaining, up-to-date, and accessible treatment of the energy-economy-environment problematique available." Vijay is a graduate of the Massachusetts Institute of Technology, where he was named a Harry S. Truman Scholar by the U.S. Congress. He was born in Madras, India, and grew up in Cheshire, Connecticut.